A Glance at the Past

by Regina Nedas

Publisher's Page:

This is a true story by Regina Nedas. The people, places, and events are accurate to my memory and other family members' memory.

Text and cover drawing by Regina Nedas.

Published by
Doctor's Dreams Publishing
www.Doctors-Dreams.com

Prepared in the United States of America
ISBN: 978-1-942181-46-0

Family Genealogy

First generation: Grandparents, Mateo and wife Gertrud (my grandparents)
Gertrud's brother: Johannes

Second generation: Gertrud's son: Lucas (my father) and Gertrud's daughter: Scarlett
Their German child Otto
Second generation: Lucas and wife Greta (my parents)
Second generation: Greta's sister: Sophilia
Second generation: Johannes' children, his son Olivier and daughter Contessa.

Third generation: Greta's daughter Christina (me) and son Simon.
Third generation: Simon married Agatha.

Fourth generation: My son with my first husband Arlo, Justin
Fourth generation: My son with my second husband Peter, Gabriel
Fourth generation: Simon and Agatha's daughters Melody and Renee

Simon's acquaintance and Renee's first husband Sven
Renee's second husband Joseph

Others:

Household helper	Anna (Gertrud) and Gabija (Johannes)
Neighbors	Zigi, Bethan
Christina's friends	Alma, Bella, Zia, David, Emma, Mia, Erick, "Cat", "Beaver"
Greta's friends	Stacy, Matina
Peter's friend	Frank, Albert
Peter's daughter	Amelia
College Friends	Lina, Vasco
Friends in America	

Lithuanian	Jania, Arturus, Lily
Iowa	Belle
Others	Adam

Introduction

In the early twentieth century, Lithuania was a quiet, peaceful, and independent country. The life there changed abruptly with the arrival of WWII, first with the invasion of the Soviets, then by the Germans, followed by the Soviet occupation.

This book contains true stories of my family and how the war changed their lives. Most of it is autobiographical, I gathered information from my family members and their friends and neighbors. Other information was received from newspaper articles, books, and television. I include the subsequent history of my family, my parents, their children, and their grandchildren in the post-war years.

The poems included were written by Greta's grandson, my son Justin.

Chapter One: Before the War

Life was simple before World War II. After that, we had systems.
  - Grace Hopper, Rear Admiral

     My family had lived for many generations in Lithuania up to the mid twentieth century. Our rural farming community was centered in a village called Satkunai in Joniskis District. This village was located by the main railroad tracks that connected Riga, Latvian's capital, through the Lithuanian towns of Siauliai and Taurage, to Konigsberg, Prussia. On a working farm lived my grandparents Gertrud and Mateo. Nearby lived the family of Johannes, Gertrud's brother.

     Gertrud was a thin, short, very beautiful woman with bright blue eyes and short hair with a strong and dominant soul. Her husband, Mateo, was an honest, hardworking man who loved his family, and always greeted his guests with a smile. He had a strong sense of humor, with blue eyes and black mustache as befit the owner of a large farm.

     They had two children, their daughter Scarlett and son Lucas. At the time of this story, June 1940, Scarlett had been studying at an agricultural school, and Lucas was studying at the military pilot training school. They'd both come home to spend the summer holidays.

     The lane leading to Gertrude and Mateo's house was lined with mature linden trees. The home was old looking, covered with a straw roof, giving it a pleasant unique look. It had a wooden porch, large enough for rocking chairs, and a solid front door that opened onto the kitchen. Few modern conveniences existed in the 1940s; imagine a kitchen with a sink, an ice box, and an old wood-burning stove. Off the kitchen was a storage room where they kept meat, milk, cheese, and sausages.

     A door led off the kitchen into the master bedroom. There, the feather bed lay covered with white bedding and a beautiful lace-decorated blanket. Next to their bedroom, there were two more bedrooms, one each for their two children.

Across from the kitchen was a large common room with a long wooden table with two wooden chairs on each end for Gertrud and Mateo. On the side of the table were wooden benches with backrests. A large kerosene lamp hung above the table. The family would gather there with the hired workers for the evening dining ritual, where they would tell stories, gossip, and discuss the needs of the farm. On some Saturday evenings, relatives and friends would arrive in one-horse carriages for an evening of feasting on fresh farm food accompanied by Mateo's homemade beer and Gertrud's wine.

Behind the common room, the woman helper, Anna, had a small bedroom, what Americans call the maid quarters. A short distance away, a small cottage sheltered their two farmhands. During the cold long nights of winter, the two farmhands would go to their families' homes, while Anna took over the duties of milking the cow and tending the livestock.

The farm had been in the family for many generations, nearly a hundred acres of fertile rolling hills. The barn housed fifteen cows, with a loft kept full of hay. Mateo was particularly proud of his three beautiful horses with their shiny coats. He'd built them a spacious barn and he brushed them down each day.

Near the barn, a pigsty housed two sows and a hog with forty little piglets snorting in the mud. A coop as big as the farmhand's cottage held chickens and roosters, supplying my grandparents with both eggs and meat. Behind the barn, a large, gray-stoned shed stored flour and grain. Beyond the farm lay hundreds of acres of virgin forest, rich in wildlife and berries.

Yardwork lay in the province of the household women. Gertrud and Scarlett kept a glorious garden with fragrant flowers and fruit trees. Behind the house, a row of huge cherry trees had just lost their spring blooms, the pink and white petals blowing around the farm like snowflakes. Songbirds and cuckoos sang out from the apple, pear, and plum trees. In one corner, Mateo kept a beehive, prized throughout the village for its rich honey.

For the cold winter nights, a sauna would be heated by firewood. There was a tradition that friends would strike each other with birch branches in the sauna. This supposedly increased blood circulation, and everyone claimed it felt invigorating.

My grandmother had two brothers. The eldest emigrated to the United States during the First World War, settling in Grand Rapids, Michigan. Although he never returned for a visit, he exchanged frequent letters with Gertrud and his other brother, that is, up until the events of this story.

Johannes, the second brother of Gertrud, had a farm only a mile away from his sister. Only a few years younger than her, he still had a full head of hair, now turned gray. His most remarkable features were his height, a good six-foot, and his intense blue eyes. He'd stare down at you with a fixating gaze, and you'd believe anything he'd say.

His wife was tall as well, a hefty lady who always welcomed guests with a cheerful smile, offering them homemade biscuits and wine. She and her old lady friends would gather cross-legged on chairs, gossip about their neighbors, and pass around cigarettes.

They had two sons and a beautiful daughter. After finishing high school, the elder son returned to manage the farm. Tall like his parents, he rarely spoke, a bit shy and modest. His brother became a veterinarian and had a clinic in the village.

Several years younger than her brothers, Contessa, the sister, turned sixteen in May, one month before these events. Added to the captivating blue eyes and height of her family, she had gorgeous golden hair, falling in bangs above her flawless features. For the previous two years, their household had been a target for hopeful young men and matchmakers – but to no avail. The daughter insisted she would know when she found her true love, and until then, she wasn't interested in romance.

Johannes' house was bigger than Gertrud's. The front door opened to an expansive living room filled with comfortable wooden furniture. In one corner the family's pride, a golden pendulum clock with an etched glass door, ticked away. Johannes wound the clock every morning.

Like his sister, Johannes had a house woman. Gabija, a fortyish plump orphan, had been with the family since she turned sixteen. She'd become one of the family, taking over many of the decisions about managing the farm and the farmworkers' duties. Any time somebody visited for breakfast, Gabija scrambled very tasty eggs, usually served with fresh cucumbers.

I remember one time, when I was about four years old, my mother and I were visiting Johannes' house. The four of us, Johannes, his wife, my mother, and I, were all sitting at a wooden outdoor table, chatting. A small, slender man with a tiny white bag hanging on his shoulder came up from the road. Johannes greeted him and asked what he wanted.

"Food, if you have any to spare," the man said.

Johannes stepped out and brought the man inside the house, calling to Gabija. He bade the man sit at the table and told Gabija to give the man anything to eat that he wanted and as much as he wanted. When finished eating, the man thanked Gabija. She filled his tiny bag with various foods and the beggar went on his way.

The two families maintained close ties, love, and respect, sharing joys and worries, dreams and fulfillment. It was a peaceful village life that flowed as old as a regular riverbed with the usual joys and daily troubles.

All that ended on June 15th, 1940.

First poem: FOR LIFE

That directionless whirlwind
with the sparkling eye of the vortex
glances at your windows
And mirrors only with fire
moonlight reflections
and the ground appears to be burning
from heat
when the stone speaks
and so then the world
turns full circle
you cannot unravel
each vein of it
storm and whirlwind
chatters
even when the rooster
starts to crow at midnight
in the dreary voice of the night
Who are you?

Chapter Two: The Soviet Occupation

Gertrud's and Mateo's son Lucas married my mother, Greta. They had a daughter, Christina (me), and a son Simon. My mother Greta told me her story of the Soviet occupation, which I relate here.

On June 15th, I heard on the radio that Soviet troops had entered Lithuania. Anxiety flooded in. I was a student studying medicine in Vilnius, the capital of Lithuania. Walking down the street to the hospital for my medical practice, I saw Russian soldiers marching in the distance with their armored vehicles and trucks rolling nearby. As their army approached, I could smell their boots and their sweat. When the soldiers marched in front of me, they looked half-dead, exhausted and gloomy. When the march stopped, many of the soldiers dropped onto the street and took off their shoes. I watched them rewrap their footcloths. I was used to seeing Lithuanian soldiers always in clean and neat uniforms. There I saw exhausted soldiers.

I knew a great calamity had befallen me, my relatives, and the whole nation.

After this formidable Russian occupation of Lithuania, the letters written by my uncle rarely came from America. The Russian authorities intercepted and read any letter coming to our town. They only allowed letters that wrote about God, the weather, and health. Otherwise, they destroyed them. Gertrud was happy to get any letter from her brother. She wrote to him to say that she hoped that one day we would be together again.

The Russian officers settled in the common room of Mateo and Gertrud's house. As it was close to the main road and railway line, it made a convenient headquarters. In addition, Gertrud spoke Russian, so could communicate with them and translate their orders to the other villagers. Over the next few weeks, they turned Gertrud's house into the army's kitchen with large boilers in the yard where their staff cooked and served meals to all their soldiers.

In early June, Lucas had returned from the War Aviation Pilot School. He and the farmhands had been cutting the hay from the early spring crop and putting it into the barn. One day, Lucas was standing on top of the carriage with a pitchfork ready to unload the hay. A Russian soldier drove onto the farmyard on a motorcycle. He pulled out a rifle and began screaming, threatening to shoot Lucas. Gertrud yelled to the Russian commanders begging them to stop this Russian soldier intruder.

One of the commanders ran into the yard carrying a rifle, "I'll shoot you if you don't leave immediately," he told the man on the motorcycle. "And if you ever show up again, I'll kill you."

The intruder turned his motorcycle around and drove away.

Through the winter the Russians ate through Gertrud & Mateo's larders, so just as spring arrived, the food products ran out. The Russian commander told his subordinate to slaughter one of the cows.

When Gertrud saw her best milk cow being led to the butcher shed, she began crying. She begged the commander to pick a different cow, any other cow, but he ignored her. The cow was quickly dispatched and made into stew meat. That evening the commander held a big party with music and dancing where the main courses were stew meat and vodka.

The Russian commander told Gertrud that the authorities would pay her for the cow. He gave her a letter, saying that she could take it to the Staff Headquarters, and she would receive the money for the cow. She took it to their office, but they refused to give her any money.

A few months later, in June 1941, the Russian Commander received his orders to retreat. As they left, the Russians took away everything they could carry, including all the home's kitchen utensils and cooking equipment.

A week later, a knock came to the door with the visitor demanding in Russian for Gertrud to open the door. She thought it might be the same commander returning, but when she removed the bolts, Russian Cossack thieves burst in. They grabbed Gertrud and tied her up. Mateo was not at home at the time. Anna escaped by climbing out the back window and hiding in the forest.

The Cossacks went from room to room, emptying all the chests and cupboards and dumping the items into sheets. They bundled it all up and rode off on horseback, leaving the house empty of all but the bound matron.

Gertrud lay tied up on the floor all night. At dawn, Anna dared to creep back in, and untied Gertrud. They hugged and wept in joy to see that they'd survived unharmed.

There was one silver lining to the Russian commander choosing Gertrud's house. Because of his influence and need for her house management, these two families avoided being deported to Siberia.

Chapter Three: Stacy: Her Memories from Siberian Exile

God is on your side? He is a conservative? The Devil's on my side, he is a good communist." Joseph Stalin *(said to Winston Churchill)*

Stacy was a friend of my mother, Greta, who lived in the village nearby.

The Russians stopped with a huge truck right outside our house and arrested me and my father. Mother was not at home at the time. They put us in a truck and took us to the railway station. They told us to get into the railroad cars meant to hold cattle. Russian soldiers with machine guns and dogs stood by each car.

They crowded the wagons so full of townspeople, there was hardly any space to sit down, then they slammed the door shut. The wagon had only one small window, providing hardly any light or air. Only a single hole was left in the middle of the wagon to do our toilet needs.

I knew many of the people on the train. They came from all walks of life. Professors, lawyers, doctors, and actors. Lithuanian military officers and their families. Farmers, civil servants, and businessmen, it didn't matter who you were, they rounded up everyone they could find.

We were carried for three months, usually with a single daily stop for food and water. Someone figured out we were going towards the Laptev Sea. At the end of the railroad line, we were loaded onto barges on the Angara River. We floated downriver for several days until docking at a small village. From there, they carried us by trucks through the uninhabited forests from Angara to the Lena River. From the Lena River, we were again carried by barges to the north, about 500 miles from the Arctic Circle, where vegetation was sparse and settlements disappeared.

There, at the end of our journey, lay the Laptev Sea, and several miles offshore, there was an uninhabited island. Neither tree nor bush, the tundra was covered with only a thin layer of moss.

The Russians disembarked 400 Lithuanians to this island. Among them were children, mothers, and grandparents. The men were taken out to work for the Russians.

In the Land of Permafrost, we were left on the island without food or shelter in October, unprepared for the rapidly approaching winter. We scavenged the island for supplies, dragging back broken logs from shipwrecks to build yurts. Large blocks of ice served as windows.

We had nothing to cover ourselves. The Russians had not allowed us to take anything. Through the nights, we snuggled next to each other trying to stay warm, finding on arising our hair had frozen to the ice. Everyone suffered from hunger and scurvy, many succumbing to the elements.

The Evenks lived 75 miles away, skilled in fishing and fox hunting. When they visited and saw us in such poverty, they offered to take us to their heated yurts. When the Russian commander found out, he forbade it. Clearly, he wanted all of us to die on this island.

Every day, our commanders sent us several miles to the upper reaches of the Lena River to look for logs. Although we wanted to drag them to our yurts to build housing, instead, the Russians ordered us to drag them to their areas so they could burn them for their own warmth. Whole families died, as well as my father, leaving me alone at age eighteen.

We found nets among the shipwrecks. We waded into icy cold water and caught fish with them. We untangled the caught fish from the net which immediately were frozen into ice. Without any fire, we ate the fish frozen. Frostbite struck many of us, wounds developing on the frozen fingers and feet, and from there, infection and death.

When spring arrived, the few of us left alive decided we had to escape to survive. Ignoring the orders of the Russians, we left the island and walked for days through the bare tundra and into the forest. After two weeks we reached the kolkhoz (a collective farm of the former Soviet Union). Here we found the male Lithuanian deportees working the farm for the Russians. They welcomed us into their living barracks, but, sadly, didn't have enough food either. They suggested we go to the village and ask for food. The first home

I came to, the residents happened to be eating dinner. I begged them for food, and they gave me their potato skins. My first food in a week, I'll always remember how good that tasted.

I told the family that I'd milk their cows if they would share the milk with me. They accepted my offer, and I shared the milk with the other Lithuanians. In this manner, scrounging in the woods for food and accepting handouts from the village, we survived through the next dozen years.

In 1953, Stalin died, and the Lithuanians who still survived were allowed to return to their country.

Chapter Four: How my mother Greta Survived World War II

We are dealing with two devils who both want to rule hell.
-Ruta Sepetys, Lithuanian-American author

After graduating from medical studies in 1941, I was appointed to work in the obstetrics department of the central hospital in Joniskis, a northern Lithuanian city. Just after I started working, the Second World War began. The Senior Doctor ordered all women recently confined with their newborn children to leave the hospital and go home. The hospital remained empty.

Soon the air-raid sirens started wailing and we heard bombs being dropped. The explosions grew louder as the bombardments kept coming ever closer to our hospital. The Russians came through our town, setting up a front line of defense that went right in front of the hospital. German planes dropped bombs on the Russian soldiers, and soon bombs were exploding right next to our hospital. The windows of the hospital rattled, as if they were about to fall apart. Our entire terrified staff rushed out of the hospital and fell into nearby ditches.

All day the bombs whistled in our ears, as if the next second they might fall right on top of us. But the bombs fell behind our hospital and us. At dusk, the airplane flights and the bombing stopped, and we all went back to the hospital. We were happy that none of our staff were injured. The Russians retreated, cutting the power lines, so when we returned to the hospital, there was no electricity.

Soon, the Russians transported their wounded soldiers to the hospital. In the dark, without electricity, we bandaged their wounds by candlelight. Within days, the hospital was full of wounded, moaning, bleeding, and dying soldiers, some with so many wounds we couldn't stop them from bleeding to death.

The most seriously injured Russian soldiers were taken to hospitals in Riga or other bigger towns in Latvia. We worked at full speed day and night. We slept in the same wards as the wounded soldiers, swapping places with the entire hospital staff when we reached exhaustion. Sometimes I was so tired that I laid down next to a dead soldier in bed. I was too tired to fear or be concerned about being so close to death, I just gave in to sleep.

On June 22, 1941, the German army entered Lithuania, pushing out the Russian army in six days. They arrived in our city on June 23. All the hospital staff stopped at the window, stunned at what we saw. Soldiers in clean green uniforms and shiny boots marched straight to the hospital. These were German soldiers, who entered, disarmed the wounded Russian soldiers, and took them to other hospitals as prisoners of war.

It was a beautiful summer sunny day. Red and white peonies were blooming. We went outside and picked these peonies, placed them in vases in all the wards and hospital rooms. We welcomed the new occupying army with flowers. We thought that this army had at least come from a civilized nation, even though it was a foreign one. The Germans were very polite, they served us chocolate and put all kinds of canned food on the table. They fixed the electricity where the Russian army cut the power lines while retreating. Life went back to its almost normal course again.

Women came back to the hospital to give birth.

We continued to do our work.

Following the Order of the Chief Doctor, I was sent to the outpatient clinic to vaccinate patients against typhoid fever. At that time, massive numbers of people began to suffer from this contagious disease.

While vaccinating these patients, I met a young man, Lucas, a student at the military aviation school, who came here to be vaccinated. We were attracted to each other, and I hoped we would meet again.

This hospital had a person working as a housekeeper. He and his two daughters lived across the street from the hospital. One evening he invited me to his house. I was surprised to find he had many guests, including Lucas and his cousin Contessa. It turned out that the householder was friends with these young people, and they met often. This time I had the opportunity to get to know Lucas better. While sitting at the table with guests, he spoke very clearly, with restraint, sometimes inserting a hint of humor. He impressed me not only with his calm, commanding speech but also with his intelligence and beauty. He had dark slightly curly short hair, and blue eyes. It was a beautiful evening of friendship. After a few more encounters, Lucas took me to his parents' house and introduced me to them.

While staying at their house, I was very shy, I did not know how to speak and act. Despite this, they both welcomed me very warmly. After this meeting, I was often invited to visit their home. They liked me and I enjoyed their friendliness. Every time we visited them, our conversations became longer and more interesting. My friendship with Lucas went on for one year.

One day, I was invited to come to their house. When I arrived, his parents insisted we sit on a bench outside in the garden. Soon the roar of a plane was heard. Then Gertrud said her son was coming and he would do the Death Loop in his plane. I was astonished! We watched with great excitement, cheering when he dove so close to the ground. I already admired him, and now I was impressed with his courage.

Once he returned from having parked his airplane, he described the sensations of making this aeronautical feat. This is how he described it.

"My classmate and I boarded the Anbo-5 plane and double-checked that our seatbelts were secure. We climbed to an altitude of 1500 meters and headed towards my parents' home. I was a squadron commander and had already completed high flight training. Even though I'd flown over 300 flights, I'd never done this procedure before, so cold ants ran up my back. I discussed with my classmate how to get out of the spin if things went wrong. I was determined to show my parents and you, Greta, that I was a good pilot and could make a Death Loop.

"Flying was chasing birds in boundless space, wanting to surpass them and show them that a human can do even more. When I started the dive, it felt like time stopped and it would not start up again until I turned up again in the high heel. When the plane completed the downward arc and started up again, I knew I'd been successful, and I was very proud.

"To do such a stunt requires a pilot to be very well trained with high flight training. To do a Death Loop requires confidence, to be cold-blooded, to look at it as entertainment."

Indeed, looking at the flight at that time, it seemed to us that there were not humans on the heights but real superhumans, fearless, with boundless courage in space, like Gods with wings.

A few of Lucas' friends decided to copy his feat. Some were successful, but occasionally the plane fell to the ground at full speed and the pilot was killed. Even after those deaths, and his mourning his lost friends, Lucas still had a great desire to fly.

After one year of our friendship, Lucas proposed to me in 1942. We got married during the years of German occupation. Our wedding was very modest at Lucas' house with his parents and relatives living nearby. After our wedding, we rented a one room apartment with a kitchen on the second floor in the city near the hospital. The owners of this house lived on the first floor. Lucas brought a bed and a wardrobe from his parent's house.

After the occupation of Lithuania by the Germans, our life became normal, just like living in previously unoccupied Lithuania. I worked in a hospital; Lucas' parents managed their farm.

At first, we believed that they would let the Provisional Government, which was enthusiastically supported, manage the internal affairs of Lithuanian life. But when it was driven out in August, it became clear that the Germans were not liberators. One occupier was replaced by another, just as cruel and destructive.

Gertrud heard that the Germans were looking for and wanted to take horses from the inhabitants. She got scared. She wanted to save all three of her horses. She took them to the storage room of the house and closed its door. One-night, German soldiers came and knocked on the door. Greta went to the door but did not open it.

The Germans asked, "Do you have horses?"

Gertrud said, "No, we do not have them, we do not keep them."

She was so afraid that the horses would make noises. However, they stayed quiet all night as if they knew that they were in danger. Having decided that the Germans would not come again, Gertrud took the horses back to the barn. No other Germans ever came to look for horses.

Chapter Five: Early Years of German Occupation

The rules of fair play do not apply in love and war.
-John Lyly, English writer

After the occupation of Lithuania by the Germans, our life became normal, just like living in previously unoccupied Lithuania. I worked in a hospital and Lucas' parents managed their farm. On the weekends, Lucas and I visited his parents and helped with various farm chores. Lucas' mother gave us eggs, meat, and other goodies before we left.

One beautiful summer morning, I was sitting in my father-in-law's yard when German soldiers entered. They got out of the cars, very polite, wearing green pressed uniforms, and proud. Gertrud spoke fluent German with them and told us they wanted water to wash themselves. She brought out dishes for washing, drew water from the well, and set everything up on a bench outside. The officers took out scented soap, washed, and perfumed with eau-de-cologne. They had a radio and turned music on and danced. Afterward, they gave us pieces of dark chocolate. After an hour, they drove off in their car and we never saw them again.

Mateo died in the winter of 1942. He'd been foraging in the forest, and came home complaining of chest pain, dying suddenly. Gertrud grieved but decided to stay and keep the farm going without him. She was a strong soul, imperious, proud, undaunted, and unbroken. The two farmhands left to fight in the war, leaving only Anna to help. One day, Gertrud asked a German officer if he could find her two workers to help her with the summer work, and he assigned two Russian prisoners of war. They were pleased to have relief from the prisoner-of-war camps and worked the farm until the war ended.

In the winter of 1942, shortly after his father's funeral, Lucas fell asleep on the cold kitchen floor, damaging his kidneys. He became very ill and had to convalesce in the Riga hospital for several months. One weekend, I took the train to visit him. When it was time to go home, I found that the train was so packed with German soldiers, no one else could squeeze in. Even the roof was full of people. The only place I could fit was standing on the train's frozen steps. As the train accelerated, I had to brace myself against its railing. Not only was it a freezing temperature, but a bitter winter wind was also blowing. My hands were numb, and I was afraid I'd lose my grip and tumble to the ground. Somehow, I managed to hold on until we reached my home station. There, I jumped off and raced home to warm up by the fire in the hearth.

When Lucas recovered and returned from the hospital, he realized he couldn't fly any longer. His flying comrades were quite sad to lose such a squadron commander, but all he could do was stay on the ground and watch them fly. His desire to be a pilot again remained with him throughout his life.

Gertrud was pleased when she found out that he wouldn't fly any longer.

"Son, I have seen many of your friends die when their planes crashed. It is sad that you can no longer fly, but perhaps it's a good thing that you're safe on the ground. In time you will come to terms with it. Meanwhile, think about the future. Remember, I always wanted to see you as a priest."

He snorted. "Mother, that was your dream, never mine. My dream has always been to carve the sky like a bird. Maybe someday I'll get to do that again. Meanwhile, you're right, I do have to look to the future. I suppose I could study to be an engineer."

Having made that decision, he settled down and after many years of study, he passed his exams and afterward worked an as engineer for many years.

Chapter Six: Germans Capture Young Men

In 1943, the Germans began to capture young men and send them to forced labor in Germany. They were even taking them from churches. One Sunday morning a German military vehicle parked near the hospital where I worked. Lucas had come to visit me, and I pointed out the German vehicle. He jumped out a window and hid in a narrow gap between two houses while the Germans browsed the houses and the hospital grounds in search of young men. They left without finding anybody.

When the Germans came for the second time, I hid Lucas in the hospital. I told him to undress and put on a patient's clothes. I told him to lie in bed like a sick patient. I saved him.

Chapter Seven: In 1944 the Russians Reoccupied Lithuania

From Stetting in the Baltic to Trieste in the Adriatic, an iron curtain has descended across the Continent.
       -Winston Churchill, Prime Minister of the United Kingdom

We lived better for four years until the Russians arrived the second time. The Second Front happened when the Germans retreated and the Russians advanced back into Lithuania.

I was working in the hospital when the Russians came. When a Russian soldier came to the hospital, he found two dead Russian soldiers lying outside the hospital building.

He asked us, "Why are they lying outside and not in the hospital?"

We told him that we hadn't seen them lying there.

"If you do not take them to the hospital," he replied, "we will shoot you all immediately." Then he left.

As soon as he was gone, all four of us employees working at the hospital ran to the housekeeper who lived and worked across the street from the hospital and hid in his basement. In the morning when we returned to the hospital, we saw that the two Russian corpses were no longer there.

This time, the Russian military staff set up their headquarters with Johannes, Gertrud's brother. Next to their house, in the former school premises, the Russians set up a hospital to treat their soldiers.

One morning, Gertrud went to the barn and discovered that Russian soldiers and stolen all three horses. Gertrud told me it would be difficult to do the farm work without them. After a month, she managed to buy a small white horse. However, in a few months the Russians nationalized Gertrud's farm and took away the cultivated land and livestock. All they left her was the house and the barn with the single white horse.

The Russians established collective farms and other state institutions where they employed people in responsible positions who had never had such positions and were incapable of doing the work. Many of them hadn't even graduated from high school. The Russian motto at that time was, "Who was nothing, they will have everything."

Homeless

I gave mine fire-
You have pouring out the bitterness of words
Like an altar of priestess
Crusader with blood
To flood.
And again there is no home
In the Eternity
Just a dusty frontline soldier
Knocks on the narrow shutters
Where the Mother lies
Already dead.

Chapter Eight: The Soviets Take Control

Demons live in many lands, but particularly in Prussia.
 -Martin Luther, German priest

(Greta's story)

In 1944, the Soviets invaded East Prussia, and set about destroying all the Prussian cities. Famine raged and the people ate whatever they could scavenge. Many died, and others were deported. Many of the orphaned German children migrated to Lithuania villages in search of food and shelter. About 5,000 German children came to Lithuania on the roofs of freight wagons, on foot, in carriages, or in boats. They were wrapped in rags, cold and hungry.

It was a beautiful sunny spring day when a child with one shoe and rags on the other foot showed up at my house. Very pale, covered with tattered rags, though he spoke in German which I didn't understand, his frightened eyes told me everything I needed to know. He held out his little hand, blue with cold.

I brought him inside, sat him down, and fed him barley and hot tea. After providing him with a bowl of water to wash his feet, I gave him a pair of my socks to wear. He was as small as a four-year-old but was actually seven. I knew I couldn't keep him with me, for if the Russian authorities found out I was harboring a German boy, they would exile me to Siberia.

I decided to take him to Gertrud's farm. After he'd warmed, I dressed him in my coat, tightened it around him with a belt, and rode him on the bicycle bar. When we arrived, Gertrud brought him into the room, had him take off his clothes, and put him into a bath. We cut his hair short and washed away the lice.

Gertrud spoke to him in German and found out his name was Otto. We dressed him in Lucas' clothes, so big he looked like a scarecrow set up in the fields to scare away sparrows. Gertrud cooked potatoes with chicken. Otto ate and, for the first time, smiled. Just a little. After he ate, Gertrud put him to bed, telling him he'd be safe. She patted his head and in minutes he was sound asleep.

At that time, the Soviets went to all the houses and looked for German children, and after collecting them, they took them away. Gertrud provided Otto with Lithuanian documents and gave him a Lithuanian surname. It was not difficult to get documents at that time. Russian soldiers came to the homestead one morning. They knocked at the door and when they entered the house, they saw a little boy and asked whose child this was and where he came from. Gertrud showed them the child's documents and took Otto to another room and closed the door. After checking his documents, they left. When the Russians left, the boy left the room, hugged Gertrud, and started crying. She pulled him close to her and comforted him by stroking his head gently.

When autumn came, Otto attended school and learned to speak Lithuanian. For many years, he stayed, helping with the farm and housework. He called Gertrud "my mother". No one asked him how he became a legal citizen of Lithuania. When he turned eighteen, he decided to go to Karelia, Russia, which is of west by Finland, to earn money. Gertrud did not want to let him go, saying how she would be alone without him.

"Mother, I am an adult and I want to earn money and to experience the taste of life abroad."

They said goodbye and Otto left. In Russia, he fell ill with rheumatism. Once he recovered, he returned to the farm and lived there happily for many years.

When he turned thirty, he decided to try to track down his sister who he'd left behind in Germany. Through the Red Cross, he found her living in West Germany. She invited him to come back to Germany and live with her, but he didn't want to.

"What kind of German am I? I don't even remember how to speak the language. I'd feel inferior. I am now Lithuanian and will stay with my second mother who raised me. I won't leave her alone."

Over time, he married a woman who already had a son from her first marriage and moved to a neighboring town. Whenever he visited Gertrud, she'd say, "Otto, I will always wait for you in my house. Please visit me whenever you can."

"Yes, indeed. Mother, I love you. I will always visit you."

Chapter Nine: Life under the Soviets

Courage is rightly esteemed as the first of human qualities because it has been said, it is the quality which guarantees all others.

-Winston Churchill, Politician of the United Kingdom

When the Soviets took control in 1944, a very restless and uncertain life began. Under orders from the Russians, village elders and members of the Communist Party drew up lists of citizens for deportation to Siberia. Neighbors turned on each other, often fingering their superiors in order to better their positions and not be deported to Siberia themselves. In this way, the best people were deported, leaders, intellectuals, and the wealthy.

Then, in 1945, mass deportations began.

Lucas and I had moved to a bigger apartment, one with two rooms and a kitchen and closer to the hospital. The landlord worked in the Security Service (KBG). His mother, a good woman, lived with him and found out from him when the deportations to Siberia would take place. The night before, she came to our apartment and told us we must hide. We decided to separate to increase the chances that at least one of wouldn't be captured. I went to stay with relatives and Lucas hid in a haystack. Somehow, we both miraculously managed to avoid exile in Siberia that year.

One day, when I was working at the hospital, a Russian soldier came and ordered me to go with him. He said there was a woman who was about to give birth at the railway station who needed medical help. Very fearful, I grabbed my medical bag and followed him. At the station, a group of Russian soldiers standing with rifles saw me coming in a white coat and one told me which wagon had the woman needing help.

When I got into the wagon, I saw many people, some sat quietly, some cried, and others sang. A woman with an already born child lied between them. After examining her medically, I finished the birth process and left the wagon to return to the hospital with sad thoughts.

Very often, a young member of KGB came to visit Contessa, Gertrud's brother's daughter. One morning, he asked her to marry him, but she refused. He was short, ugly, and rude. That evening he returned to their house. He told the family that all of them and their relatives were included in the Siberian deportation lists. Then he turned to Contessa and told her that if she wanted to save her family and relatives from being deported to Siberia, she should marry him.

"I will be back in two days."

After talking to her parents with tears of pain and heartache, she agreed to marry him, hoping that when the war ended, she would divorce him.

This is how Johannes' and Gertrud's family avoided exile to Siberia. The beautiful dreams of the girl were swept away by the storms of war.

In the second year of the Russian occupation, my son Simon was born, and five years later my daughter Christina.

After the war, I was awarded the Lithuanian/Russian medal as a first-class obstetrician-gynecologist, described as clever, disciplined, conscientious and well-versed in the work of my specialty.

Chapter Ten: My Visit Years Later

*There was a place in childhood that I remember well, and
there a voice of sweetest tone bright fairy tales did tell.*
-Samuel Lover, Irish novelist song writer, composer

Happy times come and go, but the best childhood memories
stay in the mind forever.

Many years later, I had an opportunity to visit my
grandparents' homestead, bringing back many childhood memories.
Coming up to the driveway, I could see that the linden alley, the
orchard of cherry trees, the flower garden, and the huge barn where
the horses had been kept were all preserved.

After the war, a chairman of the village had bought the
farmhouse and settled there with his family. When he answered my
knock, I told him that this house used to belong to my grandparents,
and he invited me in. His family welcomed me warmly and toured
me around. Some of it was the same, but there'd been a lot of
remodeling.

Yet even with all the changes, the house elicited a flood of
fond memories from my childhood. I recalled the love and tolerance
Gertrud and Mateo effused. I carry these endlessly warm memories
with great love to this day, remembering the love given me by my
dear grandparents.

After visiting my grandparents' house, I visited the farm
where Gertrud's brother lived. Now it held his son, Olivier, with
wife and two teenage boys. All the furniture had changed, including
the heirloom grandfather clock. We talked about Johannes and
Gabija and the delicious eggs and cucumbers she served.

Where else could you find more beautiful and sweeter
childhood memories than this?

Chapter Eleven: Post-War Years, Christina's Childhood Place

And once the storm is over, you won't remember how you made it through, how you managed to survive...
-Haruki Murakami, Japanese writer

Having survived all the horrors of the war, and to forget them, my parents decided to move to a northern Lithuanian city. This city was famous for its gypsum deposits. Before the war, tall, beautiful white gypsum deposits stood here, a lovely attraction for tourists. When the Russians entered, they blew them up and took them away.

Underwater rivers sometimes wash away the buried gypsum deposits, creating huge sinkholes. I remember one story that went this way. One night a farmer heard a loud noise coming from his pasture. The next morning, he found that a huge sinkhole had swallowed half his pasture, and his cow along with it. He named the pit Cow Hole and afterward tourists would come to look at it.

This town has a long history. In the late sixteenth century, Duke Cristup Radziwill built a Renaissance bastion castle here. At the time, it was the largest and strongest Italian-style bastion castle in the world However, within fifty years it was destroyed by the Swedes. Between 1978-1986 the city rebuilt the castle, and now it serves as a library and museum. Near the palace of Duke Radziwill, a huge park was called the Mound. Not far from the Mound, you could see the country's oldest artificial lake, formed by damming two rivers. The old town was built between these two rivers.

The city was very nicely maintained with flowers in the parks, clean streets, and nice city dwellers. A long wooden pedestrian bridge crossed the lake, leading to the palace of Count Tishkevich. At the central facade of the palace stood two huge cement lion sculptures. The original ones, cast from metal, were moved to the Duke Vytautas Great War Museum in Kaunas, the second largest city in Lithuania.

In the middle of the city were Catholic and Evangelical Reformed churches whose bells rang every morning, on holidays, and during church services. On Sundays, merchants came with cars or horse-drawn carriages to sell at the marketplace, both at the food pavilion and outside booths. Everything was for sale, such as household items, food, flowers, and livestock. Afterward, people gathered at nearby restaurants.

After we moved there, Greta, my mother, took employment in the city's central hospital. Lucas worked as a senior road engineer on the executive committee. They rented an apartment in a private house and hired a nanny to cook meals, clean, and look after my brother and me. After a year or so, my mother joined the national dance group and danced at district and republican song festivals.

My brother and I spent our childhood and teenage years in this city. We were close to each other as children. Before going to sleep, we told each other various fairy tales and chatted. Our parents raised us strictly, punishing us if we did something stupid. I was a quiet girl who almost never cried. During childhood, I was very sensitive, but at the same time stubborn.

Once we were old enough to attend school, our parents rented another place with more rooms for us in the city center. The yard of our new house was fenced with a large yard for us to play in.

Although Simon was quite mischievous in primary school, the teachers praised him for his good grades and his very beautiful handwriting. At the age of nine, Simon started music school, studying accordion and piano. A piano was too expensive, so our parents bought an accordion, specifically a 120 bass Italian Manfrini.

After five years, he graduated from the accordion class and after another two years from the piano class, with very good grades in all his lessons. The teachers told our parents that he was an extremely gifted music student.

When I was four years old, my parents bought me a bicycle. Since I had never been on one before, I didn't know how to ride one. Several tries of sitting on it and moving the pedals ended up with me falling over.

My mother said, "I will hold you at the back of the bike until you start riding. You just start pedaling and look ahead."

I figured I needed to try, or I'd never learn to ride it. Mother supported me behind the bike, and I started pedaling. After a few meters, she let go. Right away I fell, and the handlebars of the bike hit me in the forehead, producing a big gash just above my eye. Even though it was painful, I didn't cry. Mother bandaged the wound, and the next day that eye was swollen, and bruises appeared under both eyes.

There was no running water in the house. Instead, in the backyard was a water well with a roller and chain connected to a bucket. It worked as one would expect, one would lower the empty bucket into the well and bring it up full of water. It was a job that required a lot of strength. This well provided water for four families.

One day, I was five and Simon about ten, he said to a group of our friends, "If you want, I will show you how to pull out a bucket of water. You will see how I can do it, but you are all too weak to do it." Because he was only as tall as the well's handle, the children didn't think he could do it.

"What a braggart," called one of the boys. "You're too small and weak."

Simon puffed out his chest. "Let's bet a box of sweets that I can do it." They sealed the bet with cross hands.

Simon approached the well and lowered the bucket into the water. Once it was full, he struggled to pull it back up. Halfway up the well, he couldn't support the heavy weight any longer and let go.

The bucket plummeted back down, causing the handle to swing rapidly, and smashing into the back of his head. Blood poured over his head and hair.

When I saw my brother's head covered in blood, instead of calling our nanny, I ran to the hospital near our house shouting, "Momma, momma, Simon has cut his head, he's bleeding. Please, mommy. Save my brother."

I screamed many times until someone heard. One of the nurses recognized me and called my mother.

"Look, Greta, your daughter is calling for you."

Mother came rushing out and asked me, "Christina, what happened?"

I told her, and she put me in the ambulance with her, and the driver drove us to the scene. Mother gave Simon first aid and took him to the hospital. There, the doctor shaved off part of his hair around the injured area and stitched it up. The wound was bandaged, and he was taken home.

I asked him, "Do you have a lot of pain?"

"Not really, only I feel ashamed that I bragged in front of my friends and now look foolish."

"Don't worry, the pain will pass, and the wound will heal. Your friends will forget the bragging, and they'll feel sorry for you."

After the wound healed, the scar remained for the rest of his life.

At age six, I attended the first grade of primary school. The teacher, an elderly intelligent woman, sat me next to Alma, a girl I didn't know. At the time, I was modest and shy. That lunchtime, as I sat with Alma in the school canteen, a photographer came to our table.

"Girls," he said, "I want to take a picture of you."

We glanced at each other, nodded in agreement, and smiled at him.

The photographer said we would be featured in the local city newspaper, and he left. At the end of the week, my parents showed me the newspaper with Alma and me at school, titled "First graders". My parents were pleased and cut out the newspaper article and saved it.

At school, Alma and I sat together on the same bench for the entire primary and secondary school years. Sometimes in class, we wrote letters to each other or to other classmates.

Alma's parents were teachers at our school, her father taught Russian and her mother needlework. Girls were taught to knit, sew, embroider, and weave with looms. Our teacher was very bright and conducted classes in an entertaining way, involving us in educational games. She loved me, calling me a doll and placing me on her lap when reading interesting fairy tales to the whole class.

I was very happy to have this teacher and often talked to our parents about the classroom tasks. I always wanted to be a very good student and get good grades. My friend Alma was also a good student, studying hard and achieving good scores.

Once the teacher assigned homework to draw a landscape. I drew mine with happiness in my heart, the resulting drawing seemed perfect to me. When it was done, I showed it to Alma.

She showed me the drawing she made and said, "Maybe we could exchange? You take mine and I will take yours, it will be more interesting that way." Since we were friends, I agreed, and we exchanged drawings.

To my surprise, the teacher graded the drawing I gave Alma a grade 5 out of 5, and the drawing Alma gave me a grade 3. I was somewhat upset. I knew that I had agreed to the exchange, but I felt I'd been tricked and decided I'd learned a lesson not to do such a thing again. Despite this, our friendship continued.

Simon also did well at school. His teacher was impressed with his grades and his beautiful calligraphic handwriting as well as his discipline. When he returned home after school, he immediately prepared his lessons. After finishing his homework, he would play in the yard with his friends kicking the ball or throwing it in the basket. He was very fond of sports, being both agile and restless.

We had three outdoor toilets built in the back of the yard with a door and a hole in the floor. One day, while playing with our friends, Simon runs to the toilet. I noticed he didn't close the door all the way, so I ran up to push it shut. I didn't realize he had his fingers in the way. He screamed in pain.

We both ran to the hospital, where our mother took him to the radiologist who scanned his fingers. They were not broken, just compressed. The doctor wrapped them up, prescribed painkillers and we returned home.

I apologized to him, "Don't be angry with me. I didn't mean to hurt you, just to close the door."

He said, "I'm not angry, and, after all, I did not break my fingers."

My parents scolded me.

Chapter Twelve: Making Music

Music is the divine way to tell beautiful, poetic things to the heart.
-Pablo Casals, Spanish cellist

At the age of 9, Alma and I attended an accordion class at a children's music school. Piano lessons, solfeggio, music literature, and conducting, were all taught during the class. I didn't really like it. My brother and I had to share the same accordion, an Italian Manfrini with 120 basses. It was so heavy I could barely hold it and struggled dragging it to school. After studying for five years, I learned to play it well, but I never did develop a love for it.

My accordion teacher was strict. When I didn't perform well, he leaned across the table, striking my hand with his pencil. He would say, "And again, Christina, you haven't learned your lesson? Next time you come to class, bring your father."

In contrast, I loved the piano. The teacher was a nice man, who never showed displeasure. However, he usually gave me bad grades, saying, "Cristina, if I give you a good grade, you will think that you play very well and next time you will come without learning the lesson."

At the end of the semester, my grade book always showed fives except for the 3 in the music classes.

Every December, we prepared music pieces to perform at a holiday concert. Both Alma's and my parents came to every concert, and from those meetings became friends. For many years, they'd visit each other and celebrate holidays together.

One July, I participated in the song festival in Vilnius, the capital of Lithuania, playing the accordion. To prepare, I had two exhausting rehearsals every day, and my hands hurt both from the strutting and carrying the heavy accordion. In addition to the rehearsals, I had to practice for several hours each day. Despite all this, the festival itself was extremely impressive. It remains in my memory as a wonderfully created unified work of dancers and musicians. We returned home happy and with the desire to travel and perform again. Sometimes the cultural houses of some collective farms invited us to perform for the people of the villages that gathered.

After graduating from music school, I gave up playing the accordion. I wanted to continue playing the piano, but I didn't have one at home and therefore I gave up playing piano, too. I rather wanted to climb trees, fight with boys, and play sports. After many years, I tried to play the piano again, but I found I no longer had the skill.

In school I always enjoyed physical education. The most interesting exercise for me was the goat, a demanding exercise requiring balance and strong hands to lean on the goat while jumping up and over it, somersaulting back and forth, and landing nicely on the mattress behind it. After school, I attended athletics, where I'd practice high jump, long jump, basketball, disc throwing, and relay.

After my classmate Bella graduated from the accordion class, she went to study music at music college. Later, she returned to the city of her childhood, where she got a job as a music teacher in a kindergarten, and taught music in a high school. She directed the children's choir in this school.

Chapter Thirteen: House Under Construction

Home should be an anchor, a port in a storm, a refuge, a happy place in which to dwell, a place where we are loved and where we can love.
   -Marvin J. Ashton, Utah State Senator

When I started primary school, my parents decided they wanted to build a house. Even though they were professionals, their salaries were too low, so they decided to ask my mother's sister for a loan. Aunt Sophilia's family lived in a nearby village seven kilometers away and gladly lent them money.

After looking at several plots, they chose one located at the intersection of two streets near the marketplace in the center of town. Over the next year, they built a lovely two-story brick house, and finally my brother and I had our own rooms.

Now that they had a bigger house to keep up, as well as a need to repay the loan. To cut down on expenses, they bought a goat and named it Ciba. Ciba's milk was safe to drink, although I remember it had an unusual taste and smell. Everyone loved drinking this milk.

My parents had a wooden rowing boat moored at a river's dock near their home. One day my mother and I led the goat onto the boat and rowed out to Love Island in the middle of the lake. Once docked, we tied the goat to a tree and watched him delightfully eating the tree leaves. We bathed in the lake and then sunbathed on a blanket. After a bit, I decided to explore the island, but I'd hardly gone a few yards when I stepped on a large shard of broken glass. I yanked it out, and the wound began bleeding profusely.

When my mother saw me limping, she asked, "What happened? Why are you limping?"

When I showed her my bloody foot, she wrapped it tight and helped me get into the boat. Ciba was not ready to go, and Mother had to coax and smack her several times to get her into the boat.

On the trip home, Ciba made it clear she was angry. She stomped her hoof and glared at me. I talked gently to her the whole trip home. I knew that if I turned my back on her, she'd use her horns to bump me from behind. I never turned away.

After returning home, my mother removed the bandage, washed the wound, applied disinfectant liquid, and gave it a proper bandage. In a week it was healed.

Chapter Fourteen: Family, Neighbors and Fun

I'm having fun. I'm being myself. I'm doing what I love. That's all that matters. -James Charles
If you're having fun, then you are winning.

St. John's Day, June 24th, was a very popular holiday. Neighbors and friends hung wreaths woven from oak branches on house doors of those named John or Joanna. In the evening, everyone partied with songs, dances, and homemade beer. Bonfires lit up the shore.

My childhood was spent near a beautiful lake, the only artificial lake in Lithuania. On St. John's Day, we would decorate our boat and sail to the middle of the lake where we flung out small wreaths into the water. All around us, other decorated boats celebrated with songs and threw wreaths. There was a tradition that if two lovers each threw a wreath, and those touched, their love would flourish. People would search for a certain fern flower. Finding it guaranteed a year of happiness.

During the winter, my parents with friends and neighbors would go ice skating. My parents, Simon, and I would hold hands and skate down the river to the lake, its ice clear and smooth. Afterward, friends gathered at my parents' house to play checkers or cards. We ate fried pancakes and laughed until late in the night. Although everyone enjoyed the homemade beer, I never saw a drunk guest.

I remember learning to skate as a child. Time after time I would fall over, taking bruises, smiling, standing, and trying again. It didn't take long for me to have excellent balance and I enjoyed this skill for the rest of my life.

Besides St. John's Day, the citizens celebrated name days with neighbors and friends. They hung braided wreaths on the doors of the people whose name was being celebrated. Sometimes they'd bring flowers to the person celebrating his or her name-day and congratulate them, having food, music, and dance.

When a name was chosen, it was meant to describe the most prominent features of a person. People believed that names could determine what kind of life a person would have, how his fate would develop, and even his position in society. Names acquired even more significance when Christianity and Islam took hold in the world. Each person tried to give his offspring holy names and thus bless his life.

Chapter Fifteen: Life in Lithuania under the Soviets

During the Soviet occupation, the shops were practically empty. There were clothes hanging in them, but those had no style. They looked like you could put them on and go straight to the fields to weed potatoes or cut hay. Sometimes the shopkeepers would obtain items from outside Soviet control, but they'd keep them hidden. I would ask my mother to go to the store and give a bribe if there were famous products there. She hated humiliating herself that way, but sometimes after going and "anointing" the seller, she bought me some beautiful foreign clothes.

After finishing high school, my classmate Zia did not go anywhere to study. Instead, she took a job as a saleswoman in a clothing store. When I visited my parent's house during my college breaks, I went to this store.

"Hello," I said to her, and asked, "Maybe you have something more interesting, more beautiful?"

"No, sorry. All I have is what is visible."

Her attitude changed when I gave her a big box of sweets and a bottle of cognac. Suddenly red pants with flared ends made in Finland appeared. I paid for them, thanked her, and left.

We never had enough meat, either. My mother and I would go to the meat store together and get on the very long queue, taking turns every hour standing in line. People clung to each other like sardines in a can, and soon became impatient, pushing each other. When we finally arrived at the front of the line, we'd often find that only cattle hooves and bones were left. We'd frequently return home without any meat at all.

Unable to live on their wages, my parents sold the goat and bought a cow that they named Princess. Princess fed us delicious milk and helped us financially by giving us enough extra milk to sell.

At first, I was afraid of the cow because she was as big as a lion. The first time I tried to milk Princes, she scowled at me and kicked the bucket, giving it a big dent. I tried again, and just as I started to get some milk into the bucket, she kicked it again, spilling all the milk. I kept trying, and on the third try she relaxed. The warm milk filled the bucket. I soon was successful at milking, and afterward I took the bucket into the house where we would all scoop in a cup and drink the delicious vitamin-filled healthy milk.

The ancient Greeks believed that honey mixed with milk, called ambrosia, prolonged life. They attributed this drink to their eternal youth and immortality.

The cow stayed in the barn in the winter, and in the pasture during the summer. Our pasture was two miles from the house, so I'd bike there to milk the cow. When I turned 13, my parents bought me a motor bike, making the trip to the pasture much easier. During the rides, I enjoyed the wind rushing through my hair. No one else at my age had ever ridden a motor bike. Sometimes I would take it across town without informing my parents. My friends were amazed when I rode by and shouted greetings.

One evening, I rode out to the pasture intending to bring Princess home for the night. As usual, I pulled out the stake, took the cow by the chain, and told it we were going home. Instead of her usual compliance, she looked at me with an angry expression, and ran off towards the other cattle, mooing loudly.

When she reached the other cows grazing in the field, she lowered her head, and ran straight at another cow, hitting it squarely on its head. They stared at each other, and then Princess backed off and ran at her again. I grabbed the chain and tried to pull Princess away, but she just looked at me with angry eyes and made another run. One more time I tried to stop them to no avail. I saw that Princess had lost one of her horns and was bleeding.

I left the cow and rode back home to tell my parents what happened. They called the vet who picked us up in his car, bringing all of us to the pasture. We found Princess standing in the same place and mooing. No other cows were around. After examining her, the veterinarian fixed the wound on the horn. He explained that if a cow wants to butt, she's in heat, looking for a bull to mate with. He said she'd need to stay in the barn until her horn was healed.

During the summer, we made haystacks. The owner of the meadow we rented cut the grass and spread it out to dry. Mother invited some friends and neighbors to come help her rake. In the hot afternoon, we would take a break in the shade of the willow tree. We'd lie with the pleasant coolness of the air flowing through our sweat-shrunk shirts, listening to the buzzing of beetles. During the break, we drank cold milk and snacked on the food we brought. Sometimes my mother would give me a handful of raspberries. By the evening, we would have raked all the hay into piles.

The next day, a truck would arrive and load up the hay, bringing it to our barn. My neighbor and I would climb into the hayloft, take the hay handed up to us on pitchforks, and stack it inside. We'd then trample it and sprinkle it with salt so that it didn't get too hot.

One Sunday morning, I milked the cow and brought it home. Then, during lunch, my father took the car to the pasture intending to move Princess. However, on arrival, he couldn't find her anywhere.

Once he returned home, he told Greta, "Today's market day. Maybe someone stole it and plans to sell it at market."

My parents decided to drive to the market and look for our cow, however, they can't find her there either. They asked people who sell livestock if they'd seen a black-bellied cow for sale at the market that day.

One merchant said, "Yes, there was a cow like that. Someone bought it and took it home."

He described the person who sold it, and my parents then went to the police. The police wrote a report and said they would start searching for the cow.

My parents drove all over the city to the bars and restaurants and asked people if they had seen such a person and gave them his description. The last place was near the railway station. Father went there and found the cow seller. He was sitting in a pub by the bar and drinking beer. Leaving Greta in this pub, Lucas told the police that he had found the person who sold the cow. The police came and ordered him to give the money back that he received for the cow. The man emptied his pockets, placing a stack of money on the table and telling how much he sold the cow for.

The man admitted that he took the cow from the pasture and sold it. He said that while it was being led past my parents' house, the cow began mooing and didn't want to go any further, as if realizing that it was being led on an unknown path. The police put the thief in the car and told him to take them to the person to whom he sold the cow. He did, and the policemen saw the cow standing in the yard. They told the man that this cow you bought was stolen and you must return it to its rightful owners. He was very surprised. He received his money back and my parents took Princess home.

I was always willing to help my parents with house and farm work after school and in the summer and autumn. They rented a patch of land where they planted strawberries, potatoes, and sugar beets so that the cow would have this fodder for the winter. The cow ate hay, but also liked to gnaw beets. In the spring, my mother and I planted sugar beet seedlings. In the fall, when they were ripe, we had to pull them out. We rode our bikes to the beet field to pick them, setting up a tent because of the frequent cold rains. We collected beets from the black soil, cut the leaves from them, and piled them nicely: tubers next to tubers, leaves next to leaves. Some of the beets grew so large and so deep, we had to dig up the ground to get them out. The furrows were so long, they seemed to never end.

Chapter Sixteen: High School

The fall after I finished eighth grade, a new high school opened at the southern end of the city. Students who studied in the central school had the option to move to the newly built school. I found out that most of my friends chose to go to the new school, including Alma. I asked my parents if I could, too, and they let me.

The distance between my home and the new school was about 3 km. Alma lived very close to this new school, it only took her 5 minutes to walk there, but it was a half an hour walk for me. In the new school, Alma and I sat together.

In high school, I liked sports, arts, and music. In athletics, I played basketball, volleyball, and disc throwing, and participated in all the competitions. During the regional sports competition, I took first place in the disc throw. During one training session, right after I threw the disc, Alma walked onto the field, right in the way of the flying disc. I shouted to her to watch out, but the disc hit her, and she fell down. I ran to check on her and on examination, we found that her injury consisted of only a bruised hand.

During high school, I thought about what I wanted to do with my life. I considered attending a military school to become a military officer like my father. However, during the years of the Russian occupation, there was no Lithuanian Military Academy, so I had to discard this plan.

My second plan was to become a model and a designer. Fashion is art, art is love, love is peace, peace embraces the whole world. I was tall and beautiful, and walked very straight, even leaning back a little, with my head held high. Nobody taught me that. Where did I get that walk from? Perhaps some woman, a passer-by I met, cast a spell on me, saying that I was a princess in India in my past life. Who knows the secrets of the universe?

When my classmates and people around me saw me walking with my head held high and leaning back, they said, "You look very proud and unattainable." It was just the way I walked, not knowing then that models walked like that. Growing up in the Soviet system, the only modeling school was in faraway Vilnius. I yearned to enroll there, but I lived far away and was still attending high school.

My third dream was to live abroad. I envied the people I saw in movies, their fullness of life, their freedom, and their abilities to travel abroad. This desire of mine became even stronger when I went on an excursion with my classmates to St. Petersburg. I saw many foreigners there, laughing and speaking in various languages. They seemed carefree. I wanted to go away with them. Yet, I had to return home to my everyday life, realizing it was impossible to leave. That desire flew away like an echo, lost in the mountains.

During high school, I joined a weaving club where we created materials for dresses and curtains. The work was tedious, requiring considerable patience. Alma's mother was our teacher, using a loom to teach us the skill. She was a master weaver who participated in many art exhibitions with her woven fabric patterns.

During the first summer vacation, Alma and I attended a summer camp near where we lived for two weeks. We slept in a tent by a lake, participating in team sports like basketball, soccer, running, and an obstacle course. There was a kitchen where we had to cook on assigned days. Every evening was filled with bonfires, dances, and concerts. I made a lot of friends, and even now fondly remember our camping days.

In tenth grade, I joined the school choir, the national dance group, and the girls' ensemble. This choir consisted of five of my classmates and me, including my friend Alma. We practiced our songs every day, preparing for the concert held at the end of the month. On that day, the hall was full of teachers and students. The six of us went on the stage. The stage curtain was raised. We had hardly begun to sing when Alma mixed up the words. We became silent for a couple of seconds. Standing next to Alma, I turned my head behind her and started laughing. The other girls also followed me with laughter as Alma continued to sing the song alone. The hall erupted in an uproar, with applause and laughter. Everyone chanted repeat, repeat.

We finished our performance, and as the curtain fell, Alma began weeping. The audience cheered, thinking it was supposed to be a humorous act. Although we were hesitant to face the public sitting in a school hall, all the teachers and students received us very warmly and shouted "Bravo, bravo."

After the concert, we pulled the chairs against the walls, preparing for a dance party. Once the music started, we waited for someone to ask us to dance, but our boy classmates just sat because they didn't know how to dance. The other girls from upper classes were dancing and we were jealous of them.

The next day we decided to teach the boys how to dance. We brought a record player and records into the classroom. After our classes ended and the teacher was gone, we locked the classroom door with the boys in it. When they realized the door was locked and they couldn't go home they got mad at us. We did not give in to them and told them that they had to stay until they learned how to dance. We taught them several dance steps. After the lesson, we were happy since after that we would have dance partners and not be wallflowers.

One day after a dance party, Alma's classmate walked her home. He asked, "Can I kiss you?"

She laughed, said, "Goodnight," and ran into her house. The next morning Alma told me what had happened.

"Last night, my friend wanted to kiss me. He asked, 'Can I kiss you?' I ran off, but really, I wanted him to grab me manfully and kiss me. I wanted to feel the kiss." She laughed.

Afterward, they became good friends. Eventually, they fell in love and became sweethearts.

Being tall and slim, I found a boy who was also tall and knew how to dance. He often invited me to dance and hugged me around the waist. We performed slow dances with our classmates. Although he liked me, he seemed boyish, arrogant, and spoiled. He was interesting to talk to and we had intriguing conversations. When he finished high school, he went off to study at the University and later became a professor there.

With our classmates, we celebrated birthdays as well as name's days. On these days we gathered to listen to music, dance, and gossip. We would party late into the night.

At one of the parties, my classmate David was present. He was a fast learner interested in philosophy. At this party, I became interested in him and asked my male classmate Cat to go with me up to David and start a conversation. The problem was that David had a girlfriend in a lower class.

Cat was very shy, cheerful, and always smiling. Cat didn't want me to be with David because Cat wanted me for himself. I didn't realize he was in love with me, I thought of him more as a brother. Sometimes we'd hug and even kiss, but I had no desire to enter into a more serious relationship with him. We always joked amicably when we were together.

He never showed any signs of love, he only knew it in his soul. It wasn't until many years later that I found out that he had a big crush on me. I told him, "Why you didn't tell me that you loved me? There is a saying that if you love, say it right away, because if you wait, it might be too late."

A more serious relationship with David never materialized. After graduating from school, David entered the university and graduated in psychology. After many years, he was elected mayor of the city where he lived. He became a well-known political figure who wrote several books.

One year, we had a New Year Carnival at school. We dressed in short blue skirts, white blouses, black glasses, blue military berets, and carried toy rifles. With these uniforms, we danced the twist. When the teachers saw us dancing, they forbade it, saying that these dances were not allowed in school. After they left, we danced the twist with the music at full blast. During this dance, it seemed that everything sparkled, and life seemed completely different.

Chapter Seventeen: First Love

A first love always occupies a special place.
-Lee Konitz, American composer

One Saturday night, our crowd decided to go to another school to dance. It was a high school boarding school where students from many towns and villages came to study. That evening, the performance was about school life. We were fascinated by their acting and the content of the show. Afterward, we stayed for the dance.

While we were sitting and looking for dance partners, the performer of the main role of the spectacle approached me and invited me to dance. He introduced himself as Arlo. I was touched by his attention. During our dance, I praised his acting and told him that I found the play impressive. He told me funny stories about his school. After the dance, he accompanied me to my friends. I thanked him for the dance.

Every time the music played, he came and invited me to dance. I really had a great time with him all evening. Later I found out that he was well known in this school. Besides the drama club, he played the trumpet and made great grades. He told me the teachers complained about him because he treated the strict rules of school as jokes. His mother was unable to deal with him as a teenager so sent him to this boarding school. He told me that he was neat and disciplined, made the bed up every morning, put away clothes neatly, and kept his room clean.

After the dance, Arlo offered to accompany me home. Our friendship began. When we met again, we discussed our plans. We had many chats and never ran out of things to talk about. We started dating often, spending time together whenever we could. We met every week at student dances. He invited me to go see movies in the cinema. While watching a movie, we sat hand in hand munching dark chocolate-covered hazelnuts while whispering words of love. It quickly turned into a serious love relationship.

When my parents met Arlo, they found him interesting and cheerful. He told anecdotes to them in an impressive way. My parents and I invited him to come with us to a resort. At the resort, Arlo was very talkative and attentive to my parents and most of all to me. The resort trip turned out to be perfect for all of us.

Arlo graduated from high school-boarding school with very good grades one year before me and went back to his hometown. He passed the entrance exams there and started studying engineering at the University. My senior year was lonely without Arlo, but we kept in touch with daily phone calls and love letters he wrote.

Chapter Eighteen: School Friends

Good friends, good books, and a sleepy conscience. This is the ideal life. -Mark Twain, American writer

One fall day, my senior class went on an excursion to a museum. My close classmate Emma went to the back of the bus and sat on the knees of my classmate David, whom I had an eye on before. She started kissing him. While they were kissing so sweetly, we arrived at the museum. Her behavior surprised me and my other classmates. Maybe we were all jealous. It reminded me of my meeting with David and Cat.

When we returned to class in the morning, we girls organized a court with the defendant present. In the court we condemned her. How dare you kiss in front of everyone? She looked at us and smiled.

"You know what," she said. "Nobody kisses you because you are absolutely not interesting."

Emma lived near me in a four-story Bella's parents' former house that was turned into apartments with the Russians' confiscation. Bella and her parents during Soviet occupation were exiled to Siberia. After the long and difficult time in Siberia, after the death of Stalin in 1953, the family survived and returned to Lithuania to the city where they lived before and rented an apartment. Bella's parents' house was in a good location next to the center of the city and marketplace.

The next day I visited Emma and found her eating lunch.

"Do you know what you're eating?" I asked.

"Of course, I know. It's borsch and a hamburger."

"No," I told her. "You're now eating frog soup and worm hamburgers."

She imagined that was what she was eating. "Christina, please don't talk like that. You've ruined my appetite. Go home."

She pushed me out the door and told me not to come again. Afterward, we continued to be friends. Sometimes when I visited her, I'd tease her again about the food she ate.

On the first floor of this house where my friend lived, just inside the front door, there was a cellar with a hinged lid where they stored potatoes and vegetables. There were stairs to climb down to the cellar. When the lid was closed, it was flush with the floor. One time, when I came to her house, the lid wasn't closed. When I took my first step into her house, I tumbled down to the bottom of the basement. Climbing back up, I saw bruises on my hands and body. Hearing the noise, my friend came into the room. She asked me what happened, and I told her I had fallen into her cellar. She said she was sorry.

Emma married after graduating from high school. She stayed in town, bought a house in the village, and became a famous textile artist. She sold her art in Lithuania and in the Scandinavian countries.

Mia, another classmate of mine, lived not far from my house by the central street. We often walked to school together. Every Saturday I would invite her to go to school dances.

She would always say, "I don't want to go."

One time I asked her why not, telling her we could dance together.

"I will be honest with you, Christina. I wear glasses and I don't want to go to the dance with them on. The boys will laugh at me."

"You see well without them," I insisted. "Put on your clothes, and let's go. After all, you only wear glasses for reading, yes? Just get ready and we'll go to the dance."

She did and we went dancing together.

After graduating from high school, Mia went to pharmacy college and worked in a pharmacy. A few years later, she successfully graduated from law school and worked for the President of Lithuania, holding a high position in the Judiciary branch. In time she was awarded a letter of honor for her work.

One fall day, the chairman of the collective farm asked for students to help with harvesting. Several of us climbed into a truck that had some benches. There wasn't enough room for everyone to have their own seat, so I sat down on Cat's lap. After a while, I felt a stone stabbing me in my ass. I asked him what kind of stones did you put in your pants? Everyone started laughing and Cat blushed.

When we arrived at the farm, the class was assigned a field to dig beets. After digging for a while, we relaxed on the haystacks, and then we chased each other, running around and laughing.

During the winter months, my classmates and I went to the ice-skating arena, located by the city center near the catholic church. Holding hands with boys, we skated in a circle listening to the music. Having mastered the skates well, we spent the evenings chasing each other, talking, and having a good time. After a rigorous evening of skating, once home I'd have a sip of Norwegian glogg, putting me in a good mood. I'd fall asleep with a smile on my face.

Alma had a brother one year younger than us. One time the three of us were skating on the frozen pond near their house. I'd just gotten out onto the middle of the pond when the ice broke, and I fell in. Fortunately, the water in the pond was not deep. They both stood on the shore and laughed at me.

"Do not laugh," I cried. "Hurry and pull me out of this cold water."

They helped me get out and brought me to their house where I changed clothes and had some warm tea.

One time during geometry class, I asked Alma to help me solve some of the problems. She promised she would help, but,

60

instead, once she solved her assignment, she gave her paper to the teacher and left the classroom. I was angry that Alma had deserted me, and I wound up getting a bad grade.

Everybody had to take a geometry exam in their last year of high school. I knew that if I didn't pass, I'd have to go to summer school and ruin my vacation. I asked Alma to be a good friend and help me to solve my geometry task. I told Alma that I'd sit by the window and drop a string outside. Once she solved it, she would tie the answer to the string and give it a tug, so I could pull up the answer. Thanks to her, I passed the geometry exam. I always remember this act with gratitude.

My senior year chemistry teacher was very rigorous about teaching chemistry yet did it with a sense of humor. He said once in front of the whole class that I would achieve all my desires and succeed in life. I studied hard and learned the chemistry formulas and their applications so well that I was able to teach my fellow students. Later, I passed the chemistry and biology exams without any problems when I went to study at the university.

After graduating from high school, most of my classmates were thinking about which schools to enroll in, and what exams they needed to pass to get in. At that time, to enroll in higher education, you needed to have a written recommendation from a teacher.

Because this was the Soviet era, the teacher had to be careful what she wrote about each student. In my case, she wrote that I was stubborn and always firmly defended my opinion. Some of my classmates received not very pleasant character references. Therefore, I was happy to get the reference that I received.

Before graduation, everyone had to write a composition about their desires. It needed to say what the person wanted to achieve, their dreams, an ideal life partner, and how many children they would like to have. We all put our compositions into a single bottle, sealed it, and buried it in Duke Radziwill's Park.

I wrote that I was happy and proud. These traits showed that I loved myself and others. I wrote that if one doesn't love oneself, one will never love others. Walking straight with my head held high gave me confidence.

At the same time, I was boyish, I climbed trees, and I ran around the meadows barefoot. When I needed to stand up for myself, I would fight with the boys at school. According to the zodiac, I was born under the constellation of Virgo. That meant I was simple and reserved inside. This is perhaps the most complex of all zodiac signs.

I pushed myself towards art, culture, creativity, and higher goals through logical deduction. I was curious but cautious. It took me a while to trust the people around me. I thought carefully before doing anything. Rarely did a spark of spontaneity flash. I expressed myself through art.

At the same time, I was very sensitive and easily vulnerable, but I didn't cry, keeping my experiences and wrongs to myself. I never showed my weak points to other people. Left alone, I poured out my accumulated emotions.

After the Graduation Ball, we went to meet the dawn in the park. Sitting in the meadow by the tree, everyone was talking about the future. Knowing that many of us would be leaving our town, we knew this was a time to say goodbye to school and classmates.

Up until now, living in my parent's house, I was provided with everything. I grew up surrounded by love, respect, harmony, and loyalty. When someone spoke, you knew they were telling the truth and would keep their promises. Punctuality was always observed. I was happy and proud to have such strong spiritual parents who loved each other. I'd been pampered and didn't learn independence, which I felt very strongly after graduating from high school.

A few years later, we tried to find the bottle we had buried as a class. Unfortunately, construction had been performed where the bottle had been buried and it was destroyed. Our written dreams would forever remain unread.

Chapter Nineteen: My Brother Simon's Story

During Simon's final year in high school, his grades begin to deteriorate. He kept two school diaries, one with his real grades and one with the ones he made up. He often showed our parents the very good grades in the diary which he signed himself. Our parents didn't even suspect that the grades were made up until the teachers invited them to school. They were quite surprised to see his actual grades. After returning home, Simon was punished for lying.

He played the piano at school parties without looking at the piano keys. Sometimes he'd roll his pants down and strum his keys like the American Jerry Lee Louis.

After graduating from high school, Simon wanted to be a sailor, so enrolled in the Seamen's School. However, our parents convinced him that sailing was a difficult and dangerous job. He obeyed them and entered the music college in Kaunas. There, he rented an apartment, paying for it with money our parents sent for his education and living expenses. In music college, he was recognized as a very gifted student and graduated with top grades. He found a job as a music teacher at a high school of his choice and established a bagpipe orchestra.

Returning to his parents' home one summer, he met a girl who lived in our hometown, named Agatha. She lived at the end of another town, at her parents' house. This was a very crowded house, holding not only Agatha, her parents, and her brothers, but also other relatives. It was so crowded there wasn't enough room for everyone to sleep, so many of them slept in their barn. When Simon visited her, he sometimes wouldn't return home at all, and when he did, he was usually drunk. My parents told him she didn't seem like a good match for him.

"I think she's beautiful," he replied, "and I'm in love with her."

Lucas replied, "Beauty isn't everything one wants in a wife. You need to take life more seriously. Don't be in a hurry to marry. You are young and still have plenty of time. Wait and see if she is really your chosen one."

Shortly after the conversation, Simon's girlfriend came to my parents and informed them that she was pregnant, and Simon was the father. She wanted him to marry her. After they left, my father told Simon that if it really was his future baby and if he loved her, he should marry her.

Simon moved back to our hometown and lived with our parents. On Saturdays, he played the piano at various dance parties and joined the pipe orchestra in the city where he played brass instruments.

Our parents prepared a big wedding, inviting neighbors, relatives, and friends. Simon sent me an invitation, but I couldn't come because I was involved in final exams. One month after their marriage, their first daughter, Melody, was born.

Once the two were married, Agatha moved in with Simon on the second floor of my parents' house. After Agatha came to live in my parents' house, she worked as a hairdresser in a beauty shop. After some time, she found a job as an insurance agent and then decided she wanted to graduate from college and complete dairy technology studies.

When I returned to my home after their wedding, I met Simon's wife for the first time. My first interaction with her was pleasant. My sister-in-law had beautiful facial features and seemed friendly. I thought I would have a good companion and a family member.

After the birth of their first daughter, Agatha invited her aunt, who raised Agatha, to take care of the child. The aunt not only took care of the newborn daughter but also made food for their whole family and cleaned the rooms.

Agatha and I did not communicate much. Whenever I returned home from school, I liked to put my little niece Melody in her stroller to ride around the city. She kicked and waved her little hands, a cute, beautiful, and happy baby.

I continued to help my parents with the chores during the summer holidays. My mother and father had full-time jobs and after work had to take care of the cow. Agatha was expecting her second baby. Since our parents were tired, I asked Simon to help me take care of the cow. He refused. I told him that the cow must be milked, moved, and brought home in the evening. Her hay must be stacked in the barn. But he continued to refuse, both he and Agatha disappearing when there were chores to be done.

Eighteen months after the birth of their first daughter, their second daughter, Renee, was born. Both daughters were looked after by Agatha's aunt.

Simon and Agatha, living on the second floor, often invited their friends over to drink alcohol, or go out, and then they'd return drunk, soon with daily drinking-bouts. Once drunk, Agatha became aggressive and often angry with her husband.

Agatha's aunt asked Agatha not to drink, to stop screaming at her husband, and to pay more attention to the children. "You should set a good example for the girls. You and your husband are addicted to alcohol." They ignored her requests.

My father, a serious family man who did not drink alcohol, became upset with the everyday arguments. He talked about family and alcohol damage to Simon. He said, "Your girls need both parents to love them, to take care of them, and to be able to trust you. You are losing control, showing your children that you are ruining your lives, and making them feel insecure. They need love, hugs, comfort, and attention."

Simon scoffed. "We do not drink too much; it just seems that way to you."

The longer they lived together, the more they enjoyed alcohol. They drank and smoked. Sometimes, after coming home from drinking, they were so drunk that they couldn't get out of the car and slept in it until morning.

Agatha reduced her alcohol use during her studies, and when she graduated from college, the whole family celebrated. They hoped that she would change her habits and pursue a career. However, it wasn't long before she and Simon went back to drinking and partying.

One evening they were out all-night drinking. When they returned in the morning, they found Agatha's aunt dead in bed. Everyone was saddened, especially Agatha, for the aunt was a loved, respected, sweet, and always smiling woman.

Chapter Twenty: Melody and Renee

After Agatha's aunt died, Grandpa Lucas took over as surrogate parent. After school, Melody and Renee would stay on the ground floor with their grandparents. Grandpa Lucas loved them very much and helped them with their homework and played games with them. He prepared them for school each morning, even braiding their hair. Grandma Greta cooked for them.

After returning from school, Renee always complained that she had a headache. She was an extremely sensitive girl who missed her parents' attention. Often, after work, their parents would go out with their friends. Several times when Renee was downstairs in her grandparents' part of the house and heard her parents going down the stairs, she would rush out into the corridor, grab her mother's skirt, and scream in a hysterical voice.

"Mommy, Mommy don't go, I'm begging you, I'm begging you."

Her mother pushed her off her skirt and left, slamming the door behind her. Her grandparents had to hold her until she would calm down and stop crying.

Over time Agatha and Simon's drinking worsened and they became more aggressive. When they came back in the early morning hours, they'd play music. Greta would fall asleep exhausted after returning from her work in the hospital. She'd be awakened by Simon's pounding on the piano and Agatha's singing and stomping on the floor to the beat.

She would pound on their door asking them to be quiet. They didn't care.

When Agatha was drunk, she would scream and cuss at Simon. However, he'd remain calm, just laugh in front of her and go to the bedroom and lie down. One time she was so angry and drunk she threatened to jump from the upper floor window. Simon grabbed her and held her back, causing her to cut her nose on the window.

Simon asked his mother, Greta, to take Agatha to the hospital. Greta knew all the doctors and took her daughter-in-law to the surgeon, saying she hurt her nose when she fell. The surgeon sewed her nose together and the top of her nose was scarred for life.

During the summer breaks, I'd return home and spend time with the girls. One time, when the girls were in high school, I took them to the lake not far from their home where we caught fish and swam. Sometimes we played badminton or threw a ball in the yard. I have fond memories of summer times spent with very sweet and beloved nieces.

Sometimes I had the impression that Simon and Agatha were not pleased to see me back for the summer at our home. I didn't care, because I knew I was always welcome with my parents, and knew it was important to be friends with my nieces.

After graduating from high school, Melody chose to go away to college for a degree in music, like her father. While in college, she met a serious man whose parents lived in a nearby village.

One Friday evening, she came home to her grandparents and found me sitting with my parents.

"It is good to see you here, Christina," she said. "I need grandma's and your help. My boyfriend is coming to see me tomorrow afternoon, I want to pitch a tent from branches and leaves on the island in our lake near the wooden bridge."

"How romantic," I answered. "We will definitely row there tomorrow to help you set it up."

The very next morning, Melody, my mother, and I rowed to Love Island, collected tree branches, and arranged them in a triangle. We tied them on top with a rope, put leaves on top and a tarpaulin. It turned out to be a tent like Robinson Crusoe.

Melody was cheerful. "It will be a big surprise for my friend."

"Let's see what the adventures will be like on this uninhabited island tomorrow," I said.

Satisfied with our work, we returned home. It turned out that Melody's boyfriend's arrival was delayed one week, but when he arrived, they rowed to the island for a romantic evening.

Renee, Agatha's second daughter, studied at the same college as her sister Melody. She chose to be a kindergarten teacher. After receiving her college degree, Renee continued her studies for another year, living in a student dormitory.

Simon had an acquaintance named Sven, who played bagpipes. He asked Simon if he could play with him in the bagpipe orchestra, and soon was visiting the home often. He met Renee during these visits.

Sven was ten years older than Renee and worked as a police officer. He had a child out of wedlock and had mistreated his wife. Once, when he got angry, he threw her naked into the snow and locked the door. Then he divorced her.

Even knowing this, Renee fell in love with him. Often, after returning from studies on Saturdays, Sven visited her at Simon's house. Simon and Agatha didn't approve of Sven. They forbade her to see him, so she began dating him secretly.

One weekend, Renee went out to visit her friends on a Friday evening, but by Saturday morning still hadn't returned. Agatha went to Sven's house to look for her. When Renee saw her mother coming, she climbed out the window and hid in the bottle building nearby. Agatha couldn't find her.

Greta went out and found Renee hiding behind the boxes. "Why are you sitting here? Go home."

"Grandma, I am afraid to go, I am afraid my parents will punish me."

"Do not be afraid, I will intercede for you."

Together they walked home. When she came to my father's house, Renee's parents strictly forbade her to meet him. She apologized and promised not to meet him again.

Chapter Twenty-One: College

It always seems impossible until it is done.
-Nelson Mandela, South African politician

After finishing high school, I left my parent's house to study engineering in the city of Kaunas. After passing my entrance exams, I decided that I wanted to be a civil engineer like my father. During my studies, the school gaps in my mathematics appeared. It soon became clear I wasn't going to be able to pass the courses in this school and so I had to quit. Still determined, I enrolled in a different school that required fewer mathematical classes.

I met Erick during the entrance exams to the new school. We became good friends, and by studying together we both conquered the math requirements. As the semester proceeded, I got particularly good grades in chemistry and biology. Erick and I became good friends and maintained our friendship to this day.

My friend Arlo lived in Kaunas with his mother and younger sister in a big house near the city center. His mother worked as an accountant in a fashion salon. I rented an apartment close to them, and Arlo and I met almost every day. When we couldn't meet, Arlo would call me, saying, "Christina, I want to hug you, love you, and not let you go." We would talk on the phone for hours, gabbing and laughing.

One evening Arlo invited me to his house and introduced me to his mother and sister. His mother was a very presentable and intelligent woman that liked beautiful stylish clothes. Pretty soon, Arlo's mom and I became close friends. She often invited me over for tea and her baked cookies.

His sister was in high school in eleventh grade. One year later, she graduated from high school and entered the Academy of

Fine Arts. After graduating, she fell in love with a man of German origin, and they moved to Germany.

Student life suited us very well. We liked to dance at student parties, sometimes until five in the morning. We liked spending time with our friends, but we never neglected our studies. We knew we had to graduate to create our future. Arlo was an excellent engineering student, and he often helped his friends with design drawings.

For my birthday during my sophomore year, my friends and I decided to celebrate by camping in the forest. We set up tents and built a campfire in a lovely spot near the lake. In the evening by the fire, Arlo's friend played the guitar, and we sang along. Someone brought beer and liquor, and, without realizing it, I drank too much by mixing my drink with other drinks. The trees and grass started to spin around me. I decided I needed to lie down, and on the way to my tent I kept stepping into holes and falling. When I finally reached my tent, I said to myself, "Happy birthday, Christina!" In the morning, I decided I'd never drink alcohol again, and so far have stuck with it.

My classmate Alma was also studying engineering in Kaunas. Her boyfriend from our hometown moved there to be close to her and to take classes. The two continued to date and be close friends for a year. Then, Alma met another young man at the University who she liked better than her sweetheart. Soon after, she arranged to meet with her old boyfriend.

"It's over between us," she told him. "I've met someone new."

"But, Alma, I love you. Our friendship is so strong and so long. You can't possibly fall in love with someone else so quickly. Don't give up on us."

"No," she replied. "I've already decided we are not right for each other. I'm leaving you."

After saying this, she got on the bus and left him standing there. He sat on the bench for a long-time contemplating that their long-cherished love had ended. When he got up, he decided he never wanted to meet her again.

Alma studied at one end of the city and I at the other. Our friendship slowly drifted apart. We made new friends, and as our studies were taking up much of our time, we rarely spent time together. One of the few times we got together during this period was when Alma invited me to a Swedish sauna party where most of the guests were her fellow students. Her brother also attended, having come to study in the same city.

I found a small apartment in some woods near my university where I had more privacy. Arlo finished his junior year but then decided he'd had enough school.

"I'm bored," he said. "I think I'll go serve in the Soviet Army."

"This is a mistake! You shouldn't be leaving me and your studies. You are a talented student and should finish what you've started. While serving in the Soviet Army, you will not gain any knowledge, on the contrary, you will forget what you have acquired so far."

Despite my urging, he signed up to serve in the Soviet Army for two years without asking his mother. I accompanied him to the bus when he left.

"Christina, I love you," he said at the bus station. "Will you be waiting for me when I get back?"

My heart felt empty. "We will see what the future brings," is all I could promise him.

As the bus moved off, I waved, and we parted for two years. Soon the first letter arrived from Riga. He was very lucky and was assigned to serve in the capital of Latvia, Riga, which is close to Lithuania.

I had been to Riga a lot with my parents, so I was familiar with its history and architecture. Riga is an extremely beautiful historical city, its old town included in the UNESCO World Heritage List. The city is particularly famous for its abundance of Art Nouveau and 19th century wooden architecture. We'd walk along the streets of Riga, and the seaside, enjoying their delicious fresh fish.

After he left, I wondered if we'd be able to keep up our friendship from a distance for such a long period of time. I still couldn't understand why he decided to join the Russian army. Everything seemed to be going well for him at the university. I felt alone and betrayed.

I received letters from him almost every day. I read them and remembered with nostalgia the days we'd spent together. Sometimes when I would go to student parties, other men would offer me friendship, but I refused them all. After telephone conversations with Arlo, I started to believe that we would see each other in Riga and discuss our future together. I believed my first love would come back to me.

After a few months, I began visiting him in Riga on a regular basis on weekends. I'd leave Friday evening to be in Riga in the morning. In the train cabin, there were two wooden seats at the bottom and two at the top. Upon entering the cabin, I would be greeted by three complete strangers, always friendly and good people. The conductor would bring hot tea, pour it into glasses, and place it in a metal container insert. The tea was free, and if you wanted cookies, you could buy them from the conductor or go to the restaurant in the middle of the train.

The conductor provided bed linen and I slept comfortably, arriving in Riga by morning. From the train station, I took a tram and walked several blocks to the barracks. Sometimes Arlo wasn't allowed to leave the barracks, in which case I had to go back to the train station and wait for the next morning until he was released. The barracks allowed me to stay and sleep in a specially designated guest room only once.

One evening, I lit a small candle that I had brought.

"Arlo," I said, "In this candle's burning flame, let's dream and, being both in the darkness of this room, swear by our loyalty and feelings that we are now and that we will be together again. Let this candle burn until it goes out. When it goes out, kiss me. Let's sink into our romantic short, crystal-clear night."

After visiting for the weekend, I would go back to the railway station on Sunday evening and spend the night sitting on the bench there to take the morning train back to the University.

One time when I went to visit Arlo, I'd just gotten off the train when I heard him shouting my name and saw him waving to me from the tram. I had to run to get on the tram with him.

"Why are you taking the tram?" I asked.

"That's how we go to the barracks after the exercises early in the morning," he explained. This time they allowed him to leave the barracks for the whole day and he only had to return in the evening.

We took the tram to the center of Riga. Arlo talked about its history as we walked through the main streets of the old town. After visiting and talking, he returned to the barracks, and I went to the railway station to spend the night.

That evening, sitting on a bench at the train station, I was about to try to sleep when an elderly man sat down near me and started speaking in Russian.

He asked, "What train are you waiting for?"

"No train. I have to spend the night in Riga, and without anywhere else, I sleep in the station. In the morning I'll take the train home."

The man was surprised. "I imagine it's uncomfortable sleeping in the railway station. I can offer you a room where you can sleep near here. My sister's apartment; she's not at home now."

I was very grateful for the offer and followed him down the street to a tall apartment building. We climbed to the fourth floor where he unlocked a door and let us into an empty corridor with several doors leading to other rooms, with the only opening to a small kitchen. He said all the doors were locked in this apartment, but we could lie down in the corridor.

"I will lie down at one end of the corridor, and you at the other," he said.

He dropped some coats on the floor on either end, and he laid down near the exit door and I laid down at the other end of the corridor. He turned off the light and I tried to sleep.

I found I couldn't sleep; something was disturbing my heart. The fellow had promised me a room, and instead, I was locked in a corridor with him. I got quite scared, wondering why I was so trusting. I heard a splash and my companion laid down next to me. I jumped up and told him that I was feeling nauseous and asked for a glass of water.

He got up, turned on the light in the kitchen, and brought me water. I told him that I'd sit there and drink water. He went back to his coat at the other end of the hall. I sat by the light until morning. When I got ready to leave, he woke up and said he'd accompany me. He unlocked the door, we went downstairs and said goodbye.

I considered how I had been too trusting, and I had gotten myself into a situation where things could have gone very badly. I shook myself and chased away the bad thoughts. A sunny, beautiful morning had dawned.

After two years of service, Arlo returned from the army. I met him at the train station. We were happy to be together again. We kissed and enjoyed a long hug.

"Christina, I can't believe that I'm back home with you. Thank you for waiting for me faithfully."

We hugged and kissed again.

At first, after his return, everything seemed back to normal. He resumed his studies at the same University and lived with his mother. Yet, he seemed too busy to see me, saying that he had many projects to do at school. Soon I felt something wrong in our relationship. When we met, he seemed sad and tense.

"What's wrong?" I asked.

"Nothing. I am just not in a good mood today."

I wondered what had happened to that sincere smile and those endless conversations. He became more reserved. After spending two years in the army, his thoughts and his behavior had changed, perhaps more mature, and manlier. Despite this, I remained in love with him, but I felt his coldness and a change in his thinking. Perhaps he thought that he could recover his earlier feelings by marrying me. I accepted his proposal with joy.

Chapter Twenty-Two: Wedding

Happy marriages begin when we marry the ones we love,
and they blossom when we love the ones we marry.
- Tom Mullen, American novelist

Arlo asked his aunt who lived in America to send me a beautiful wedding dress, telling her my measurements. She sent a beautifully tailored white dress of an extremely interesting style that fit my tall and thin physique perfectly. A long train draped across the ground embroidered with white guipure and beads over the shoulders. When I put it on, I looked like a queen.

We married three months later. My parents arranged for a large wedding with all our friends and relatives in attendance, including Arlo's mother and sister. My friends and Arlo's student friends were bridesmaids and groomsmen, and my classmate Alma was a bridesmaid. We went to the registry office and then the church where we married.

After the ceremony, we went to the photo studio to take pictures. When my friend Alma saw us heading towards the front door of the photo studio, she told me not to enter that way. She said a lot of people were watching and would be jealous. She suggested we go through the back door.

I was shocked. "What are you talking about? At a wedding, the bride always wants and must be the center of attention. She doesn't go like a servant through the back door."

With my head held high, I entered through the front door. We took pictures and returned home to celebrate our marriage.

Shortly after the wedding, I learned from his study friends that Arlo had been dating other girls after returning from the army. I figured he probably just wanted to flirt when he was still unmarried.

One of them was a famous Lithuanian singer. Their friendship was short-lived.

After the wedding, we went to the student office and filled out an application to get a room in a student dormitory. We were assigned one, where we settled in. It was a single room, so small that it barely fit the couch where we slept, with two chairs, and a small table. We had to share the bathroom with other students living on the hallway. The kitchen was in the middle of the dormitory floor and shared by all the students. Most of the time we ate in the student canteen.

One evening I asked him, "I heard from your friends that you used to date girls after you got back from the army. You were doing it behind my back. I feel so stupid that I faithfully waited for you to come back from the army for two years."

"It's not true," he insisted. "I've always loved only you. They were just friends. Really! You must trust me."

"Yes, I believe you," I answered. "Let's look to the future, let's create our new life."

I disregarded those gossips, and we continued to live happily, both seriously concentrating on our studies.

Chapter Twenty-Three: Birth of Justin

On an autumn evening, a small, wonderful earth bud, our son Justin, was born. He arrived in the constellation of Libra in a small town in northern Lithuania. My mother was working that night at the hospital, which helped calm me as I knew she'd be there to help with the delivery.

It was a long labor, and finally at 9:45 in the evening I heard his first cry. "Mother, I'm here, Mother, I'm here. Can you hear me? Accept me into this world as I am now and as I will be."

My mother laid him on my chest, a beautiful newborn swaddled just after birth. My father, Lucas, came in to congratulate me. We three chatted late into the night.

The next day Arlo came by bus to visit his son, delighted at how beautiful and healthy he was. After visiting for a few days, he returned to his hometown to continue his studies.

Justin and I stayed at my parents' house for a month before returning home. I tried to resume my studies, but with a newborn crying at night, attending lectures became difficult. Arlo's mother occasionally took care of him while we were in classes.

I became interested in cooking which I had never been interested in before. I read a lot of cookbooks and tried to make a meal based on the recipes.

There is a saying that a man's love goes through his stomach. I don't know if it's true, but after reading various cookbooks, I decided one evening to surprise Arlo with a creative masterpiece. Inspired by the spring sun smiling through the window, flowers blooming, and while my son slept, I rolled up my sleeves and rolled out dough for an apple pie. To my surprise, the cake baked perfectly. The whole room smelled like freshly baked apple pie. My heart laughed and melted with happiness.

I woke up Justin with my laughter. He looked around and then went back to sleep. I turned on quiet music, sat down, and enjoyed my first cooking masterpiece.

When Arlo returned from class, he asked, "What smells so good in here?"

"This is my apple pie," I said proudly, showing him my masterpiece. "Sit down, I'm about to feed you some."

He washed his hands and sat at the table saying, "I am very hungry."

I gave him one piece of the delicious pastry which he ate promptly and asked for more.

"Where did you learn to cook this? I'm astonished that you created this wonderful delicacy."

I answered him, "You are my inspiration as is our little prince." Justin was awake, happy, smiling, and waving and kicking with his legs and small hands, as if agreeing with me. "Both of you inspire me to do great things."

Arlo drew projects in the student study room because our dorm room was so small. Our fatigue continued for a long time, sleepless nights affecting our studies. We started skipping lectures and had to get up without enough sleep. When we did attend, we sat through them unfocused and sleepy. We were compelled to return home and rest as soon as possible.

I called my parents and asked them if they could raise our baby until we graduated. Arlo had one year left, and I had one and a half years to write and defend my thesis. They gladly agreed. They arrived with their little car, Bug, in a few days. Upon arrival, they visited us for one day and then took our little one away. It was painful to watch him go. We knew every day we would miss watching him grow and his shouts of joy. Whenever possible, I went to my parents' house by bus, about four hours away, to visit him.

Chapter Twenty-Four: My Father's New Car

In the Soviet times, it was not possible to freely buy carpets, furniture, or cars. You needed to get an allocation. My dad Lucas had a small Russian-made Bug car. As a good and honest worker and a long-serving chief road engineer, he was given a new Russian car of the brand Ziguli (Lada). The car had a shiny new red color. After paying the money and with the greatest joy, he brought it home to show Greta, who was delighted.

After a long discussion, they decided that my brother Simon needed the car more than they did because he had a big family. Simon was overjoyed, unable to believe that he had a new car. Agatha had kept up her license, and she drove the new car, including taking her brother and other relatives on rides. However, she would never take our parents for rides, even when she lived on the second floor of the house.

One time when I came to visit, I saw the beautiful car in the yard with Agatha at the wheel, her father beside her, and her children in the back seat.

I asked my dad, "How did Agatha get this beautiful red car in the yard?"

Father explained how the car had been assigned to him, and how he had paid for it and given it to Simon.

"Why are they sitting in it?" I asked. "Are you going to go somewhere with them?"

"Not that I know of. Let's go to the yard and ask."

When we went out to the yard, the car was gone. They left without saying where they were going or when they planned to return. A month later I found out that they'd taken the family on a two-week, 2500-kilometer vacation to Yalta on the Black Sea. I was disgusted that they took this trip without informing us.

My father Lucas was chief road engineer, a respected man in his hometown. One day, he was offered the opportunity to be mayor of the city. After consulting with his wife, he said. "Thank you for this offer, I will stay in this job. I enjoy this work and the responsibility that comes with it".

One time while pouring new asphalt on the street, a manager asked Lucas to pave his yard. My father refused, saying it wouldn't be honest. This was just one example, but because of this and similar actions, all the townsfolk knew him to be honest and treated him with great respect.

That was everyone, except for Simon and Agatha. Angry with their insults and abuse, my father threatened to sell the house and they would have to move out. Shortly after that his sickness resumed and the sale of the house was postponed.

Chapter Twenty-Five: Diploma Defense of Arlo

When Arlo finished his studies, he performed a successful diploma defense with drawings and was awarded his degree. After his graduation, he received a job offer in a city near the Baltic Sea. The offer included a studio apartment in a newly built house. We discussed this offer with his mother and my parents and decided to accept the position.

The apartments built in the Soviet years were not spacious, the only advantage was that they came with amenities. After arriving in this city, we received the keys to the new apartment, which was on the second floor. Through the door, we entered a hallway with one large room on the right side, the door to the kitchen on the left side, and a bathroom with a toilet in the middle between these rooms. This apartment reminded us of a student dormitory room, only with a larger square footage and a kitchen nearby.

We rolled up our sleeves and over the next few days, cleaned our new apartment. Then, we decided to see the city center, visit the shops, and explore the more interesting places. We bought a sofa, bedding, and a few things we needed for our household. The city itself was interesting for its architectural buildings and was located near a large seaport.

We were both happy and talked about how the three of us would live beautifully together, albeit in a cozy small apartment.

With half a year left until I graduated, I left Arlo alone and went back to school. I believed that he would work hard while he waited for my return.

Once back at school, I found I had free time between lectures. Sometimes I would visit my son Justin at my parents and other times visit Arlo. As I didn't have a car, I traveled by bus.

After completing my studies and successfully defending my thesis, I returned to our apartment. I went to the grain product packing combine in that town to look for a job and was offered a position as an engineer in the flour workshop. Arlo seemed happy that I had found a job, which was to start in one month. Meanwhile, I returned home to pack up my belongings.

Chapter Twenty-Six: Surprise

"Trust is earned, respect is given, and loyalty is demonstrated. Betrayal of any one of those is to lose all three".
- Ziag Abdelnour.

After packing up, I decided to surprise Arlo by returning without letting him know I was coming. I arrived around six in the afternoon, climbed the stairs, and knocked on the door. When no one answered, I figured that he hadn't returned from work yet.

In front of our apartment building was a railway station. I sat down inside where I could see the windows of my room, watching for the light to come on in the room. As time passed, I became a bit bored and remembered that I had a former classmate nicknamed Beaver working in this city as an engineer. He'd given me his number, so I called him, but he didn't answer.

After a bit, I fell asleep and dreamt that Arlo was embracing me. He hugged me in his strong arms, and then kissed me, and whispered sweet words of love. When I opened my eyes, there was still no light in the window. Already it was nine pm in the evening. Sorrow and uncertainty crept into my head. I was getting hungry and thirsty.

Finally, around eleven in the evening, I saw a light in the window. I took my rucksack and flew towards that light like a butterfly. I ran up to the second floor and was just about to ring the doorbell when I heard a woman's voice inside.

I hesitated, hoping maybe I'd imagined it because of the long wait and my fatigue. I listened again. Then I heard laughter and music. Impulsively, I rang the doorbell, my heart beating like church bells. I heard firm footsteps coming to the door. When Arlo opened the door, he wouldn't let me in.

"I have a guest," he said.

I pushed past him and entered, finding a woman half-undressed on the couch.

"Get out!" I yelled. "I'm his wife."

She grabbed her clothes and her purse and ran out the door, slamming it behind her.

I slugged Arlo on his jaw with all my strength. Then I hit him again on the other side of his jaw.

Rubbing his jaw he said, "Nice! And a very strong shot, Christina." After saying this and laughing, he grabbed his coat and opened the front door.

Turning to me he said, "Everything is over. I don't love you anymore and don't want to live with you." Then he walked down the stairs and out of the building.

With tears rolling down my cheeks, I called my parents. "My family was destroyed tonight. I found Arlo with a half-naked woman in my house. I don't know what to do next."

My parents told me to try to stay calm. "We'll come with our car tomorrow. Don't make any plans or do anything rash."

I thanked them and tried to calm down a little. It was now past midnight, and I hadn't eaten since noon. However, when I opened the refrigerator, it was empty. I found a bottle of cheap cherry wine and began drinking.

Thoughts raced through my head. What was to be my future, now? I realized I had to be strong and self-confident. When I went to the bedroom, I found the bed dirty and disgusting. If I had anything in my stomach, I would have vomited. I sat on the bed and listened to the trains rolling by.

When I finally fell asleep. I dreamt I was walking in a meadow at night. The moon shone brightly. I tripped over a dewy meadow flower and saw Arlo his face bright and cute. I wanted to scream. A cold wind picked up, and everything became obscured by fog.

I woke to the sound of Arlo unlocking the door at two o'clock in the night. He undressed and lay down next to me. I slapped him again, but he didn't hit me back.

He said, "I'm in love with this other woman. When I close my eyes, I only see her. No one has ever loved me like she does, kissed me like she does, caressed me like she does. Christina, everything is over between us. I truly and firmly declare this to you."

I didn't say anything back to him. Although I thought I wouldn't be able to fall asleep, time, fatigue, and the dark of night overcame me, and I slept.

In the morning, the doorbell rang. When I opened the door, I found my parents, my son Justin, and Agatha. We all hugged. Justin was already two and a half years old. I raised him in my arms, kissed him, and told him how wonderful he was.

"Mommy," Justin said, "can I live with you and my grandparents together?"

"Yes, only together."

Arlo came in from the bedroom. He didn't show joy on seeing Justin and didn't take him in his arms, not even saying a single word to him.

My father Lucas greeted Arlo and spoke in a reserved manly manner. "I already know this situation from yesterday's conversation with my daughter. I want to talk to you like a man. Have you really decided to leave your family and give up your beloved wife and son? Until now, your friendship with my daughter has been faithful and long. I believe that your infatuation with another woman is only episodic and temporary. There is nothing serious about your relationship with her. Is it worth violating such a long friendship and love to give up everything you both wanted?"

Arlo answered, "Yes, I am true to my feelings. It's over with our family, I love another woman. She is currently a restaurant waitress. I will send her to the university and nurture her. I met her every day while going to eat at the restaurant where she works and fell in love with her as soon as I saw her. What thick and beautiful hair she has. I have been dating her for quite some time. I decided very seriously to leave my family. I also want to tell you that she is divorced, she has a daughter from her first marriage. Her husband was a tractor driver and used to beat her."

After these words, Arlo took his jacket and said, "I'm leaving, you won't dissuade me anymore. Nobody will change my mind. Before I leave, I want to inform you that your daughter is a beautiful dead doll. Put her in the window and admire from afar."

Lucas tried to hold him back, but Arlo pushed him away and walked out the door. Justin cried and Greta took him in her arms.

Let's discuss outer beauty and how much it has to do with inner happiness. There is a saying, "Don't be born beautiful, but be born happy." What is beauty? Beauty is a gift. It is mind, wisdom, and goodness. When our soul is transparent, we attract with our inner self. From that comes the beauty of a woman.

Chapter Twenty-Seven: A Night with Another Man

Needing to get out of the house, I thought about my friend Beaver. I remembered the first time we had met. I must have been nineteen and had been invited by my friend Alma to join some of her classmates at a student ball in a Swedish sauna. He was there with his girlfriend. I think I hadn't seen him since.

I gave him a call and this time he answered, agreeing to meet with me at a coffee shop. Over pastries, I told him my situation and asked him to try to talk sense to my husband Arlo. He agreed to give it a try and I listened in as they talked. However, Arlo cut him short, saying he'd already decided that he wasn't going to live with me any longer.

I was about to cry, and, trying to cheer me up, he suggested I come spend the evening at his house. His wife, coincidentally also named Christina, was out of town.

His apartment was larger than the one Arlo and I shared, with a nice view of the river. We sat at his table eating borsch.

"Do you remember the first time we met?" he asked.

"I was thinking about it earlier today. It was at that sauna party, wasn't it?"

"That's right. I'd come with Christina, the one who's now my wife, but at the time we'd just started dating. When I saw you, I thought you were the most beautiful woman I'd ever set eyes on. I stood up and announced to everyone that I liked you more than my girlfriend."

He took a spoonful of food, swallowed it, and washed it down with some champagne. "Do you remember?"

"Yes. You were drunk and made me feel very uncomfortable," I said. "After your speech, I went to another room. At that time, I was faithfully waiting for my high school sweetheart, Arlo, to return from the army."

"Well, that was a long time ago. Now I'm happily married and you're in a mess. Arlo seems determined to end the marriage. What are you going to do?"

I began to cry, and he gave me a warm hug. Over champagne and toast, we talked and talked. About midnight, Beaver put on slow dance music, and we held on to each other and swayed to the sad songs. The champagne had cheered me up and when he suggested I spend the night with him, I agreed.

We lay next to each other in bed, and he hugged me.

"I know everything looks bleak now," he said, "but don't worry. You're a beautiful, intelligent, attractive woman. Someday you'll meet a man who will truly be worthy of you and love you dearly. Believe and wait, life will change for the better."

As he snuggled against me, I could feel his masculinity being pushing against me. Lying next to a man who wanted me was very tempting. Then I remembered how angry I was about my husband being with another woman and I didn't want to do the same thing to Beaver's wife. I pushed him away. We slept all night in the same bed without touching each other.

In the morning, I thanked him for his understanding, conversation, and kind heart. I returned home sober and calm.

Chapter Twenty-Eight: Leaving Arlo

After returning home, I found that Arlo hadn't returned, my parents and Agatha were still there waiting for me. Agatha offered to go with me to the restaurant where the lover of Arlo worked and talk to her. My mother also wanted to go along. As we walked down the street, I saw her coming towards us. As we got closer to her, Agatha shouted profanities at her.

"Don't do that," I told her. "It's rude and unnecessary.

Agatha replied. "Was it polite for her to sneak in and destroy your family?" And she continued to curse loudly.

"Stop, please. You've done enough." I grabbed Agatha's arm and turned us around. I glanced back and saw Arlo's lover standing stunned on the sidewalk.

I told Agatha, "You can't force someone to love you. Everything must flow from your heart. The world is what it is. It is neither right nor wrong. Since my husband betrayed me, I have to force myself not to condemn him but to choose an alternative path. What should I do next? If I can only achieve his loyalty by coercion, then the relationship will be worthless, even worse than infidelity."

Back at the new apartment, I sat on the sofa trying to decide what to do. Although I had a good job in this city and an apartment, I didn't know anyone besides Beaver. And what if Arlo brought that woman back here? I couldn't have tolerated that.

A broken pot cannot be put together. Scars will remain. Can you trust a broken pot? The answer is no!

I decided to give up my job and live at my parents' house. I was sad that the love I had with Arlo that was fostered and nurtured for such a long time had completely collapsed, but I realized it was absolutely over.

Arlo finally returned as I was finishing packing my things.

"Before I leave, I would like to ask what happened to you, Arlo? Why did you change so much? Have you always been keeping your feelings secret from me? Or did something happen to change your affection? It's now clear that you're a labyrinth of words, a secretive manipulator, and a man not bound by his promises."

I continued, "I could never go to the mountains with people like you. From the first failure, you would break down and leave me alone in the unknown. I am leaving now and closing the door on you forever."

He never said a word as I walked out the door carrying my suitcases.

When I returned to my parents' house, they gave me a large carpet, a present that was supposed to be for my graduation. Since I was now going to be living at their home, we decided to place this carpet in their house.

Chapter Twenty-Nine: My Friend Erick

Once settled back in my parents' house, I felt depressed. I decided I needed a friend to talk with and called Erick, a comrade from my student days. When we were students, we always sat by each other in the classrooms and helped each other study. We remained good friends even after our studies. He was happy to hear from me.

"What's up?" he asked.

"I'm not doing well," I told him. "I broke up with Arlo and now I'm back home staying with my parents."

"Sounds like you could use a friend, huh? I could stay for a few days to cheer you up."

He came from the next town over and stayed with us for four days. He played with my son, and we walked around the city where I showed him the famous places and museums. After brightening my mood, he needed to return home to his job where he was the chairman of a collective farm.

"If you have some free time, how about you come visit me?"

"Well, I don't have a job, so maybe I should take some time off. How about I come on Saturday?"

"Great, here's my address. Oh, better yet, call me when you arrive, and I'll meet you at the bus station."

That weekend I packed a small bag and traveled to his town. From the bus station, we walked to his residence.

After dinner, we sat by his fireplace and talked.

"Do you remember, Christina, during my studies, you teased me that I didn't have a girlfriend and I would remain an old bachelor? You jokingly told me that you would introduce me to somebody. You will be surprised by what I am going to tell you. At that moment I was thinking only of you."

I was quite surprised, as I hadn't any idea that he was attracted to me. "Why didn't you ever tell me this before, Erick?"

"How could I? At that time, you were dating Arlo." Reaching over he took my hands. "Christina, now that you are alone, please come live with me. I love you. I will provide you with everything. I will support you for I have a good job. We will be very happy together and I promise I will love you faithfully."

I considered his proposal for several minutes. I knew Erick was very good-natured and never angered. Although he didn't like dancing, he was honest, sweet, and overall a very good person. I liked him a lot, but I didn't love him and knew I couldn't live with him in that way.

"Erick, thank you. You're very sweet and your offer makes me very happy to know that I can still be loved like that. However, I'm not ready to get into another relationship so quickly. My wounds need time to heal. But I'd like to continue being your friend. Can you understand that?"

His smile was gentle and reassuring. "Of course, I can be your friend like before. Please understand this. Christina, whenever you want and can, please come and visit me, I will always be waiting for you."

"Thank you, Erick. I will definitely come, I promise. While I live with my parents, I will invite you to come by as often as you can."

After this meeting, Erick visited us several times at my parents' house. He enjoyed interacting with my son, often bringing him a toy. It was good to have a friend.

Chapter Thirty: A Job in the Countryside

Within a few days of being home, I found a job in a nearby village. Deep in the countryside, it was perfect for my peace of mind, a setting designed to distance myself from all worldly life. It took me one and a half hours from home to work by bus.

I had never lived in a real village. At first, it was strange until everything gradually settled down. People there were simple, kind, and sincere, totally different from the city. The work seemed complicated to me at first. Tractors rumbled, cows mooed, pigs squealed. Although I grew up in a small town, village life was quite different.

During this period, I was constantly bothered by sad thoughts. Nothing could cheer me. I kept asking myself, what does life consist of? From good and bad moments, betrayals, deception, bad and good friends? Or do men do bad things from lack of education and ignorance? I think men need to be made jealous. Could they then appreciate and love their girlfriends and wives? Probably yes.

I had been blindly in love with Arlo without seeing so many intelligent and interesting male students around me. They had offered me friendship and showed great attention. I had been faithful and saw only Arlo on my life path. It was a great high school crush. Arlo played the main roles in school plays and played the trumpet. He was loved by girls in school. Why do girls and women reject men who are worthy of true love and choose those who are not worthy of attention?

A few months after I moved into my parents' house, Arlo called me. He said that he would like to come visit his son. I told this news to my father. Being a sensitive man, very loyal and devoted to his family, he felt distressed about Arlo's impending visit. He told me that Arlo better not come, he didn't want to see him.

I told him not to worry, that Arlo wouldn't stay long.

When Arlo arrived, he brought sweets for his son.

That evening, just as he was leaving, he took my hands and looked into my eyes. "Christina, when I see you, I feel good. When I go back to the town where I live and work and see my current girlfriend, I will also feel very good. It's confusing."

I laughed. "I'm not interested in polygamy."

I opened the door for him and told him to get out. "Good luck with the rest of your life."

For the next year, I shut myself down. Just work – home – home – work. Except for an occasional visit from Erick, I only talked with my son and my parents. Every day, I'd get up at five in the morning and take the bus to the village. I was a specialist there where I organized work in the office and fields. If the workers worked well, I sometimes would buy beer for them. Occasionally they told me, "Christina, buy a beer and then we will go to work."

When winter arrived, I had to get up in the cold and dark. Waiting at the bus station, I wore my woolen sheep coat that had been given to my mother by a relative who wore it when she was in Siberia. It was so old I'd had to sew on patches.

One winter day, I had to go to a second facility four kilometers away. Waiting by the bus station, I saw that the next bus wouldn't arrive for another four hours, and the wind was blowing making me shiver. I thought maybe I could get a ride and raised my hand as a gravel truck approached. It stopped, and I asked the driver if he could drive me to the site. He agreed and I gave him directions. Snowflakes began to fall, and the roads became slippery. Suddenly, the truck veered to the left side of the road. The driver tried to gain control, but he couldn't stop it and the truck rolled into a ditch and turned upside down.

All kinds of things fell on me. I smelled gasoline and hoped that the truck would not explode. The driver asked me if I was hurt, and I told him besides a sore shoulder I seemed okay. He tried to open his door, but it was stuck in the snow. The same was true for my door. Soon enough, people stopped by the side of the road to help us, and they cleared away enough snow to open both doors. An ambulance stopped by the road and asked us if we needed medical help, but we both declined.

The truck driver apologized for the accident, and I reassured him I understood it wasn't his fault. He said he'd call for a tow truck. One of the men who had stopped offered to give me a ride and I was able to complete my tasks for the day.

The next morning, I visited the doctor, and he performed a shoulder scan. Fortunately, my shoulder wasn't broken, only badly bruised.

After this incident, I decided that I would rent an apartment in the village for the winter. The next day I found a room in a house where a young handsome bachelor lived, an agronomist. He had a two-bedroom home, living in one room and the other had a bed, a table, a chair, and a lamp. It seemed perfect!

"When could I move in?" I asked.

"Whenever you want."

The next day I brought a few things and settled in. I wondered if women of the village would soon start gossiping about us. After all, I was divorced, and he wasn't married. However, because our aspirations, views, and goals were completely different, there wasn't even a hint of romance between us. In the evenings, we talked and watched TV together.

Although it was pleasant and convenient, I didn't live there for long. The constant sounds of cows mooing and tractors rumbling annoyed me. After a couple of weeks, I thanked him that he had allowed me to live there and went back to my parents' home.

Chapter Thirty-One: Getting my Driving License

The best way to predict the future is to create it.
  - Abraham Lincoln, The 16th president of America

While living with my parents, I started attending driving courses. In the beginning it seemed to me that I would never pass. The courses included a lot of things I didn't understand. However, I was determined and self-confident and kept at it.

Simon taught me how to drive. In the beginning, everything looked complicated. After two days of driving everything was clear, and I was driving.

Having learned both the theory and the practical, I passed both driving exams on the first time. At the same time, I received my motorcycle license.

Chapter Thirty-Two: A Trip Abroad

I have found out that there is no surer way to find out whether you like people or hate them than to travel with them.
-Mark Twain, American writer

While working in the village, we employees were offered a trip abroad to visit two socialist countries, Bulgaria and Romania. I filled out the forms, passed all the censorships, and was awarded with the trip. This excursion was scheduled to last a week and a half.

Our first stop was in Bucharest, the capital of Romania, where the guide lectured us about the local culture and history. The tourist bus took us to Bran Castle, the mysterious abode of the vampire Dracula, a national monument and landmark. Many films have been made about the legend of Dracula. It is a 14th century castle that stands near the city of Brasov. The next stop was Sofia, the capital of Bulgaria. There we visited many art galleries, museums, and markets. We also visited the Alexander Nevsky Cathedral with its beautiful domes.

After spending a night in the hotel provided for us in Sofia, we drove to another city called Gabrovo in Bulgaria. It is called the "Humor Capital of Bulgaria," with jokes about tailless cats and the hospitality of the people of Gabrovo. The people of Gabrovo like to make fun of themselves. They are said to stop the clocks at night to prevent the clock parts from wearing out. A half hour after we settled into our hotel, the lights went out, and we thought it was because of their sense of humor. Sure enough, after a short time the lights were on again.

In Bulgaria, the mountain air, the southern sun, the Black Sea, and the excellent beaches fascinated me. The leader of our group, the secretary of the Communist Party, wouldn't allow us to communicate with people of other nations or go anywhere without his permission. I knew that if I didn't follow all the rules, he would write a bad report about me, and I wouldn't be allowed to go on any other excursions. Every evening, we would sit with him in the hotel and watch him drink schnapps until he got drunk and went to bed. Then we'd ignore his interference and go where we wanted.

Bulgaria was an extremely beautiful country. I could see entire plantations of red roses by the roads. Rose oil was one of their main products, so much so that they called it "liquid gold." Their roses had a milder scent than roses from other countries where oil was also pressed. I bought small bottles of rose oil for my family as Bulgarian souvenirs.

A few months later another excursion to Italy was organized, this time to Italy. However, my application was denied. I never found out why, but apparently there was something in the biographies of my grandparents and great-grandparents that worried the authorities.

Chapter Thirty-Three: Neighbors

Next to my parents' house, was a small house with a single room and kitchenette. They were quiet neighbors for many years until the wife of the owner died. About the time I went off to college, he remarried. Soon after they married, the newlyweds had a child and named him Zigi. People started to visit that house very often, especially after the market on Sunday. They ate and drank, or maybe just came to escape from their family. Hosts and guests began to relax not only on Saturdays and Sundays but for the rest of the week. Women came there to look for their husbands and usually brought them back drunk. One day, the inscription "Bar" appeared on the side of the house, written with chalk by a woman who found her husband drunk here. The owners ignored this and continued to debauch.

Once, the housewife of this house ran to Greta's house crying. She saw Greta working in the garden and asked for her help.

"Please Greta, come by my house and see what's wrong with my son."

Both ran to house. There, Greta found the three-year-old boy lying on the bed breathing but not reacting to the environment. She took his pulse which beat very strongly. Greta leaned over Zigi and smelled alcohol.

"What did you give to your child?"

"Just a little vodka."

After waiting for the boy to recover, Greta told the woman never to give him vodka again.

Zigi was the same age as my nieces Melody and Renee. My son Justin was a few years younger. My father enjoyed playing with the children, and soon all four spent time with him. They'd prepare performances for us during the evenings dressed in costumes. They recited poems and sang songs. They all had good voices and acting talents.

After graduating from high school, Zigi decided he wanted to be an actor. He went to Vilnius, the capital of Lithuania, and attended every performance in a theatre. However, Zigi did not become an actor. Fate dictated that he eventually immigrated to the United States. He always talked about his mother with love and adoration. He grew up to be a serious and good man.

Chapter Thirty-Four: Spring in the Collective Farm

Either you will reach a point higher up today, or you will be training your powers so that you will be able to climb higher tomorrow.
- Friedrich Nietzsche, German philosopher

Spring finally arrived and I was glad that I had my license. The farm had a motorcycle that the chairman of the collective farm assigned to me to drive around the village and organize the workers.

While working, I met the zootechnician who inspected the farm animals. She was a very friendly woman with a warm spirit, divorced, and raising a son. Soon we were spending a lot of time together not only at work but also at leisure. We both liked to read books and dress stylishly. She always had a good sense of humor and met me with a smile.

She lived in a neat and tasteful two-story house on the farm and often invited me home for lunch where she'd serve homemade bread accompanied by fresh raw milk and honey. Sometimes she invited me to spend the night. I was grateful to her for her sincere friendship and the pleasant days we spent together. Having her as a friend made my life interesting and complete.

While living at my parents' house and returning home from the farm in the evenings or on my free days, I started to weave carpets. The carpets came in various sizes and were made from jute or other natural fibers. I employed the macrame technique, which was a popular art at that time.

I participated in various city and district art exhibitions and aspired to receive the title of folk master. To receive the title of People's Artist, an artist must participate in the Republican Art Exhibition held in Vilnius. I communicated with the folk craftswoman who oversaw giving the invitations to participate, and she said my creations were beautiful and creative. However, she decided to go against me and my art and did not invite me to participate in this exhibition. Rather she chose her daughter, my classmate Alma. So, instead of me, Alma received the title of folk master.

As the Women's Day holiday approached, the women in the office wanted to organize an event. They invited me to their meeting and suggested I prepare an exhibition of my artistic works and I accepted with pleasure. The women decided to prepare a performance for the occasion. I offered to play in the spectacle, and they suggested I could have a main role.

"What will it be about?" I asked.

"It will be about love."

"When will I get to read the script?"

"Tomorrow," answered my zootechnician friend. "We'll also want to prepare a feast for after the performance and everyone will need to help."

I happily collected my artwork and hung them in the village office hall. These included a dozen large macramé wall hangings as well as many small textiles. The next morning, my friend handed me the play's script. I discovered that there were only four characters in the play. I would play a woman named Ugne, another would be a man called Ainis, and two actors played my parents. I learned all my words and became so involved with the play that my disposition turned happy.

Upon entering the hall on the evening of the Women's Day celebration I see people looking at my artwork as they waited for the performance to begin. They praised my artwork, saying that I'd prepared the exhibition beautifully. I thanked them and left the hall to prepare for my performance.

The stage was set with four chairs around a table holding some food, a bottle of whisky, my perfume, and a mirror. Pictures and a clock hung on the wall. A record player was placed on another table against the wall. The curtain opened with all four of us at the table.

The performance had a humorous theme. Ugne, a city girl, fell in love with a village boy, Ainis. Ainis refused Ugne's advances.

He said, "I do not need you, and I never will. You are a beautiful but arrogant city girl, and I am a country boy and I only like modest country girls."

My father wanted me to get married and tried to persuade Ainis. He poured the whiskey into Ainis' glass.

"Let's have a drink, son-in-law. If you think too long, you will never get married. My daughter is an excellent hostess, and well educated. Throw away your foolish principles and empty ambitions."

While they were talking, I took my lipstick and powder and applied my makeup. Seeing this, Ainis became even more upset. He got up from the chair and started walking around the stage.

"No, I really do not want your daughter. No, thank you."

After hearing this, I said, "My dear, think about it and change your mind."

I got up from the chair and put a romantic song on the record player. I approached Ainis and he smiled.

"I am in love with you Ainis," I claimed. "Where will you find another girl like me?"

"Why did you fall in love with me?" he asked.

"I don't know," I said. "But if you reject me, you will be sorry for the rest of your life. I could always find a rich city boy that is good looking and with better manners than you have."

"I'm not attracted to you because you're just a spoiled city girl."

"Very well," I said, "Then I've changed my mind and I'm no longer interested in you, either."

I turned off the music and walked towards Ainis. When I got closer to him, without saying anything, he hugged and kissed me. We turn to the audience, standing in each other's arms, and exclaim together, "We love each other. All our vices are smothered by love."

The audience laughed and applauded.

After this performance, I got a lot of male fans. Many asked me out, but I rejected all the proposals as I wasn't attracted to any of them.

For my work clothes at the collective farm, I sewed a khaki overall with pockets and braces. It was a simple garment that accented my slim figure.

When the chairman of the collective farm saw me in the outfit, he said, "Christina, you need to work here, not show fashion."

"You needn't worry," I told him. "I can work hard and still dress with fashion."

Once summer arrived, I put on shorts and rode my motorcycle through the fields with my long blonde hair down, having fun. The sun was shining, the birds were chirping, and the air felt fresh and clean. When the tractor drivers saw me riding the motorcycle, they shouted and waved their hands.

"Christina, Christina, come to us. We love your shorts."

Nobody wore shorts at this time. I waved my hand and drove away to my work.

One time when I had ridden the motorcycle to town for lunch, the engine froze. I had to get a truck from the village to load up the bike and drive us back to the workplace. The chairman said that the workshop would fix it.

During this summer, one young worker started flirting with me. He invited me to his home to meet his parents. I already knew them, as they worked on the same collective farm where I worked. The young man's admiration for me didn't last long. When a young specialist came to the village to work there, she lured him away from me. I did not feel bad but was happy. I never thought that anything would come of his attraction for me.

It turned out I saw him one more time. After completing his studies at an agricultural college, he broke up with his girlfriend and signed up to serve in the Soviet army. After a few years in the army, he came back and visited me. We had a short chat standing by the fence where he talked about his experiences in the army. We parted, wished each other good luck, and never saw each other again.

As the fall approached, I'd been living at my parents' house and working at the collective farm for a year. During this period, it appeared that someone had waved a magic wand and opened my eyes. All my sadness and my feelings for Arlo had magically disappeared from my heart. I realized that it was a pity that my youth had been wasted on him. My only other regret was that my son had to endure the loss of his father.

While I was happy living with my parents and my son, I didn't like living with Simon and his wife. They wanted to control my parents and me. In fact, I felt that they wanted me to leave the house as soon as possible.

I went to the collective farm and informed the chairman that I was quitting my job.

He looked at me with surprise. "Christina do not leave, we need you. You worked so well and have been excellent at organizing our work. All the collective farm workers like you."

"Thank you, chairman, I need to change my lifestyle, as well as my clothes."

He laughed. "Really Christina, you inspired all of us and set a good example with your clothes and your behavior."

Thank you, Chairman. We will see each other again. I wish you health and success in your life."

Chapter Thirty-Five: Looking for a new Life

Believing in yourself is the first step to achieving anything.
-Steve Jobs, American business magnate

I was determined to start a whole new life. I was so happy, it felt like the sun was shining again in bright colors. Yupi ja je, yupi ja je!

I decided to look for a job in a community college. It felt good to know what I was aiming for. I set a motto for myself: Purpose, confidence, and victory. I saw it in my eyes, and I set my goals. Guided by this motto, I told myself that my goals were high, and I had to achieve them. I would be a teacher in a community college. I saw myself walking nicely dressed and being a cultured woman while working with the students and the teachers there.

I started riding buses from one district to another looking for a job. I went to a community college in the northern city and went straight to the Head of School office. I told the director what I wanted.

He listened to me very politely and said, "I am very glad to see you here. But you know you have one weak point."

"You are seeing me for the first time, so how can you know this? What is it, Director? Please, tell me."

"The problem is," he said, "you are a beautiful woman, and we have a lot of men working here. Your presence here would be distracting and might result in seducing them. For this reason, I cannot hire you."

In my mind I thought, "I will start with you first." But instead of saying it, I said goodbye and left.

I realized my body was young and beautiful, yet my mind was naive, my heart cowardly, and my character modest. This was the first burnt pancake. Well, I wasn't about to give up.

The next day I went to a community college located in a park near the lakes outside of the capitol Vilnius. I faced the same story again. The same words come out of the mouth of this director. I asked myself what was wrong with me? Why can't I have my dream job? What kind of spell was haunting me?

When I returned home, I was upset, and told my father what had happened.

"Do not get discouraged, Christina. I have a good friend in Vilnius whom I helped before, and he will help me this time. I'll call him tomorrow."

In the morning, his friend listened to my father's speech with great interest.

"You know, Lucas, you are my good friend, and I will help you in this matter. I respect you a lot and I believe that your daughter must be as responsible and dutiful as you."

My father's friend told him to have me come to see him. I drove to the specified address, bringing one of my macrame art pieces as a gift. It was a round large textile work to be hung on the wall with a large metal button placed in the middle of this work.

When I walked in the door, I greeted him, and right away he asked me what subject I'd like to teach. I told him botany and biology, preferably in a college in the southern region or a southern city.

He wrote a referral and gave it to me. He told me that he really liked the piece of art I gave him. I was very happy, arriving home with a big smile on my face. I embraced my father, saying, "Yes! We did it father."

Father told me that Arlo is here, having brought sweets for our son, Justin.

I went to the next room and asked Arlo, "Where have you been? It's been so long since your shadow's been here your son has already forgotten your face."

After visiting for a few hours, Arlo prepared to leave.

"Christina, I want to apologize to you. I want to live with you again. Please, give me another chance. When I see you, when I feel your closeness, I want to be with you again and love you."

"I have a new life already without you," I answered him.

"I think if you think about it, you will change your mind and forgive me for all the evil I caused. You really did not deserve all of that."

I told him to leave.

The next week I received divorce papers. We both signed them and finally we were divorced.

Within a week, I went to the community college with my reference letter.

The director read it, smiled, and said, "Yes, we need good specialists. We accept you. However, we will need you to go to Moscow for training. Can you leave by the end of this month?"

I agreed. On his desk I saw that he had the same last name as the chairman of my former collective farm. I asked, but they weren't related. The director and his deputy were extremely nice and cultured people, as I later got to know them better after working there.

When I arrived back home and told my parents of my new job, they both rejoiced.

I embraced my father, saying, "Without your help, my dreams never would have come true. Father, you did it! Only through you did I get my desired job. I want to tell you that the community college director is going to send me to Moscow for training and I'll have to leave you and my son within one month."

"Do not worry, go, we will be very happy to raise Justin. He will be cared for and loved."

I told them that the reason I had to go to Moscow was to pass the disciplines of pedagogy and to get a defended diploma and a master's degree. "After I pass all the exams, I will come back and work here. I will write you letters and call often."

We all hugged and said goodbye.

"Take care of yourself," my parents said to me, "and stay healthy!"

"Yes, I will."

Chapter Thirty-Six: Moscow

I went back to the community college to get the necessary documents from the director, and a referral to the Moscow Timiryazev Academy. I bought a ticket and left by train to Moscow. There were four of us sitting in one cabin on the train. At night, as always, I preferred to sleep in the upper bed. In the evening, the conductor brought free tea and cookies. When the evening came, I went to the middle of the carriages to the restaurant.

Sitting at the table and eating, I looked out the window as the train took me farther away from all that I'd known in life. The pursuit of my goal once again dominated my thoughts. I felt the fullness of life, my eyes glowing in happiness. I was confident that everything would be just fine in Moscow. At the same time, I felt fear with a kind of sadness. I was leaving my beloved family and would be away from them for a substantial time.

After eating I returned to my cabin. I put bed linens on the second floor of the cabin, and after a good night's sleep I got off the train in the morning in Moscow. Everything around was new and different. A taxi took me to the central building of the Academy, where I showed my credentials, and the administrator told me where to find the student dormitory and the room assigned to me.

There I found the two young women who I'd be sharing the room with. They smiled kindly and we introduced ourselves. One girl was from Russia, but the other, Lina, was from my country. I was pleased that I would not be the only student from my country, and Lina and I became friends.

The very first night, I fell asleep quickly, but woke up with the feeling of being bitten. When I turned on the lights, I saw that the bed was full of black round bugs. I woke up the other girls and asked, "What are these?"

They told me that these were bed bugs. They examined their bodies and found red marks all over. After that restless unusual night, we bought bedbug poison and put it under our mattresses in our beds. After a few days, the bugs disappeared. However, every morning, there were cockroaches running around our food. We didn't have those in my hometown. They were much harder to get rid of, but at least they didn't bite us.

Our student dormitory was undergoing restoration in the corridors. One had to go down a long corridor to get to the washroom.

When the academic year started and we came to lectures, a young man approached me and introduced himself, saying that he was a student here and he spoke my native language. He said that he lived in the same student dormitory.

"How nice that there will be three of us from our native country together with local and international students," I said.

One evening, as I was walking down the corridor, an African man with a beard like Mephistopheles grabbed my hand and said, "My girl, wait. Wait girlie."

I had never seen a single African before, but I was not surprised or frightened. I pulled his hand away and went to the bathroom to wash up. On the way back, I met many students from Africa.

The next morning, when I went to the washroom, I saw a young African man. He showed his snow-white teeth and said good morning in Russian. The washroom was shared by all, both by male and female students. I replied, "Good morning," and smiled.

I saw small children of mixed races running around the dormitory living with their Russian mothers married to Africans. I wondered what fate awaited these children and wives when their African parents and husbands finished their studies and brought them back to Africa. I wondered if they would be sold to a shah.

In one case one woman fell in love and married an African. After going to Africa to live, her husband told her that she was too old for him, and he married a young girl in Africa. So, she returned home with her children.

As a blonde with blue eyes, several Africans wanted to get to know me as soon as I arrived. I didn't want to get into big friendships but when they invited me, I went to their rooms together with Lina. They always politely received us, prepared dinner, and played popular music. We listened to music by Abba, Rod Stewart, the Eagles, the Beatles, and more. We danced and laughed. After having a good time, we thanked them for the evening.

An African student lived in the next room. He seemed to me to be seriously in love with me. I did not know how to politely tell him that I wasn't romantically interested in him, so I started to avoid him. He still wouldn't leave me alone. One evening he knocked on our door with a bouquet of flowers. I sat him down and made him a sandwich. We spent our evening having fun and joking. I asked him if I could touch his hair. It was soft, fluffy, and curly.

The first weeks of my studies in Moscow were difficult because my knowledge of Russian was poor. Although I had passed the mandatory Russian language exam when I graduated from high school, I hadn't used it again and had mostly forgotten it. All international students had to study the Russian language in their first year, and then take courses in their chosen specialties. It took about two months before I was fluent, which my friends said was quite impressive.

The dormitory canteen served tasty pancakes for breakfast that melted in my mouth. They looked like crepes stuffed with a delicious filling. I had never had such delicious crepes in my life. I was sorry I did not ask for the recipe. In the evenings we drank tea with baked potatoes and had group discussions.

I met a lot of good people in Moscow, not only among Russians but also foreigners who studied in the city. Lina and I often took the bus from the student dormitory to Red Square in the center of Moscow for a walk. One time there, we met a Jew and an Arab from Israel. They studied at a Moscow Communist Party school. Pinned on the lapels of their jackets were badges with Lenin's image. We asked them why they had those badges.

"Our school told us we had to wear them, so we pinned them on the back of our jackets."

Another time, Lina and I went to the student sauna which was very close to our dormitory. We saw a lot of African girls in the sauna. Their naked, beautifully grown thin figures looked like perfectly formed bronze sculptures. I could hardly take my eyes off them.

A few months later, Lina and I were invited to a wedding between a white and an African student that took place in our dormitory. On the day of the wedding, the hall was filled with students from different countries, including Cuba, the Czech Republic, India, Germany, Poland, and Russia.

After the ceremony, there was a dance where I made friends with a Cuban named Vasco. I gave him my room number and the next day he came to visit me, inviting me to come to his room. He introduced me to his brother who was also a student at this Academy. Both were tall, Vasco with blond curly hair and his brother with dark straight hair. I started dating Vasco during my free time from lectures and he bought Lina and me tickets to various theaters, concerts, and museums. We had a splendid time together.

One evening, Vasco bought tickets for us to see the famous Russian singer Visocki who performed at the Taganka Theater. Visocki sang about his love of a French actress Marina Vladi. He told how he had met Marina Vladi for the first time at a party. Being shorter than her, he had to stand on tiptoe and whisper words of love in her ear, telling her that someday she would be his wife, even though they were both already married. It was a beautiful love story.

He told how the Russian authorities wouldn't allow him to fly to Paris to see her, and when he called her on the phone in France, the operator disconnected them. He described how he was put in prison for this song which the authorities said was against the communist regime. His father was an ardent communist and went against his son.

Another time, Vasco took me to the concert of the famous Russian singer Ala Pugachiova, where she also sang about broken love. Pugachiova was married to a Lithuanian circus artist, and they had a daughter. He gave her his father's Lithuanian surname and first name. Ala's Pugachiova's song "Arlekino" was the most successful in the concert. Whenever I hear it, I remember the best time I spent in Moscow.

I am grateful to all the students of that time who gave me such a great opportunity to see so much Russian culture, where I would not have had time to stand in lines to buy tickets for events.

Studying foreigners had separate stores from Russian students where the products were much better. We saw Russian students from our dormitory buying food from local stores, such as flour, cookies, and canned goods, and sending them to their hometowns, explaining that these food items were not available in their home stores. We were surprised that their home life was so difficult.

In the central streets of Moscow, I saw all kinds of meat in meat shops, but the further I went from the center, the shops were almost empty with nothing worth buying.

One day Lina went to a shoe store located in the very center of Moscow. The shopkeeper wrote the number one hundred and thirty-five on her wrist and told her to return in the evening. When she went back, she had to stand in the line for several hours until her number was called. She returned to the dormitory early in the morning with her purchase.

One fall weekend, my mother came to Moscow for a training course for three days. I met her at the train station and accompanied her to the hotel she'd booked with her colleagues. After checking in, we went to a restaurant in the city center. Sitting down at our table, we saw cockroaches walking across the tables and curtains. Needless to say, this spoiled our appetite.

After eating, we went to Red Square. The next day we met again. I showed her some of the museums and historical sites in Moscow. In the evening, we went to shops called Cum and Gum, although we didn't buy anything. The next morning, I rose early and went to her hotel to accompany her to the train station. We hugged and she thanked me for showing her a good time in Moscow.

In Moscow, the metro train stations were absolutely beautiful. Each stop had different big and attractive sculptures. Sometimes when walking down the street or waiting for the subway, people asked me if I was an actress or a dancer. They said my posture was so very beautiful, I looked like a dancer.

When I returned home from college during the holidays, I brought champagne, oranges, and bananas, goods not available in Lithuania. Everything in my country was hard to find, often requiring a bribe to get the items you needed.

One weekend, Lina and I and a few other students took a train to St. Petersburg. There we visited the world-famous Hermitage Museum Petrodvorec where Tsar Peter the Great lived. It was an amazingly beautiful place with an impressive park with fountains. I noticed that the museum employees treated local tourists differently than the foreign visitors. For locals, the guards sat on chairs and gave instructions in a strict tone without a smile. At one point, I lost my group and had to enter the museum a second time with foreign visitors. When I entered with the foreign group all the guides stood

119

and greeted us in English. They nodded and smiled, politely explaining about rules and the exhibits.

When I left this museum, I thought about what injustice this was. I felt for the first time a great envy that the foreigners were treated so much better.

After the museum, we went to the edge of the Baltic Sea by St. Petersburg. I saw a huge cruise ship docked by the shore. Women stood proudly smoking on board. All were nicely dressed in hats and chatting with each other. The waiters brought them drinks. I wanted to be on that ship and experience the feeling. I wanted to be free and travelling with them – but I realized it was only a dream.

Not long after coming back, I was surprised to see a letter from Arlo. How did he find my address, I wondered. I was shocked and opened his letter.

"Christina," he wrote. "We need to talk. I miss you so much. I apologize again for the wrongs I caused you. I need to see you as soon as possible and discuss our situation. Please, come back to Lithuania. I will meet you anytime. I think we should start all over again. I will wait for your reply.

"Signed, Arlo"

Reading this letter made me think about my past life. That evening, I wrote him this reply.

"Dear Arlo, thank you for your letter. I am surprised by your desire to see me. If you really still love me and love burns in your heart, I invite you to buy a ticket, get on a train, and come to meet me in Moscow. I will be glad to meet you here. Please let me know the day and time of your arrival. At the moment, I can't come to Lithuania. I have exams to finish. I won't sacrifice my career which I've fought for so hard. Also, I won't betray myself and my parents. I won't jeopardize my future based on one letter from you. I have a chance to take the first step toward the beginning of my new life. I will wait for you here. Signed, Christina"

I never received an answer from him. A few months later I learned from Arlo's friend that Arlo had married the same woman who worked in the restaurant, and she was expecting a baby. After a few years, he got a divorce from her.

When I completed the training courses, I had to pass my exams. The first exam was in psychology. This course had been difficult, and I was frightened of the exam. When I entered the exam room I sat down in front of the teacher. I started telling him my psychology knowledge. He stopped me, saying he wanted me to speak in Lithuanian. I was surprised!

I spoke about everything that came to my mind and he followed my speech attentively.

"Your language is very beautiful," he said.

He thanked me and asked for my gradebook. I submitted my gradebook to him, and he wrote the highest grade on it. I was surprised and thanked him. I left his room in a cheerful mood with tears streaming down my face.

After the psychology exam, Vasco invited me to go to the theatre for a performance about the myth based on the Greek mythology named "Icarus". The myth tells of Icarus and his father Daedalus who lived on an island. Daedalus, the most cunning sculptor and architect of the time, wanted to fly out from the island. Daedalus created wings for himself and his son Icarus from feathers bound to a thick cloth covered with wax. Daedalus warned his son not to fly too high, as the sun could melt the wax-covered wings, or too low, as the waves of the sea would wet the wings. Icarus rose too high, the wax melted, the feathers scattered, and Icarus fell into the sea and drowned. Daedalus reached Sicily safely where he built a temple to Apollo and hung his wings there as a gift to the Gods.

Vasco graduated from the Academy and prepared to return to Cuba. He invited me to come live with him there. I refused, telling him I didn't know the language, didn't have a job, and didn't have

121

the needed documents for departure. More importantly, I had to finish my schooling here. Then I'd return to my home and family in Lithuania. I told him that I would always remember him and our friendship. "You are the best friend I met here," I told him.

I hugged and kissed him. I accompanied him to the airport where we had a tearful goodbye.

While living in Moscow, I met a Polish student who was the friend of a German student. After she left Moscow and I returned to Lithuania, I went to visit her in Poland at her invitation. She took me to beautiful Polish cities named Sopot, Gdansk, Gdynia. She lived in Torun with her husband. The extremely beautiful Copernicus Cathedral in Torun remained in my memory. We corresponded with letters in the Russian language.

After completing the two-year program and defending my diploma, I was awarded the master's degree. Besides all the knowledge I gained and the increase in my professional profile, it opened up more opportunities to get a job.

Chapter Thirty-Seven: Love

Love is the poetry of life and the Sun.
- Belinsky, Russian critic

Returning home from my schooling, I found that I loved myself and respected my feelings. Love is a miracle medicine. Many people speculate to this day as to who wrote the first book about love. Nobody knows. Perhaps that person had not experienced the feeling of love himself and only imagined it as it should be. But indeed. Is love a miracle cure? I believe that love is the greatest drug.

First of all, you have to love yourself. Loving yourself can change your entire life. This is not vanity, arrogance, or conceit. Not loving yourself is just fear. Love is a miracle that fills the heart like an overflowing cup with respect and gratitude. This is the miracle of our body and mind. Love can be very diverse. It has a broad concept of feelings. You can love many things, the beauty that surrounds you, knowledge, the process of thinking, the joy of being in this world and loving it, the universe, your body and its functions, animals, and plants. Love embraces the whole world.

Chapter Thirty-Eight: Returning Home

I was happy to return to Lithuania after passing all the exams and having a good time in Moscow. Before leaving I had arranged for a job at a community college where I would start working in the fall teaching botany and microbiology. I went straight to my home where my parents and my son were waiting for me.

Thinking about starting my new life, I'm considering whether I should get married again. I asked my mother for advice.

"You know, Mother, I'm considering visiting my friend Erick. He liked me from my student years. Now I am thinking of going to him and proposing marriage to him.

"Definitely go," Mother said. "As I remember, he is a good person. You will have a sincere, good friend, and not only a friend, but at the same time a lover and a husband."

I went on the trip with great enthusiasm. I thought that when I met him, I would tell him first: "Hello, old man I am with you."

I got off the bus in his village and then realized I didn't know how to find him. I met a man walking along the road and asked him if he knew where the chairman of the collective farm lived.

He said, "Walk along the main road, after reaching the first street, turn right and he lives in the third house on the left."

"One more thing I would like to ask you. Is he still unmarried?"

"Oh, he is already married and raising a son."

His words hit me like thunder from a clear sky. I thanked him. I turned around on one leg, crossed to the other side of the road, and waited for the bus to take me home.

I later found out that he married a woman who worked at the farm with him. Although they had a son and a daughter, the marriage wasn't a happy one. After a few years, Erick left her to live with his mother. After a few more years, his wife filed for divorce and Erick continued to live with his mother.

Erick and I met many years later in a restaurant near his village. He told me that if he had known that I would come to him and want to live with him, he would never have married her. "I would have waited for you for many years."

I told him if you didn't make an effort to find me before marrying that woman, then your love was just infatuation.

"No Christina, it is not true. I wrote you letters at your parents' address but you didn't answer a single one."

"Erick," I replied, "I didn't receive any of your letters. Probably Agatha took the letters from the mailbox and destroyed them after reading them."

Erick said that he thought that I didn't want to communicate with him anymore.

"That wasn't true," I said. "You were my best friend and always will be." I bent to him and kissed his cheek.

Chapter Thirty-Nine: My Father's Death

In family life, love is the oil that eases friction, the cement
that binds closer together, and the music that brings harmony.
-Friedrich Nietzsche, philosopher

Shortly after I returned from Moscow, my father became ill.
He'd had kidney disease in his youth, and soon after my return, he
died from it. Life is sad when you lose a loved one.

Arlo and his mother came for the funeral. After the service,
many guests came for dinner at our house. When we finished our
dinner, my mother prepared bedding for Arlo and his mother.

Agatha came to the bedroom and asked Arlo, "Why are you
staying here? We don't want you here."

Arlo said, "Calm down Agatha. We did not come to visit
you. We came to pay our respects to a dear person with whom I
spent a lot of time. His memory is dear to me. Why are you so
angry?"

"I do not want to see you here," Agatha shouted.

My mother left the room and asked me to come to the
bedroom and stop Agatha from embarrassing us. When we got to the
bedroom Arlo and his mother weren't there.

I asked Agatha, "Where are our quests?"

"Gone."

My mother and I ran outside to look for them. They were
walking toward the bus station. We asked them to come back to the
house and stay with us. They answered no, your daughter-in-law told
us we had to leave. We'll stay in this bus station till the morning.

My mother said, "Please, Agatha doesn't speak for us. I am
embarrassed for her actions and beg you to come and stay in my
house."

They thanked us for the kind offer, but they did not come. My mother left and I stayed with them till the morning when they left. I was quite angry at Agatha.

I always remember how sweet and tolerant my father was. He instilled in me the feelings of conscientiousness, duty, punctuality, and keeping one's word. His greatest dream was to fly in the sky to carve the space without feeling any fear. Whenever I see planes flying, I want to wave at them, thinking that there is my dad's spirit flying. He was an extremely respectable person who shouldn't be forgotten. He loved his wife and family with all his heart and was devoted to his grandchildren. My love for him will never fade. His dream of selling his house and moving somewhere else faded and he could not live peacefully. So many of his dreams did not come true. Losing her beloved life partner devastated my mother.

Chapter Forty: Simon and Agatha

My mother had to take over all the tasks and all the household chores. She sold the cow Princess and continued to help the relatives living on the second floor of the house. She continued to try to help her son to make his life easier.

The residents of the second floor came up with the idea of growing tulips in two of my mother's rooms on the ground floor. When I returned home to visit my mother, I saw a field of tulips in the two rooms.

I went up to the second floor and asked, "How does your conscience allow you to oppress my mother like this?"

Simon answered, "My mother does not need to have so many rooms now that she lives by herself. One room is more than enough for her."

I became furious with them. My mother asked me to keep quiet and not talk to them about this. She said she was fed up with all the squabbles. "I want a quiet life."

When the tulips were ready to bloom, Simon and Agatha delivered them to sell at different cities and markets during various holidays. Mother did much of the work, including picking them, wrapping them in bundles, and putting them in boxes.

One morning when Simon's car was loaded with tulips, he asked our mother to go to the market with them and help sell tulips. Mother agreed.

When Agatha found out that Greta would also be traveling with them in the same car, she angrily told her husband, "If your mother goes in our car, then I will not go! You go alone with her."

Not wanting to get angry with his wife, Simon obeys his wife and leaves with her. To have peace at home, my mother went to the market by bus and helped them sell the tulips. She returned home by bus exhausted.

Mother never complained when she performed hard tasks. Never.

Simon had a German shepherd. One week when he and his wife went to St. Petersburg to sell tulips, their dog fell ill, refusing to eat. Mother took him to the veterinarian who said that he had canine distemper. No medicine would help the dog. Mother became scared. She knew that her son left a healthy dog behind and asked her to look after the dog. If he returned from St. Petersburg to find the dog dead, he'd be angry. Mom gave it high doses of penicillin and little by little, the dog got better. Thus, when Simon and Agatha returned home, they found the dog healthy.

After a few years, they came up with another business idea, brew beer and sell it. Good business indeed. The questions were, who would make that beer, and who would sell it? They said that they would brew it in the basement and sell it through the window on the first floor.

Shortly after they started, Agatha began causing problems. Having already drunk a little beer, she wanted to go to the cellar and pour herself more. When her husband saw that she had already drunk enough, he locked the cellar. When she saw that, she got very angry with him, took a broom with a wooden handle, and left through the door, walking around the house talking loudly and shouting for him to give her more beer.

No one would give it to her. She smashed a piece of glass in my mother's first-floor kitchen window with the broom handle. Seeing this, her husband told her sternly to go to her room.

"Sleep, do not go around asking for more beer, and do not break windows."

Early the next morning, while Simon and Agatha were still sleeping, the customers were already knocking on the window, thirsty for beer. Mother got up and sold them beer.

I came to visit my mother that weekend. When Saturday afternoon came, I invited her to go with me to a spring dance in the town by the lake. We had fun, danced, and went home happily. Agatha saw us coming from the window on the second floor.

She stated, "Two lonely women come from the dance, one a widow, and another divorced," and laughed cynically at us. We went to our rooms in silence.

Chapter Forty-One: Alma's Brother's Wedding

My classmate Alma graduated from engineering college and was assigned to work as an engineer in a meat factory. During the Soviet years, people working in such places became rich, for they could steal meat from the factory and sell it. No one tried to catch them. They gave a bribe to the guard at the gate. If an ordinary laborer got caught doing this, he or she would be severely punished. Engineers and directors who stole meat or other items could save enough money to buy a house and other expensive items.

My friend Alma built and moved into a new summer house. Sometimes she invited me and treated me to some delicious meat products. She would pack some meat pieces for me to take home. I was always grateful for her generosity. On one visit, Alma invited me to a Swedish sauna. Her brother and some former students were there. Her brother didn't talk to me but just looked at me strangely as if he wanted to say something but didn't dare.

When the government changed in Lithuania, the golden door mostly closed for the individuals who took state property. Alma received a docent degree and got a job as a teacher at the University.

During one summer, my mother and I were invited to Alma's brother's wedding which was held in rented premises in the village by the lake. We arrived late to the party and saw that there wasn't anywhere for us to sit at the tables. The guests were already eating.

In one room were the groom's guests, some of whom I recognized. In another room I didn't recognize any of the guests, deciding that these must be the bride's guests. The bride was sitting in the second room by herself with her guests. I wondered where the groom was. I suggested to my mother that we go for a walk to explore the surroundings.

While walking along a path, I found the groom sitting on a bench by himself.

"Why are you sitting here alone? Why are you looking so unhappy? Why would you frown like a flaxen brush?"

He looked at me but didn't answer. We left him with his thoughts.

Nearby we saw his mother coming toward us. She saw me wrapped in a French designer scarf with small raised red flowers falling over my shoulders.

"Oh, Christina, how beautiful your scarf is, but its fringes are so shabby."

I did not say anything. I took her statement as a mocking and ambiguous compliment. We left them and moved on to the wedding celebration. Most of the guests had finished eating. We found empty chairs where we sat down and ate.

I found out that Alma's brother met his bride on a train excursion to Romania. The bride lived in the capital of Lithuania, and the bridegroom was from a small town. Her father was a professor, and her mother worked as a nurse in a hospital. The bridegroom's parents were teachers.

After the wedding, my mother told me that Alma's brother, having learned that I was divorced, told his parents that he was going to propose to me. When the parents heard this, they stopped him.

"Son, think carefully. She is divorced and has a son. Her character is not good. She is stubborn and always has strong opinions and defends them."

"Mother, those issues don't matter to me. I love her. I liked her when we spent time together as children and as adults. I remember during my sister Alma's wedding, and after it was over, we guests went to sleep in the hotel rooms reserved for us. I was in the same room with Christina. We had two separate beds in this room. In the evening when she was lying in bed, I jumped from my bed to hers.

"She threw me out of that bed saying, 'What have you come up with now? You are like a brother to me.'

"I wanted so badly to hug her and tell her that I loved her, but she threw me out of bed. Mom, I will marry her. She is beautiful, knows her worth, and is a serious woman."

"Think, son. You met a girl from Vilnius on the train. Admittedly, she is without a figure but probably will be interesting and rich. Her parents are intelligent, they have many competent friends in powerful positions. If you marry her, your future will be bright. Your father could buy beer cheaper from the brewery where he works. He will send beer to you in Vilnius. You will set up stalls there and hire people to sell the beer. You will make a great living."

"I can do the same when I am married to Christina."

"No," his mother insisted, "She has no place of residence, she lives with her parents after the divorce. Think carefully, my son."

He obeyed his mother and married the girl from Vilnius. My mother said that's why he was looking so sad at his wedding party, sitting alone on a bench with his thoughts.

It was like in the song of the famous Russian singer Alla Pugachiova. The bridegroom was a king but fell in love with a young, beautiful, talented but poor singer. He told his knights that he would marry her.

"I will marry, I will marry."

The knights told him he couldn't marry her, it would be scandalous. So he married someone else. In his retinue he saw the poor singer girl standing near him, he was heartbroken that he was not with her.

Chapter Forty-Two: My New Beautiful Life

If you want your life to smile at you, give your good mood first.

-Benedict de Spinoza, Dutch philosopher

After leaving my parent's house in autumn, I started a new job and a new life. I brought my son Justin who was then six years old. Everything was new here for both of us.

The director of the college arranged for us to have a two-room apartment in the student dormitory on the first floor where the teachers lived. I dedicated one room as the bedroom where I put two beds. The other room I made into a living room. After giving a bribe to the furniture seller, my mother received furniture made in Germany, two light brown armchairs with an ornamented texture, a sofa, and a bookshelf. There was a continuous lamp array at the bottom of the shelf. The desk had a soft swivel chair next to it. On the living room floor, I laid the carpet my parents had gifted me for my graduation.

We had to share the bath and kitchen with other teachers, both located in the middle of the first-floor building. The layout was the same as during my studies in the student dormitory. The difference was that we had a private entry hall in our apartment with a sink and a toilet. Our building was surrounded with trees and flowers. Justin loved our new home.

Every morning, I took the bus with Justin to his kindergarten. Once my classes were finished, I took the bus back to pick him up. It seemed that after great efforts all my dreams had come true.

The people of this region were proud. The first months my work was very hard due to the new rhythm of my life and living conditions. It seemed to me that the teachers were watching me. I think that my posture and pride seemed strange to them. After a few months of work, they saw me as a friendly, pleasant colleague. We became a pleasant and friendly team with whom I got along, and we understood each other perfectly. We worked together for thirteen years.

A year later, Justin finished kindergarten and started attending the first grade of elementary school, 3 km away. He bravely took the bus by himself both ways.

Years later, one of my students told me that she used to see me and Justin walking hand in hand around the community college area. After getting married and having a son, she named him after my son.

One day, a student knocked on the door of the class I was giving.

He said, "Teacher, your rooms are burning and full of smoke."

I asked my students to stay in the class until I came back. I gave them some tasks to do to keep them busy. I ran home and when I opened the door, I saw Justin standing with a sooty face and crying. The apartment was full of smoke. Justin ran to me and hugged.

"Mother don't be angry. I lit a match in the toilet, and it lit the curtain on fire."

I saw the blackened walls and black webs hanging around the curtains. Holding him close, I said, "Don't cry, what is important is that you are alive. Calm down and let's go and wash your sooty face."

Later, I asked my students to help me clean up. They came after the lecture and gladly helped.

Various concerts came to the community college. One of the singers was one of my favorites, and when I told Justin he said we should buy flowers to give to him.

"You've come up with a great idea," I said. I bought a bouquet of red roses. At the day of the performance, we sat in the second row. The concert ended with a big ovation. We all applauded and asked him to sing additional songs. At the end, Justin ran to the stage and handed the bouquet of flowers to the singer. He thanked him and a happy Justin returned to his seat. Perhaps this is what inspired Justin to want to sing, act, and perform on stage, a desire that remained with him his entire life.

One summer weekend Aunt Beta, a famous children's television host, came with her performance program to our town. A lot of people with their children came to see her, and I took Justin. After her performance, she interacted with the children. She asked them various riddles.

After the riddles, she asked, "Can any of you children sing for us?"

Justin stood up, raised his hand, and said "I will sing. I am going to sing a song about the wolf and the goats."

Aunt Beta gave Justin the microphone and he sang. Everyone applauded him. The people sitting next to me said, "This child will definitely achieve a lot in life."

I was also very surprised when he sang the whole song with courage and no confusion. I congratulated him for a song well sung.

After four years of elementary school, Justin wanted to attend a children's music school. I asked him what kind of instrument he'd like to play.

He said a saxophone.

I went to Moscow and bought one for him.

Because the instrument was so heavy, after my lectures I'd take it on the bus to his music school for his lessons. After music lessons, he returned home by bus with his instrument.

While living in this city, I participated in many art exhibitions. I found out that there would be an exhibition of dry flower bouquets on the premises of the art center. I told them that I wanted to participate. I made several bouquets and put them in big bags and displayed them at the exhibition. Out of all the bouquets in the show, one of my bouquets won first place. I received an affidavit of a first place and a small award. At other times, I participated in exhibitions with various pieces of my textile works, carpets woven with the macrame technique, and pictures cut out of paper.

I participated with various groups of artists who introduced me to different art forms and gave me opportunities to participate in many art exhibitions.

One summer day I went to the farm where my friend Erick was chairman. When I arrived at the village, I went to the office and introduced myself. I asked the secretary where I could see the chairman.

The woman told me Erick had left for the regional conference that morning and would not return until late in the evening.

"And where can I see the students who are working here? Do you know something about them?"

"Yes, I know," she said. "They are always punctual at work and perform their duties well."

"Where could I see them and talk to them?"

She drove me to the field where they were working. When I approached them, the students were happy to see me. I discussed with them about their work there. At the end of the summer, the students finished their practices, and I wrote good reports on them.

In college I admired my colleagues, and we respected each other. Sometimes we organized music and dance parties. It was good to spend time with them not only at work but also in pleasure.

While working at the college in the fall, collective farm specialists invited students to help with the fall harvest. When I and the students arrived at the collective farm, the brigade-leader approached one of the students and asked him if he was the leader.

He said, "No," and pointed towards me.

The brigade-leader approached me and asked, "Are you the teacher here?"

"Yes, I am responsible for this group."

"How can it be that you are so young? You look like those students."

I thanked him for the compliment.

I also taught part-time students at the college, those who worked at the same time that they were studying for a diploma. I taught them botany and microbiology. To get their diplomas, these part-time students had to pass exams in all the subjects we were teaching, including my subjects.

After passing my subject exams, they invited me to a restaurant in the evening for dinner and refreshments. They presented me a flower bouquet. We discussed their jobs, hobbies, and other interesting subjects. I wished them all good luck and we parted.

"If you need me, feel free to contact me," I said. "We will meet again at the next session."

Chapter Forty-Three: The Mountain Climb

To accomplish great things, we must not only act, but also dream; not only plan, but also believe.
- Anatole France. French poet, journalist, novelist

During my second year, we organized an excursion to the mountains for the summer vacation with my student group. At the excursion office, we learned that there was a trip from Kabardino Balkaria (Russia) through the mountains to Georgia. A tour guide was appointed for us. We loaded winter and summer clothes into large backpacks as well as non-perishable food and canned goods. After flying to Kabardino Balkaria, we took a bus to the mountains and spent one night in a school, sleeping on the wooden floor with our backpacks for pillows.

In the morning, we took a bus to the mountain where a local mountain guide was waiting for us. After putting on our heavy backpacks, we started to hike up the mountainside. Being afraid of heights, after seeing the huge high mountains up close, I wanted to go back. But there was no going back, only forward. We walked up the steep mountain slope through the rock formations. There was no trail, the guide forging a path where the stones were stacked more evenly.

Climbing wasn't easy with a heavy backpack on my shoulders. The views around were stunning, especially the vast expanse of the mountains. The guide warned us not to look back, only forward, and follow him. After a few hours of hiking, we reached a narrow, long, uneven, mountain pass. On one side there was rock, on the other side deep below we could see a small bluish lake and mountains. The water of the lake was emerald.

We walked through, one by one in silence, clinging to the rock. I kept my gaze focused forward, hoping to get through this mountain pass as quickly as possible. Happily, we all reached a smoother road where we could rest, have a drink, and take off the heavy backpacks. The worst part of the mountain track was over.

After sitting down, we took out homemade sandwiches from our backpacks. They were absolutely delicious. It was much tastier than what we ate at home. I walked away from everyone to dream. I felt the joy and peace of the mountains. I wanted to dance and jump. The views of the mountains were amazing, breathtaking.

While dreaming like this, I saw a backpack rolling towards me. The backpack, being heavy, gained momentum quickly. I tried to catch it and it slammed into my arms, nearly knocking me over, and rolled past me, right down the side of the mountain. The guide climbed down and retrieved the backpack, returning it to the girl who carelessly misplaced it.

After resting and eating, we changed our clothes for the colder weather we'd soon be encountering. Our guide encouraged us to stand up and continue walking again. He warned us that we had a long way to go before it got dark and we reached our resting place for the night.

As we climbed higher, the vegetation thinned. The green decreased and patches of snow could be seen. In the evening, we reached a big tent in an area without greenery, with only snow. The guide told us that this was where we'd be sleeping and that we'd be up at four in the morning. Inside were plank beds. We were eager to rest from the fatigue we experienced.

One man warmed up the tea outside. I went outside, took my tea, sat on a rock, and listened to the absolute quiet. Breathing the fresh mountain air, I thought of how mighty the mountains were around us, and how little man was before them. Exhausted from the day's hike, I went into the tent and fell asleep quickly.

In the middle of the night, we were awakened by the noise of strong winds. It roared, whistled, and shook our whole tent with its blowing. It seemed that our tent might collapse and take us down the side of the mountain. Everyone gathered in the center of the tent floor, scared, listening to the wind's rustling.

Eventually, the wind calmed down and all became completely silent. We returned to our plank beds again to sleep for a couple of more hours. Four o'clock in the morning came too quickly. The guide was already up and waiting for us all as we went outside.

I ate some dark chocolate to increase my blood sugar, knowing we still had a long day of climbing up through the snow. We put on our backpacks and left. The snow was fluffy, and our feet stuck in it, making our climb slow. I could barely put one foot in front of the other.

After eight hours of climbing, we reached the peak of the mountain. The guide warned that when going back down the mountain, we shouldn't slide on our backs because the sharp mountain edges would be injurious. He explained when going down, firmly press your heel into the snow. Don't forget to put the gauze masks on your face because the strong mountain sun will burn them as much as fire burns. Painful blisters will result. One girl in our group did not obey the guide, she wanted her face to have a nice brown burn.

The guide said goodbye as we would now be led by our own tour guide. Our boots were strong for hiking in the mountains. Although we went slowly, we discovered that it was much easier to go down than to climb the mountain.

When we reached the bottom of the mountain, we no longer felt the weight of the backpack as our shoulders had gotten used to it. After stopping, we changed back to summer shorts. The sun was scorching, and we no longer felt the cold. We took pictures of ourselves lying in the snow half-naked.

As we descended further, we came across flowing mountain streams with water clear and cold. We dipped into the cold water for drink and washing. We splashed each other and laughed.

After a short rest, we continued our trek, knowing we had to reach our hotel in Georgia in the evening, still with a long way to go. It was after nightfall by the time we reached the hotel. We could finally take off our backpacks, eat and rest. The face of the girl without the mask had burned. She was in so much pain that we had to look for a medical personnel to help her. Luckily for us, the staff at the hotel included a nurse.

At the hotel, we met tourists who had traveled by other routes and shared our experiences with them. In the morning, our tourist bus took us to the capital of Georgia. After staying there for two days and exploring the interesting historical places of this city, we happily flew back full of impressions and experiences from our trip.

I was proud to make it to the top of the mountain despite the difficulties. Can mountain hiking fundamentally change an individual? I think so. Cooperation is revealed in a mountain trip. If you want to experience the character of the man you love, go to the mountains. You will definitely decide after that whether it is worth continuing your friendship with him.

I learned many lessons in the mountains. To be successful at a difficult venture, one must be stubborn and persistent, hardened. Without these qualities, it's impossible to achieve good results. One of the biggest difficulties of mountain travel is the intense physical exertion. One needs a strong body and a clear head. In the mountains, one can improve their health but can also be injured. Sports provide energy and help maintain mental balance. I liked various sports. What bothered me at the beginning of the trip was the fear of heights. Later, I felt no fear, as if I'd merged with nature.

Also important was preparation and planning and listening to the instructions of the tour guide to achieve the goal. Our good tour guide and mountain guide helped us to overcome this mountain track. We united in the mountains as if we became one family.

We went up the north side of the mountain and came down the south side. Mountains eliminate the state of stress. A greater connection with nature emerges. To travel is to experience a trance. When you enter this state, you stop thinking. This state seems to lull you to sleep. It also appears when you immerse yourself in the creation of a work of art, the same feeling as when you are in nature. This state is very pleasant. The more I walked up the mountain, the more I relaxed. Not without reason it is said. To improve your health, go to the mountains at least once a year.

Chapter Forty-Four: Meeting Peter

Man is initially indeterminate, that is, he is nothing at first.
He will become something only later and be what he makes himself.
-Jean-Paul Sartre, French philosopher, novelist

About five years into my teaching at the community college, I participated in an art exhibit with my macramé. When I visited the show, I saw a man admiring my artwork. I told him I was the artist.

"Are you an artist too?" I asked him.

"Yes." He showed me his beautiful, precisely carved wooden statues and bowls. We introduced ourselves, his name was Peter.

Peter was tall, with dark curly hair and dark skin, and dressed in a long black leather coat with a red scarf thrown over his shoulder. Black shoes and blue jeans finished the outfit. He looked like the famous designer Halston, only with a red scarf instead of white. I was impressed by the combination of his outfit and his artwork. After talking a little, we parted.

Not more than a few months later, another exhibition came in which I participated. Here I showed my knitted coats, gloves, hats, crocheted napkins, and paper cut pictures. Peter was there.

"Christina, I see that your artwork this time is completely different. I find the different compositions interesting, created with precision."

"Thank you. I'm pleased that you appreciate them."

We discussed art for an hour, and then exchanged phone numbers and addresses. Peter lived in a small town about 30 kilometers from where I lived.

Soon we started talking on the phone, and then he visited me, bringing a bouquet of roses. We talked and I made dinner. After the meal, he offered to wash the dishes. He communicated pleasantly with my son Justin.

Peter started to visit often. One evening after his arrival, I was sitting in the living room on the sofa, and he on the armchair reading a newspaper. I wanted to get his attention, so I ran my thumb through the bottom of the newspaper and sang a song called "Ciao bambino sorry," following the lyrics of the song by the French singer Mireille Mathieu.

He stood up, dropped the newspaper, and shook convulsively.

"What happened to you?" I shouted. "Did I do something wrong?"

"Don't you dare ever do that to me again," he said.

"Sorry. I just wanted to make a joke. I certainly didn't mean to offend you. I don't see that what I did was so wrong."

After being silent for a few minutes, he told me that he was leaving. I escorted him to the door and wondered what had caused him to get so upset.

The next day, early in the morning, the doorbell rings. I open the door. Peter is standing there with a bouquet of roses.

He said, "I feel badly for my behavior yesterday. I'm sorry and promise it won't happen again."

I informed him that he couldn't stay because I had to go to work. He kissed me on the cheek and left.

From then on, whenever we were together, he was on good behavior. We became close friends, seeing each other from time to time at my place in the student dormitory.

He told me that he had a daughter from his first marriage who was the same age as Justin. "I divorced from my wife because she was unfaithful to me."

I briefly told him about myself.

I asked my son, "How do you like him?"

"Mother, I think he suits you. You and he have common interests."

I called my mother and told her that I had met an artist at the exhibition who interested me.

She answered, "I am planning to visit you soon and I hope to meet him."

Soon she came to the student dormitory. Peter brought flowers to give her. I served dinner and after everyone had eaten Peter washed the dishes. He told jokes and was very nice to my mother. It seemed to me that he made a good impression on her.

A month after we met, he proposed to me. I told my mother about it.

"Christina, is this really the husband you dreamed about?"

"I think so," I said.

I asked, "Peter why did you not introduce me to your parents? Do your parents know that you want to get married with me?"

"No, it doesn't matter to them. I will tell them about it later."

I found that to be strange. I thought maybe their family relationship was not close, so I didn't pay too much attention to it.

I accepted his proposal of marriage. I told Peter that I will live and work at the community college until Justin finishes elementary school but will often come to his house. He agreed.

Chapter Forty-Five: Meeting Peter's Parents

Life is not looking at each other, it is looking in the same direction.
-Antoine de Saint-Exupery, French writer

Our wedding was very modest. Peter came to our dormitory with his daughter and with his four best friends. My mother, Justin, and I greeted them. We married at the registry office. Afterward, we celebrated at the student dormitory. At dinner, Peter gave a speech, saying that now that I was married I could reduce my working hours or not work at all.

He said, "You will be inspiration for my artwork, and the queen of my town."

Those sweet, strong-sounding words rang in my ears like cathedral bells. When I listened to them, I felt the greatness of life and peace in my soul.

He continued, "Both of us will be able to communicate with each other through our art creations. Christina, I promise to love you, to be strong in my soul, to consult with you on all the issues that arise in our lives."

I thought to myself, what beautiful words. Would our life really be the way he painted it? If this was true, the joy of life and the fullness of life would return to me.

After dinner, Peter, his daughter, and his friends went home.

The next day, when I went to work, I told my colleagues that I married Peter yesterday. I brought them lunch, candy, cake, and champagne. They congratulated me with a song.

After the wedding, Peter invited me to come by train to his house to introduce me to his mother and father. Peter met me at the train station and took me to his parents' house. They appeared to me to be kind, lovely people.

Peter's mother was offended that he did not tell them earlier about the wedding.

"Son, it seems you do not need us anymore."

"No, Mom. It just happened quickly, we fell in love and got married. Do not be angry with me."

Peter's father, being a Russian soldier after the Second World War, fell in love with a Lithuanian woman and married her. He remained to live in Lithuania. His language was broken Lithuanian. Later, after getting to know them more, I found out that both parents were communists. My family, on the contrary, had different views. At that time, I was in love with my husband, and I did not pay attention to it.

After meeting his parents, Peter invited me to his house. It was a small house with a chimney on the roof. The front door opened onto a small kitchen with a brick stove heated with firewood or coal. Water was brought from the well in buckets. Behind the kitchen, there was a living room with a folding sofa, a small table, and a small display holding various things. A small bedroom had a narrow bed and a round table with four chairs.

The large yard held a broken, crooked barn which Peter told me used to be an animal slaughterhouse where he stored his household items. Behind the barn was a small garden. I thought about how different my grandmother's house was from this one, larger and prettier.

In his living room, he had spindles and wood carvings hanging on the walls. He told me his house served as his workshop. He said people bought his work for weddings, baptisms, and birthdays.

"Sometimes I have a rich customer who orders artistically carved furniture with various small ornaments. Mostly, though, I make the small items you see here."

I told him he was a very talented man.

The next day we flew to the Russian resort town of Sochi on the Black Sea for a week's honeymoon. We went to their huge market where we shopped and bought exotic fruits. Peter seemed only interested and items for himself, not paying any attention to me. I figured he probably lived alone for so long that he was used to buying for himself. I told him to wait and we could look at the goods together.

"Oh, of course, of course."

After that, we shopped together. Yet he continued only buying clothes for himself without seeking my opinion and not asking me if there was anything I wanted to buy. I began to wonder if I had made a mistake by marrying him so quickly. Peter showed neither attention nor love to me.

In the mornings, we went to the sea to sunbathe. One day we walked around a wonderful botanical garden. Peter walked with his head down, daydreaming and unhappy. The week in the beautiful resort town went by quickly.

On the day we were to return home, an important Russian commander died, and all flights were suspended. We went to the airport to try to find other flights and found long lines of angry people, pushing and shouting.

Peter told me to go stand in line.

I asked, "Why don't you go to stand?"

"You're better at it. I will sit here in the corner." He sat down on a chair. I stood in the long line for several hours. As I stood, I wondered why he was such a weak man that he never came once to replace me in line, never relieving me so I could sit down. I received the tickets, and we went back home the next day.

A week after we returned, my mother said she wanted to come see Peter's house. When she saw the building, she was surprised.

"Christina, how can you live in such a small house like this? After the first divorce your dreams were different."

"Mother, I fell in love with the man and did not care where I would live. He is a famous and recognized folk master in wood carving. He is known not only in our country but also abroad."

She looked around and sighed. "Well, as you say, it is your life, if you are happy, I am happy."

A sad smile washed across my face as I considered whether I really was happy. I wondered if I really loved him and whether he loved me. I realized I probably had jumped on this cart too soon.

"So far, we have been living together for a short time. Sometimes we live in harmony with spiritual support of each other and mutual understanding. There are other days when I do not understand what is happening with him. Maybe he has some kind of nervous disease, and he does not know it. I am happy when he does not have these bad days. We rarely see each other, and sometimes not every weekend. Our common life will begin when Justin and I move into this small house and live together."

"Well, I hope you have happiness," my mother replied sadly.

My mother decided to make us lunch. She put paper and some dry small firewood in the stove and lit it. Smoke poured through the oven door, filling the kitchen.

She looks at me and says, "What is this? The chimney is really clogged," she says. "Probably crows have made a nest there. How can you cook?"

I asked Peter if the chimney had ever been cleaned, but he didn't know. Living alone, he never cooked.

"Well," Mother said, "I will make a broom from birch tree trunks, tie them together, find a wooden pole, put the tied birch tree trunks into the pole and make a broom. I will go up on the roof with this broom and put it in the chimney and clean it."

I doubted she would do all that and went to the bedroom to lie down. Sure enough, while I was resting, she walked to a nearby woods, collected branches, made a broom, placed a ladder, and climbed onto the roof of the hut. She pushed her broom down the chimney and began scrubbing. Several screeching crows flew out, saying that you disrupted our warm and peaceful life.

Peter's friend Frank came to our yard riding his bicycle. He laughed loudly on seeing my mother on the roof.

"Who is on the roof?" he shouted. "Am I dreaming or watching a movie? I see a woman on the roof with a broom. Is she a witch? But she's not dressed in black and riding the broom. Therefore, she's not a witch, probably she's Christina's mother."

She climbed down from the roof to greet Frank, her face and hands covered with soot.

Frank shook his head in astonishment. "I have never seen such a thing in my life that a woman would climb on the roof to clean the chimney."

Mother said, "The chimney was blocked and had to be cleaned."

She returned to the kitchen, relit the fire, and, voila, smoke was drawn outside.

There was no place to sleep in the evening for three people. Mother and Justin lay down in the narrow sofa in the living room. By morning, they felt that they'd hardly slept. In the afternoon, we accompanied my mother to the railway station. We went back to our community college, where the next day I had to go to work and Justin to school.

Peter had a very good voice. He was tall, thin, and good looking. He had an eloquence around him. He knew how to joke while telling interesting anecdotes. He spoke softly and was always cheerful in the company of friends. He didn't drink or smoke.

Some weekend nights, we'd go dancing. We both loved to dance. Women watched us with envy when we danced. They simply adored him.

We were invited to a big party with well-to-do people. I wore a nice blue short dress with one shoulder, a fashion I found in a magazine and had a seamstress sew it for me. At the ball, the director of the factory invited me for a dance.

He asked, "Who cut off one of your sleeves from the dress?" Probably it was his sense of humor.

Having free time, Peter tore down the old barn and built a wooden two-story house with wooden folk motifs and oak carved front door. I called this our "House of Fairy Tale." The interior of the house was covered with wooden boards. On the first floor, there was a living room, a kitchen, and a w.c. with a shower and toilet. Peter built a spiral staircase to climb to the second floor, where there was a small lounge and two bedrooms.

In April, the teachers organized an excursion to the drama theater in Vilnius. Peter agreed to join us. When he arrived at my house the morning of the show, his shoes were filthy. I offered to clean them, but he refused. On the bus ride to the theatre he wouldn't talk, just sat with his head drooped into his hands.

"What's wrong?" I asked, but he wouldn't talk to me.

The teachers sitting behind us asked if something was wrong with my husband. I answered he was very tired.

When we got off the bus, he wandered off and only joined us after everyone was seated in the theatre. The whole performance, he sat with his head propped down. When I tried to talk to him, he told me to go away and shut up.

I felt uncomfortable for myself and my colleagues. I wondered why he was acting this way. We returned late to my home without saying anything to each other. When he got on the night train to go home, we didn't even say goodbye.

152

Peter called me the next day to apologize.

I told him I was disgusted with him and his behavior. "How can I accept your apology when you keep repeating the same actions?"

"I promise you that I will control my emotions."

On his last week in elementary school, Justin's teacher assigned him to give a speech to the class of high school graduating seniors. Just before the last bell that the seniors would ever hear in that school, Justin entered their classroom. He stood at the blackboard and told them that he would be your last teacher in this school today.

Justin began his speech with this poem.

Beloved class graduates
I am closing the blackboard of this class
And opening the class of your new lives
Even though you are all tearing
Do not think about parting from each other.
But rather think about the stormy life that will carry you forward.

Today I have been assigned to be your last schoolteacher in a school that is celebrating its centenary, so sit up straight, put your hands on your desks, and listen carefully.

Remember your spelling rules, your mathematic equations, your history, and most of all, friends you leave behind.

Since you answered all my questions well, you showed me that you have learned a lot during these twelve academic years. Good luck to all of you and come back to the school every now and then to say hello to your teachers. Class period is over.

The students stood up and called "Bravo, bravo," to the teacher and themselves.

Chapter Forty-Six: Moving to a Small Town

Once Justin finished elementary school, we moved to the new House of Fairy Tale built by Peter. I borrowed a car with a trailer from Peter's friend and brought my furniture from the dormitory. We put my German furniture on the second floor where Justin lived. On the first floor, armchairs and a table were placed in the living room. I hung a round carpet of my macrame art that had a huge metal button embedded in the middle over the sofa. I hung my crocheted curtain made of linen threads on the window. In the middle of the upstairs wall, I hung a Rembrandt reproduction, "The Union of Earth and Water," which I bought in the St. Petersburg Hermitage Art Gallery while studying in Moscow. A modern textile rug I made from jute with various colors and with macrame ropes also got hung on the wall.

For the living room, I made a wedding garden out of straw and hung it near the stairs. After cutting out various paper clips with Roman motifs and framing them, I hung them on the walls. On the kitchen window I hung a curtain I knitted from white linen threads with a grass carp arrow. In the kitchen, there was a small white sideboard for storing dishes and a stove heated with wood or coal. By the window, there was a small wooden table with two chairs carved from wood with ornaments. Behind the kitchen, there was a water boiler to store and heat water. If the water boiler filled with too much water, it started running over your head when you went to the toilet. Hanging behind the toilet were shelves covered with my batik-dyed and hung curtain.

My friend Alma came to visit me. When she saw this curtain, she asked me to give it to her.

"I will make a very nice skirt from it," she said. "You can paint another curtain."

"Take it if you like it," I said. "You are my good friend."

I gave it to her and replaced it with a plain white sheet. I never did paint a new curtain in batik style for the spot.

Close to our home were soldier barracks, where, at times, they had target practice. My German shepherd always barked when he heard their gunshots.

Peter demolished his grandmother's house and built a large wooden building with patterns for his workshop. The interior shop was never furnished.

Next to the living house, Peter attached a shed as a storage place for firewood and coal. He installed two wide wooden boards inside the shed and put some of his work tools on top of them. The shed door was crooked and needed to be repaired. I thought that when I bought a car, I could park it there.

When my mother visited us, she complimented us on the beautifully designed and furnished house. However, when she saw the mattress lying on the floor of the second floor she was surprised.

"What is this? Where is your bed?"

"There is no bed," I answered.

"Can't you buy one? If you do not have money, you have a master of woodwork. Why can't he make a normal bed? How do you wash the floor? You know that there must be dust under it."

She went outside and brought back logs that she placed under each corner of the mattress.

"Now it will be possible for you to wash the floor under the mattress."

Seeing this unusual design of hers made me laugh.

After building the house in the middle of the yard, he dug a pool and filled it with water that summer. When the water warmed up, we went swimming, but this happened rarely because summers were usually cold and rainy. I planted flowers at the end of the pool.

I took a picture of the pool full of water and the blooming flowers I planted. After developing the flower photo, I was startled

155

to see that the arrangement looked like the face of Satan, similar to that shown in the movies or described in books. The face was elongated, with horns, a long-pointed beard, and symmetrically arranged ears and eyes. His ironic smile was twisted. I showed the photo to my mother and friends who were with us. Some saw it immediately, others didn't.

I enrolled Justin in grade school and in a children's music school. The music teacher advised Justin to buy a clarinet, saying that the saxophone was too heavy for him. I sold the saxophone and went to Moscow again and bought a clarinet. Justin liked it. He attended the bagpipe orchestra and soon participated in various festivals and after a few years played at the Republic Song Festival in Vilnius.

I didn't want to give up my job at the community college. Every morning, I rushed to the train and then the bus took me near to the college. With my low salary, I didn't have enough money to buy a car. Sometimes the bus didn't arrive on time, and I was late for classes. This upset the college director who gave me notes and warnings. It became a difficult situation. Finally, I had to find a second job.

I found a new one as a housework teacher in a school near where I lived. I taught girls sewing, knitting, cooking, color matching, ethics, and aesthetics.

Chapter Forty-Seven: Peter's Cousin's Wedding

Love is like a spice. It can sweeten your life, - however, it can spoil it, too.
- Confucius, Chinese philosopher

After living in this town for a few months, Peter's uncle invited us to his daughter's wedding where Peter introduced me and Justin to him. I liked him right away and accepted his invitation to be the maid of honor. I had already prepared Melody's wedding, so planned to repeat the same, adding some new nuances.

Justin, now eleven, and Peter's daughter came with us to the wedding. As I was conducting the wedding ceremony, Justin came up to me and sat down next to me.

"Mother, may I sit here and be with you?"

"Of course," I told him.

Seeing this, Peter approached and shouted, "Justin, you see that mommy is busy. Get away from her."

Upset, he obeyed him and left. Peter could have said, "Son let's go and sit together and talk and have some food together." Then Peter walked away.

My mood was spoiled. The wedding house was so full of guests that there were no empty chairs. Peter busied himself telling stories. Not Peter, his mother, or his father paid the slightest attention to Justin. The sister of Peter's mother saw that Justin was trying to sit some place and she invited him to sit by her.

"Come, my boy, and sit by me," she said. "There's enough room for both of us. You must be hungry, eat." She hugged and kissed him.

"Thanks, Aunty," he said.

I was very grateful to see that she was an understanding and friendly woman.

On the second day of the wedding, Peter and I were sitting across from each other at a table. The music began and I asked Peter to dance with me.

He answered, "Go take a shit."

I was shocked! The people sitting next to me and next to him became silent. I felt very uncomfortable. Never had I heard such dirty words in mixed company. I got up from the table, apologized, and went outside. The music was playing loudly, and I wandered onto the dance floor. My matchmaker invited me to dance. While dancing I could not forget my husband's dirty words. I tried to be cheerful and not to show my sadness. The matchmaker thanked me for yesterday evening in which we both performed. He was glad that he met me and that we had made the wedding feast with all the traditions that the bride and groom requested.

I replied the same to him and thanked him for last night's meeting. While we were talking Justin approached us.

"Excuse me mother," he said. "I am going home."

"Okay, son see you there."

When he left, I continued to dance many more dances with the best man and other guests. Eventually, Peter came to me and told me we had to go home.

"Wait," I said, "I still want to dance. Can you wait for me or perhaps dance with me?"

"No, I do not want to dance."

"Well, I don't want to go home yet."

He didn't answer, just turned and left. Once again, he ruined my mood and my evening. I thanked the hosts, guests, and matchmaker for the great time I had and left.

I went back home slowly, dragging my feet. I went to the kitchen and made myself a lemon drink. I talked with Justin, undressed, and went to sleep.

Chapter Forty-Eight: Sugar Beet Weeding

One of my former students offered me an opportunity to weed one hectare of a sugar beet field.

"You get a big bag of sugar if you weed the field," she said. "I will choose a good field for you that has few weeds."

The offer was tempting for I wanted the sugar to cook jams and compotes, so although I wasn't enthusiastic, I agreed.

When she showed me my assigned weeding field, I got scared at seeing the very long furrows. They were so long, I couldn't see their ends. I invited my mother to come and help me.

"Let's take the weeding hoes right away," she said. We took our bikes and went to the train station. When the train arrived, we put our bikes on the train. After getting off the train, we biked to the beet field. We weeded all morning and then took a lunch break with sandwiches we'd brought. We discussed that we wouldn't be able to finish the job in one day and decided to sleep in the nearby barn rather than go all the way home. The barn was standing right next to the area of the beets field. That night, we settled in and drank milk and ate leftovers. After a successful sleepover, we returned to weeding at dawn and worked until dusk. Both of us were exhausted when we returned home on the train.

When we entered our house, I noticed that Justin had a bloody nose.

"Justin, what happened?"

In between sobs, he said, "Peter had told me to warm up the zeppelins (food) but instead I ate them cold. When he saw that I wasn't listening to him, he shoved me into a corner. He pressed me against the wall and put his knee into my stomach. He forced my mouth open and stuffed a zeppelin in my mouth. He yelled, 'Now you will see what will happen to you for not listening to me.' My heart started beating and I got scared. My eyes started to tear. I could not say a word since the food was in my mouth. He then punched me in the nose and dropped me down on the floor. He slammed the door and left."

After hearing this, I found Peter sitting and watching TV. I asked, "What happened, what kind of conflict did you start here? Don't you dare touch him again. I will file a police report on you on this incident. Why are you treating my son like this? He had to endure your dirty words, fists, and bullying."

In the evening Justin approaches Peter saying, "Dad, I brought you candy."

He took the candy not saying anything to him.

It was difficult for Justin to live like that since he needed love and affection. I felt I was failing him as his mother and responsible for his safety.

A month later, the brigade leader called asking if I'd weed the beet field again. I invited my niece Renee to help my mother and me do the weeding. She agreed to come and help us. This time instead of sleeping in the barn we went back home and then returned the next day by train and bikes. Again, it took two days to finish weeding the furrows. Renee stayed with us for a week before returning home.

Another month passed and the brigade leader asked me to come weed for a third time.

"No, I'm sorry, I can't weed a third time. If you can, hire a woman to weed the field and I will pay her for it."

"Don't worry, I'll take care of it."

In autumn, the brigade leader called to say that I should come and pick up a bundle of sugar.

Chapter Forty-Nine: Stepfather in Lives of Children.

When a stepfather comes into the family, the child has to decide what to call him. In order to create a warm relationship, the stepfather must communicate with and pay attention to the child, including engaging in activities. Early investment of time will create a loving and trusting long-term relationship. Joint activities bring the family together. They should participate in fun leisure activities and do housework together. Expressing opinions in open conversation is especially necessary.

An adolescent child may find it difficult to accept a stepfather and adjust to having him in the home. It takes patience and time. A stepfather must provide children with a strong sense of security. To be his strong partner, they need to provide respect, love, and communication.

The stepfather should be a good friend of the child, not a competitor or a rival. A child feels trauma when he is humiliated and insulted every day. Saying to the child that he is stupid and cannot do anything does not accomplish love or understanding with him. A victim of bullying shuts himself off and experiences difficult feelings, long-lived fear, anxiety, and tension. It could be a risk factor for the emergence of various mental disorders.

When a stepfather comes into a family with children of different parents, the rules at home must be the same.

A stepfather must have self-control and avoid being angry. He must remember he is dealing with a child and show patience. Do not humiliate him. Children need hugs and kind words. Ask how they are doing, how are they feeling? It is difficult for the child to live with a stepfather who won't respect the child. The stepfather must know that the value of kindness given to the children will give them a great connection in the future.

Chapter Fifty: Birth of a Son

After two years of marriage, I delivered a second son, Gabriel. I had looked at various pictures of beautiful and healthy girls in magazines and thought that I would have a girl.

My mother was working in the hospital and helped me with the birthing, that happened at 5 hours and 35 minutes p.m. My mother handed him to me, and said, "This is your beautiful son." I held him close and gazed upon his beautiful face. He was a very cute and healthy baby.

Peter came to visit us at the hospital but couldn't touch us due to the sanitary conditions. We talked through the window, and I showed him our son Gabriel.

Peter was nicely dressed. He wore a blue corduroy jacket, white pants, and black holiday shoes. All the nurses were paying attention to him through the window. I was pleased with his looks and his clothes. He seemed to me very happy that everything was fine.

Children are born out of love. We want them, we are waiting for them, and need them. They do not ask to come into this world. They come from the labyrinths of love. Our love for our children must be nurtured as they grow. Parents should spend a lot of time with their children. It's also important for them to have friends to play with. We teach children to see the life in nature that surrounds us, animals, birds, and plants. We must instill healthy interaction and joy in everything. We create a benevolent warm connection with children by loving them. They will always remember our participation with them when they grow up.

After returning from the hospital, I stayed with my mother until Gabriel was four months old. Gabriel was healthy and a good sleeper.

Chapter Fifty-One: Peter's Profession

A sad home is a home where love does not laugh.
  -Giuseppe Giacosa, Italian poet

Throughout our life together, Peter had enough work. His clients were satisfied with his precise artwork. I'd ask him how much money he was paid for his work, but instead of telling me, he'd be rude.

"Why do you care?" he'd say.

"Because we're one family, raising two sons with a life together."

"How much I received is my business alone."

Without saying anything more, he'd walk away mumbling.

He always treated his friends and visitors politely, and with jokes. People would ask me, "How could you not love such a talented person?"

"Yes, some days when he is in a good mood, he is pleasant. You never know when and from which direction the wind will blow and when he will turn on you."

When he got angry, he was mean. When I saw that he was upset, I'd walk away, not saying a word. Usually, I'd go to another room and do some work. Every time we went out to visit our friends, I'd swear to myself that I would never go anywhere with him again. But then I'd realize that if I didn't go, his friends would condemn me. They didn't know he was a chameleon. They only saw the good side of his character. With them he was always a pleasant interlocutor and never got angry when talking to them.

I never saw his money and didn't know how much he made. I continued to make meals for the whole family and buy food with the money I earned. Our financial affairs were completely separate.

Due to the household expenses of raising two children, with no financial help from Peter, I had to increase my hours, working two jobs in different cities.

When Peter's parents came to visit, I always prepared a meal for them, and we would chat. Although they were calm when they arrived, before leaving our house, they would quarrel with each other and never leave our house together. Peter's father would got angry and left the house first, followed by his wife. He would always incite problems by turning everything she said to its opposite side.

Peter's parents had four children, two girls and two boys, of which Peter was the oldest and appeared to be the most talented. Peter's brother was a teacher in another city. His wife told me that she cried often because of his nasty behavior. The older sister worked as a saleswoman. She had nervous spells and sometimes fainted. The second sister was a quiet woman who had an unfaithful husband.

In our kitchen we had an old refrigerator that often broke down. Taking pity on us, my mother bought us a new refrigerator. When it arrived, Peter commented that it was much bigger than the old one. He didn't offer my mother any money for the purchase and didn't even thank her.

I really needed a car. My mother told Peter that she would contribute to a car purchase if he would pay for half.

Peter answered, "I don't have the money, or even if I did, I wouldn't give it to your daughter. If you want to buy it, you'll have to buy it yourself. It's your business."

I suggested to my mother that she and I could pool our money to buy a small car. We found a car that had been rebuilt with parts from two other cars. It was only a few thousand dollars and ran well. Having the car made me very happy as then I could drive to work instead of having to take the bus and train rides, and I could visit my mother during vacations and holidays.

After buying the car, my mother and I drove to my house and parked in the yard. I went inside and told Peter, but he ignored me and the car. I opened the shed door and found it empty, so I parked my car inside. Unfortunately, the shed's door was too wide, crooked, and slanted to close properly. I asked Peter to fix it.

He answered, "I don't feel like fixing it. Fix it yourself." He waived his hand and left.

My mother heard him and said we could fix it ourselves. We went outside and I gathered up the ladder, hammer, and nails. While my mother held up the door, I climbed the ladder, carrying the hammer and nails, and started to nail the door.

I heard a voice behind us saying, "Hello."

I turned around and saw Frank laughing.

"This isn't a job for you," he said. "Come down from the ladder and let me fix that."

He fixed the shed doors. We thanked him and invited him to go to lunch. He refused, stating that he had to talk with Peter.

The next day when I came home from work, I saw Peter carrying a wide wooden board from the shed across the yard into the newly built house. I entered the shed and saw that the board he'd taken was a shelf I had used for my car accessories. Peter came back to the shed and tried to pull another board from the wall.

"Peter, don't take these boards. I need them to hold my car tools, oil, and other things."

He answered, "Do it yourself and you will know what it means."

What can I say after hearing this? Fighting or pushing? Not really. I went inside.

On the same afternoon, Peter came up with the idea that he needed to cut some grape stems before autumn. When he cut the grape stems, juice flowed. I came outside and asked him to stop cutting.

I said, "They give a good harvest and are tasty for everyone to eat."

He ignored me. I left him and returned inside.

He lit the grape vines and they erupted in flames, burning the fingers of his right hand. He ran into the kitchen and washed off his hand, wrapping his fingers in a towel. He ran out the door saying he was going to the hospital.

I got in the car and stopped by him, telling him to get in the car and I'd drive him to the hospital. He waved his hand and wouldn't get in the car. I parked the car by the hospital and sat in the waiting room while the doctor helped Peter. When he left the doctor's office, his fingers were bandaged. He ignored me and walked towards home. Driving after him, I invited him to get in for a ride home, and this time he did.

Chapter Fifty-Two: Justin's Adolescence.

During the summer holidays, I decided to buy a small trailer to help Justin who wanted to collect antiques. We'd drive to nearby villages to visit our friends and relatives and collected many items. One friend gave us Russian samovars, irons on which tea was brewed. From my uncle, we received a long wooden table made without nails, an ancient bed, a child's wooden cradle, and kerosene lamps. We brought everything back to my mother's house and placed the objects in her pantry.

We both collected silver coins. Justin's grandfather gave Justin his collection from his silver money album.

Justin took two of the kerosene lamps from his grandmother and placed them outside by the wall near the entrance to our house. He placed a few more of his antiques in his room on the second floor.

On his way out from the workshop, Peter saw the ancient antiques that Justin collected and kicked them away. After returning from school, Justin asked why his things were thrown in the yard. I said that Peter kicked them. One kerosene lamp was bent, and on the second one the glass was broken. He gently took them to his room without saying anything to Peter. I felt sorry for him.

After various disagreements with his stepfather, Justin began avoiding home. After preparing his homework he went out with the street children and came back late. I went to look for him and when I found him, asked him to come home.

I started checking at night to see if Justin returned home. Once I woke up at two in the morning and went up to the second floor to see if he was in bed. He was not there. I woke up Peter.

"Justin's not home."

"He will come home when he's hungry." He turned over and went back to sleep.

I nudged him. "Please, help me go find him. I am afraid to walk alone in these dark streets."

"I am not going anywhere, let me sleep."

The streets were empty, all was quiet except for barking dogs. When I came to the railway station, I saw Justin crouching on the bench.

"Justin, let's go home."

"Mother it's hard for me. Peter does not like me, makes fun of me, calls me all kinds of words, and says that I am ignorant, a loser, and can't understand anything. Peter does not respect my antiques. I've tried to be good to him."

We hugged, kissed, and we both went home.

While walking home I said to Justin, "You're a good son and a good student. I am proud of you."

Justin began having nightmares. He often woke up at night shouting, "Mommy! Grandma help me!"

He'd sleepwalk and shout as he climbed down the stairs. I'd take his hand, and say, "Justin, wake up."

When he woke up, I'd ask him what he dreamt.

He'd describe terrible dreams. "That mill wanted to catch me and drag me inside him. I couldn't get out."

"Calm down, it's just a dream, calm down."

After a bit, he went back to sleep. This dream repeated several times a year. The very last dream came after when he turned sixteen. That night, he climbed down the stairs with his eyes wide open and again shouted, Mommy! Grandma! Help me!"

I jumped out of the bed, and we went downstairs. He was still shouting and shouting.

"Justin, wake up." I took his hand and rubbed it.

He didn't wake up and walked around the room with his eyes open and shouting the same words. It was winter, and the yard was full of snow. In order to wake him up I took him outside barefoot. He walked through the snow barefoot five meters and woke up.

"Do you feel the cold?" I asked.

"I don't feel anything."

After a couple of minutes, he felt better and walked back inside. I warmed up some tea and gave it to Justin. Eventually, he went back to bed.

To deal with his grief, Justin immersed himself in creativity with music in his ethnographic ensemble, singing folk music and playing instruments. He expressed his unhappiness by writing poems and performing in plays on stage prepared by his talented literature teacher. He felt happy to have temporarily escaped from the humiliation and violence of his stepfather. When he returned home, he often found his stepfather's face full of anger, accompanied by hissing and insults.

Ensemble members often came to our house with the ensemble leader and his dog. Everyone sat in a circle on the carpet in the living room laughing and singing. My cat lay down in the middle of their circle, and the leader's dog sat next to him. The leader created a song about his dog that all the members sang titled, "Children, me, and our dog are playing in the meadow." Hearing this, the dog must have thought "What a beautiful song is written about me." Everyone was so cheerful, and happy, and Justin would forget all the discords and wrongs.

Justin received very good grades in both schools, never being absent a single day. I longed for him to live in an environment of coziness and warmth, that he could wake up to live without experiencing harsh internal winds.

He started not to return home at night. I went to his friend's house who told me that Justin and two of his friends had gone to the village. I drove to the address he gave me and knocked on the door.

The house woman let me in and took me to the bedroom where Justin was asleep.

I asked Justin, "Why didn't you tell me you were going out with a friend?"

He just looked at the ground without answering. I told him to get dressed and not to do that again.

Life in our home was unbearable. There was no respect, love, or harmony in our home, all overwhelmed by Peter's egoistic self-love. Justin was afraid to be alone with Peter.

I felt trapped. I had to work two jobs to pay for our expenses.

I decided at school break to send Justin, now thirteen, to live with his grandmother. At grandma's home he would get the love and pampering he needed. The first week went well, and then Agatha and Simon returned from a trip. At first, all three had a good time, but then Agatha and Simon invited Justin to drink alcohol with them. When he refused, they started mocking him. He hugged his grandma goodbye and took a bus back to school.

Chapter Fifty-Three: The Willow Grasses

Besides working two jobs, I cooked our meals and created my artwork. I usually went to bed after finishing everything around midnight. Meanwhile, Peter slept until noon and stayed up until three a.m. watching TV. He often laughed loudly, his method of being passive-aggressive by waking us from sleep.

I collected various bell grasses from long-stemmed bell-shaped cereal crops, as well as dried flowers. From them, I made flower arrangements and taught my students how to make beautiful flower arrangements, choosing pleasant color compositions.

One day, a delegation from a Russian school came to visit our school. When they saw my willow display, they were fascinated, having never seen anything like it before. They asked me to sell them some of the arrangements.

"No, I'm not selling them," I told them, "But if you like them, I will give them as a gift. Please come to my house where I have plenty."

They came and I gave them all the willows I had. I was happy that people appreciated my art.

No one has ever become poorer by giving joy to others.

Chapter Fifty-Four: The Camping Trip

The next summer, Peter's friends invited us to go on a river trip. Our friends had a large military inflatable boat as big as a tent. Peter and I had a rubber two-seated boat with two oars.

I arranged for my mother to come and take care of Gabriel who, at three years old, was too young to go. Justin was eager for the adventure.

I asked Peter, "Can you promise to be nice to Justin?"

"Yes, Christina, I promise you."

When we got to the river, I suggested we leave one car at the end of the trip and the second car, which was full of food, boats, and equipment, at the starting point of our trip. When we arrived, we placed all the equipment, food, and water on the big boat, with Peter's friends and Justin, and Peter and I got into the small one.

At the beginning of our rowing, the river was calm. The weather was warm and sunny. The riverbanks were covered with beautiful vegetation. The beauty and clean air lifted our spirits.

After a while, we saw a house and decided to stop and ask if we could buy milk. The owner kindly filled up our bucket and refused to take any money. Instead, she asked us to pray for her cow to remain healthy and give more milk. We thanked her for the milk and her kind heart.

As we rowed further, the river widened and its flow increased. The two boats became separated, and our little boat got caught in a whirlpool, dragging us to the shore. Although Peter and I rowed hard trying to get out of the current, it dragged us under low-hanging branches that caught at me and started to pull me out of the boat. I became frightened, knowing I wasn't a good swimmer, and we didn't have life jackets.

Peter saw and grabbed hold of me. In a few minutes, we broke free of the current and rowed back to the middle of the river.

We caught up with the other boat that had stopped on the opposite shore to wait for us. Justin was smiling ear-to-ear.

"Did you have any problems with your boat?" I asked.

"Oh no, it's quite stable with lots of space inside," Frank told us. "Justin is our boat captain."

We rested and explored the shore and snacked on sandwiches and water.

Back on the boats, we met other tourists rowing on the river. The currents increased, and we came upon a rapid with many protruding stones. The turbulence splashed into the boat, soaking our faces and clothes.

Peter got angry. "Stop throwing water on me."

"I'm not doing that. Can't you see that the water is simmering and bubbling from the rapids?"

He got so upset that he stopped rowing. I glanced back and saw him sitting with the oar on his lap, eyes closed.

"Peter, I need your help rowing. You can see the river is very strong."

He didn't answer.

Our boat was heading directly towards a huge protruding sharp stone.

I shouted, "Peter, you need to row. The boat's heading straight to that rock. Help me, I'm begging you.

The stone was getting closer, and I knew if we hit it, we would capsize. Still, he refused to help. I rowed left and right, left and right, with all my might and all by myself. Somehow, I managed to avoid hitting the rock.

I glanced back and Peter continued to sit with his eyes closed and did not say anything.

"How dare you jeopardize our lives? What's wrong with you?"

He remained quiet and seemed to be in shock. After that, the river calmed down, and I did too.

Our friends who had been ahead of us had watched us almost hit the rock. Without Peter's help, I rowed to their boat.

"Christina, you are a strong and brave woman," Frank said. "We were watching and feared you would capsize."

"Mother, I saw that you alone rowed," Justin said. "I was very scared for you."

It was dusk by the time we reached our camping spot. We set up our two tents and sent Justin to gather dry tree branches. Soon we were sitting around a campfire and discussing our adventure. The other woman and I prepared dinner, baked potatoes, tea, milk, and some canned goods. Everyone was hungry and dinner was tasty. Exhausted from the first day of adventure, we all went to sleep early.

The evening was not cold. I put a soft blanket on the bottom of the tent and the three of us lay down dressed, Justin in the middle. The tent had just enough space for the three of us with a single wide warm blanket. In the middle of the night, Justin woke me up.

"Mother, I'm cold. Where is our blanket?"

Peter had wrapped the whole blanket around himself. I pulled on it, trying to get it back, held it tightly, and wouldn't give it up, while pretending to be asleep.

"Peter, we're cold and we want our blanket back."

He didn't respond.

Justin and I put on all the clothes we had in the backpack. I hugged Justin saying we would stay warm till morning.

I got up early, made a campfire, and warmed myself up. I also made tea for everyone and sandwiches. After everyone woke up, we had a snack, folded our tents, got into the boats, and continued rowing.

For the rest of the morning trip, the river remained calm. When we reached where we'd parked our car, we went ashore, loaded up our materials, and drove to the other car. Soon we were on our way home.

Chapter Fifty-Five: Melody's Visit

During the winter, my niece Melody came to visit us during her student vacation. There was a lot of snow and we decided to go country skiing. I dressed warmly and took my son Gabriel who had a sled with me. Melody and Justin put on their skis. We spent the day enjoying skiing and sledding, returning home at dusk happy and tired.

In the morning, Melody woke up early and was sitting in the living room reading a book when Justin began coming down the stairs. Peter came up behind him and pushed him down the steps. Justin tumbled down, sustaining a bruised arm and a bloody nose. Melody jumped up to help Justin. Peter, seeing Melody, ran up to Justin and said he was sorry. I think he only apologized to Justin because Melody saw the fall. If Melody hadn't been there, Peter wouldn't have apologized, he would have just walked away.

Chapter Fifty-Six: The Distressful Life with Peter

My mother gave money to an acquaintance to obtain a furniture voucher for foreign furniture not otherwise available to her. With it, she purchased a huge display piece with glass doors, inside mirrors, and many drawers. She also bought a sofa covered in bright red velvet, armchairs, and a coffee table. Placing it all in the living room, she decided that the sofa might be damaged by the humidity and offered me that and the display case.

"You need this, you don't have anything in your living room besides an old sofa."

"But, Mother, the furniture is beautiful and fits in your room perfectly! Keep it and enjoy my purchases."

"Do not argue with me," she insisted. "I want you to take the two pieces to your house. I will keep the armchairs and the table."

I hugged her and said, "Mother you are wonderful. Thank you."

My acquaintance delivered the furniture to our house.

Peter was upset to see the new furniture. He said, "I am not going to pay for it. This bill is on your shoulders."

I answered him, "It appears that everything is on my shoulders."

Peter asked Frank to help him carry his folding sofa to his workshop. My old armchairs and a small round table fit nicely with my new decorations. The room became beautiful and upscale.

It was nice to spend evenings there. In the display case, I placed porcelain dishes and dinner settings that my parents bought in Riga and gave to me as a present. I also set my Italian breakfast set that I saved from my first marriage and silver-plated cutleries my mother gave me.

When guests came to visit us, they praised our decor. They said, "What a lovely home you have. There are many beautiful works of art here."

They also loved our antique clock with carved ornaments and interesting designs hanging on the wall. Sadly, I did not enjoy this furniture for long.

Every day, Peter came from his workshop with dirty and dusty pants and lay down on the sofa.

I frequently asked him, "Please don't lie on the couch with your dirty clothes. Change your clothes or put a sheet on top to protect it. The sofa will become dirty and then we will have to throw it out."

Peter ignored my requests. He also liked to put sharp objects on the sofa and throw his work clothes all over the house.

I talked to my mother and my children about it. They agreed with me that the sofa would be destroyed.

I said, "We'll have to sell the sofa and the display together. Both have value now, but not for long." I placed an ad in a newspaper. People from another city came, inspected the furniture, and bought it.

Selling the furniture made the room look empty. Peter brought his old sofa back from the workshop and we placed it in the living room in the same place where the new sofa used to be.

All that remained of the coziness of the room was an ancient clock given to me by a person who knew that we collected antiques. Mother asked Peter to make a big display case to replace the former one.

"You could add your carved wooden patterns on it," Gabriel said, standing by Grandma. "Now the room and the wall look empty. We need to fill it with furniture. You could do it."

Peter grabbed the antique clock off the wall and threw it on the floor, shattering it.

"Why are you so angry and mean?" I asked. "It was such a beautiful clock."

Peter screamed, "Shut up! You don't understand anything," and stomped out of the house.

We picked up the clock pieces from the floor as tears rolled down my cheeks. It was one thing to destroy a clock and another to humiliate and disrespect a person. Why did he have to be so angry? We took the broken clock from the floor and hung it back on the wall. I wanted to run away, but there was nowhere I could go.

For the next two days, Peter and I didn't speak to each other. Finally, he apologized.

"We'll see how it goes," I answered to him. "It seems that your mean actions are increasing daily."

Peter tried to glue the clock pieces together and built a large wooden display case with glass doors. Eventually, I put back my beautiful dishes.

One day I took the train to the city to buy food for the family, returning home with bags full of groceries. When I arrived, I found the door of the house locked. I knocked but no one answered. I knew that Peter was there. I waited ten minutes and I knocked again. Still no answer. I brought a ladder to the house and set the ladder so I could climb to the second-floor window where I saw Peter lying on his bed. I knocked at the window, yelling for Peter to let me in. He ignored me. I knocked harder and called louder, but he just turned away from me and covered his head.

I sat down on a wooden bench by the house and waited for him to open the door. An hour passed before he finally unlocked the door. I picked up my goods and went into the kitchen without speaking to him.

Peter received an offer to work in Germany to restore the house of a rich German family. After working for two months, he returned satisfied and cheerful and brought back various foods, such as yogurt, hazelnuts, and chocolate butter. He treated us with these delights. We celebrated his success, and he was kind to everybody.

After he finished his job in Germany, I offered to make a deal.

"I will find you clients who need a good craftsman and tell them you're a designer who has restored houses in Germany. I will make sketches of doors, furniture, and houses to help you market your work to potential clients."

He answered bluntly. "If you don't have enough money, you should do all the work yourself, and leave me out of it."

The next day I said to him, "You just had a successful job where you earned a lot of money. This is your family and I've been paying for all the household expenses. Please give me some of that money so I can buy food for you and the family."

He sneered at me. "No, I will not. It's my money, not yours."

"You know I don't earn much as a teacher, even working two jobs. It's impossible to support our family with my salary alone. I can't afford clothes and other things the children need. There's so little money, I can only afford to buy two bananas a week."

He retorted, "The household expenses are your responsibility, not mine."

"Very well. From now on, if you don't give me any money, I'm not going to feed you."

He threw his head back and laughed. "That's fine with me. I'll go to my mother's house to eat.

After that, he ate every meal with his mother. Probably she thought, "What a lazy woman he married."

As soon as he started to eat at his mother's house, Peter bought food for himself only. He went to the store and bought sausage, butter, cheese, and bread, placing his food on one shelf in the refrigerator. He showed the children and me which was his food.

"All the food on this shelf is mine. Do not touch or eat my food. Got it?"

Of course, when the children opened the refrigerator, they cut of pieces of his food without telling their father.

When Peter saw that his food had been eaten, he asked, "Who ate my sausage? Christina, tell me."

I said I did it because I didn't want him to punish the children, especially Justin.

Soon, my mother came on a visit bringing a suitcase full of all kinds of homemade sausages, hams, sweets, and apples from her garden. I explained that the one shelf was for Peter's food, so she placed all that she brought on the other shelf. However, when Peter saw the food there, he ate as much of it as he could.

I said to Peter, "When you fell in love with me, you promised me a perfect life. Sadly, during our marriage you've never come close to keeping your promises."

Upon hearing that, he grabbed me and shoved me and hit me.

Peter said, "I'm going to beat you up. You'll have bruises by your eyes and then you'll love me more."

I glowered at him. "Don't even try it. I am not the kind of woman who will take your blows. Your thinking is insane. If you ever do this to me, I will tell your actions to everybody I know and file a police report. Do you understand that? Do you get it?"

After my words, he pushed me to the floor and walked out the door. I lay still and silent for several minutes, wanting to cry, but holding back the tears.

I moved from the floor to the couch, my whole body aching. Then I fell asleep. When I woke up in the morning, I examined my body and saw bruises on my arms and legs. I went to the kitchen and saw Peter sitting and drinking coffee. I said based on the bruises on my face, arms, and legs, I was thinking of calling for an ambulance.

"Peter, I believe that you are a chameleon: schizophrenic and psychotic. You've had a nervous breakdown. I suggest you go to see a psychiatrist. He probably could help you. Your problems can't be solved by you, since you do not know what your problems are."

He replied, "No, you're the one who should go to see a doctor."

"How can we live together if we cannot stand each other?"

He looked at me as if I'd just said the grass was purple. "You can't stand me? What is it that you don't like about me?"

"Really?" I began listing the times he had been selfish, how he never shared his money, how he treated my son, how he made promises and broke them.

After a few minutes of listening, he interrupted to say, "I am not a radio," and he left.

After these events, I reassessed my life. I analyzed my goals and the problems I faced. I realized that due to the Soviet occupation and its loss of so many freedoms, I had limited ability to succeed. This applied not only to my home situation but even more, the iron curtain stopped any chance of my mobility outside the Soviet Union too.

I realized that the poverty in which I lived was a big factor in my limitations. I couldn't buy a house or a decent car, or even make enough money to support my family.

One other consideration weighed heavily on my decision. I had to ensure that Justin went to college and Gabriel succeeded in grammar school.

Clearly, Peter was my biggest and hardest problem. He was narcissistic, greedy, controlling, had poor anger control, and worst of all, mean to my son. He had lured me into a trap by acting so wonderful and then dragged me into a nightmare.

182

Realizing that my life with Peter was causing all of us unhappiness, I determined that I would leave him on my terms as soon as possible. I decided I'd have to create an escape plan.

I came home one day and told Peter that I planned to leave him.

"Certainly, I will not hold you from going. When my first wife left, I helped her carry her things out to the car, but I will not help you.

I replied, "I know that good people often do not receive thanks for their kindness and are not able to be bad even when it is indicated. This is me. I should be mean back at you, but it's not in my nature.

"What do I get as a woman from you? Your understanding care or love? No! Instead, nothing but terror, humiliation, and fights. Who can suffer such absurdity? I can tolerate you only because by nature I am good and strong.

"I am a woman with strong family values. However, life with you throws, twists, and turns me. I did not expect such a horrible experience being with you. I do not deserve such a life."

He shrugged and turned his back on me.

Chapter Fifty-Seven: Appearance of Ghosts

Our house was built on the foundations of a former slaughterhouse and was haunted. Not every night but very often after midnight ghosts appeared. They made sounds like somebody walking down the staircase. Often, I was awakened by this creaking sound. One night I opened my eyes to see the shadow the size of a big man. He had a long black coat covering his body. The shadow flew straight at me from the door. I jumped out of the bed and turned on the light and the black shadow disappeared.

Peter slept alone on the second-floor mattress. I slept on a sofa in the living room.

One night, when my mother was visiting and sleeping on the second floor with Justin, I was awakened by a loud sound, "Buff", near the first-floor window. I sat up and listened. Silence. The dog didn't bark.

I turned on the light and went up to the second floor and asked my mother, "Are you sleeping?"

"No, a strange sound woke me up. What was it?"

"I have no idea," I answered. "Everything is quiet now, so let's try to go back to sleep. Maybe it won't happen again."

I went back to sleep. After a while, the same sound woke me again.

I sat up trying to figure out what it could be. Maybe it was the devil I had seen in the developed picture by the pool. Or perhaps it was the souls of killed animals. Or maybe the sound came because Peter filled our house with suffering and violence.

We were living in a cursed house.

I thought about the nature of Satan. I'd been taught that Satan would steal people's souls by convincing them that they were weak, worthless, and never would succeed, creating hopelessness.

Although he thought he was more powerful than God, in reality, he was a creeping coward. I realized that Peter was my Satan.

I thought I had married the prince of my dreams who came riding on a white horse speaking beautiful words and making magical promises. He promised to save me from my sadness and bad memories. But, no, it was a trick. He was a prince of darkness who had turned his black horse into a white one and turned himself into a handsome young man and came to propose to me.

Chapter Fifty-Eight: The Snake.

A wide square ditch ran near our house. Passing by it with my son Gabriel one day, we saw a grass snake stuck in the bottom. Every time the snake tried to climb out of the ditch, he fell back again.

Gabriel said, "Mother, let's get two long sticks and help him get out."

We found the sticks and successfully rescued it, releasing it to meander across the yard. He settled behind the house in the garden where wooden boards piled up against the fence. Every morning Gabriel and I went to see how our grass-snake was doing, usually finding him warming himself in the sun by lying on the boards.

One morning we did not see him, and again, the next morning the snake couldn't be found. Gabriel asked the neighbor's child if they'd seen the grass snake. They showed him our grass snake lying dead on the street near our fence.

"Who killed him?" Gabriel asked in a sad voice. His friend told him that his grandfather killed the snake. The grandfather was walking down the street after work and saw the snake meandering in the street.

Gabriel returned home in tears. "Mother, mother our snake was killed by my friend's grandfather."

I hugged him and promised to read to him legends about grass snakes, telling him that they were sacred in American Indian culture.

Chapter Fifty-Nine: Problems with my Brother's Wife

People should be beautiful in every way - in their faces, in the way they dress, in their thoughts, and in their innermost selves.
  -Anton Chekhov, Russian writer

During the summer holidays, I'd always visit my parents' house. Because I couldn't find or afford beautiful clothes in the stores, I sewed my own clothes from templates I cut out from the German magazine "Burda". It featured various clothing designs. My credo was to be stylish.

Whenever I visited my parents, Agatha was mean to me. It seemed to me that she was jealous, especially when she saw me with what seemed to her to be extravagant clothes.

Jealousy is a destructive force. It increases the release of stress hormones, blood pressure, and weakens heart immunity. Jealousy might cause fear and anger. Because of her jealousy, I never invited them to our house.

Because of her jealousy and often being drunk, Agatha incited her husband against me. She would send him downstairs to fight with me. Simon scared everyone with his aggressive behavior. He screamed and waved his fists.

My mother said, "Christina, jump out of the window, I'm afraid he's going to hit you. More than once, not only me, but also my nieces had to hide from them, often spending the night with my neighbors. His actions often ruined my summer vacations.

I wanted to call the police more than once. My mother asked me not to because, as she explained, when I left, she still had to live with them. I agreed not to call.

Chapter Sixty: Bazaar

One Saturday my mother and I went to a market in a different city. There, I saw my classmate Bella sitting and selling.

"Hello Bella, what are you selling?"

She answered, "Prima cigarettes. My business is going very well, many people are buying my cigarettes."

When we returned home, I asked my mother to go to a store near us. and buy a carton of Prima cigarettes. The following Saturday we drove to a different market to sell the cigarettes. After finding the market, we paid to be a vendor and found a good spot to sell cigarettes. We couldn't understand why no one would buy our cigarettes.

After two hours, a policeman approached us and told us that it was illegal to sell cigarettes in this market. After he left, we took our carton of cigarettes and drove home. We had spent the money unnecessarily on cigarettes, travel, and market fees. The next day, Mother went back to the store where she purchased them and asked the saleswoman if she could return the cigarettes. She accepted them back and gave us a refund. It was not a successful business!

I know that somehow and somewhere I had to make more money. I decided to call my neighbor. He weaved various works of art from wicker, like furniture, small baskets, and plates. I went to his house and asked him to teach me how to weave with wicker.

"Sure," he answered.

The next morning, I returned to his house, and he taught me how to prepare the wickers and how to weave them. He explained to me all the working techniques. I bought from him a bunch of wickers and began weaving, first a small item, and next a bouquet of flowers. Soon I was weaving tall floor vases and baskets. I placed long stems of weaved flowers in all of the tall vases.

My mother came to visit, and I suggested we go to the market and sell my woven items. The next Saturday we took several of my pieces and sold a half dozen, enough to make me happy.

At the end of the day, we discussed how else we could sell them, and came up with an idea. I would make the baskets and ship them by bus to my mother, and she would sell them in the market. We had a customer who would buy all the baskets, put live flowers in them, and sell them in a different market. After work and on the weekends, I intensively weaved the baskets. When I made thirty of them, I put them in a big bag and took them by to the train to the bus stop in the city. From there, when the bus arrived, I gave the driver a tip and asked him to deliver the bag to my mother's home. She received the bag and on Saturdays went to the market to sell them. That way I made extra money on top of my salary.

One Monday morning, a woman holding a bunch of flowers knocked on my door. She asked me to make three flower baskets for a funeral. I told her that I could have them ready by five. She provided her phone number and I promised I'd call her when they were ready.

At this time Gabriel was in kindergarten and Justin in school. Just Peter and I were present. I put all three baskets on individual stairsteps as I made the flower arrangements. When finished, I was quite pleased with the results.

As I was admiring my compositions, Peter descended the stairs. Although he could have walked around them very easily, instead he kicked all my baskets down. All the flowers fell out and were ruined.

"Look what you've done! I have a client coming to pick up these flowers and pay me for my work. Why have you destroyed my beautiful bouquets and ruined my work?"

He answered, "They were in my way. You don't have the right to be angry."

I sat down and held my head. "I really can't understand how you can be so mean. I've never met such an arrogant, vindictive, and impulsive person."

I collected the broken flowers and cleaned the messy floor. Now I didn't have enough flowers. I drove to the market and bought more, returned home, and had to make everything from the beginning. When my sons came home, I asked them to make food for themselves.

Eventually, I finished my work. The woman returned on time, liked my compositions, and paid me. However, the amount didn't cover the purchase of the new flowers.

I hated Peter for what he'd done. For the next month, I refused to talk with him. It was clear that the longer we lived together the angrier he became. As before, I remained sleeping on the first floor on the couch. He slept on the mattress on the second floor, even though he was gifted in his woodwork, he never made a bed for himself. When he would come down the stairs in the morning, I closed my eyes so I wouldn't have to see his face.

Chapter Sixty-One: Teaching in a Rural High School

I set up a wicker weaving club at the high school where I was teaching. My students and I participated in various art exhibitions where we showed our wicker pieces, as well as our embroidery, knitting, and flower arrangements. After our exhibition, I expected the school director and teachers to praise us for our work. But they never did.

It appeared to me that there was something wrong with the school. Compared with the teachers at the community college where women and men dressed well, the ones at this high school showed no interest in art or dress. I thought it might be because the school was in a small town where people were closed off from the rest of the country. Seeing this, I wanted to teach students to be creative and to express themselves.

I saw some student girls had sewed pockets on the front of their school uniforms' black aprons. Some of the teachers opposed these changes.

"Christina, do you think the students should place pockets on the aprons? Aren't the aprons considered a part of school uniform?"

"Yes," I answered, "but the pockets are the same color as the aprons and are useful for the students to keep small items. Besides, it gives the girls an opportunity to show their personality, to be unique. In my opinion, personality should be developed at school, not crushed. Students need to stand out from others and from the surrounding monotonous environment with their uniqueness."

My artwork hung in the corridors of the school. In the assembly hall, two large round plates made of wicker hung near the stage. I hoped these artworks would stimulate the imagination of both the students and the teachers.

In this small town, it was difficult to change the old-fashioned thinking of the teachers and they resented me and my fellow artist, the music teacher. We never stayed in the teachers' room for long. We'd pick up the journals for our classes and quickly leave.

The wife of the school director was a tall, well-dressed lady, who would wear red indoor plush slippers when she came to the classroom to teach the students. I'd never seen such a disrespectful dress in any other school. While I recognized that a woman has the right to be unique, in this school looking beautiful wasn't considered important.

While working in this high school, I was invited to participate in an exhibition of achievement in Moscow. To my surprise, my artistic work was evaluated and received the highest score and I was awarded a Medal of Art. They sent the medal and recognition letter of award to the director of my school.

The director called me into his office to let me know I'd won the award. However, when he looked in his drawer to give them to me, he couldn't find them. He had me come back every morning as he looked for them, but he never found them, so I never got my certificate or my medal. They were lost in obscurity. Perhaps the director gave them to someone else for his own benefit.

There was a lot of graft during the Soviet era, as well as oppression. At the beginning of the Soviet occupation, the Soviet party officials followed local citizens who went to church. If those citizens had important positions and were seen in church, the next day they received an announcement that they had been terminated from their jobs.

When the country's independence movement started, the government changed its views. The party secretary and directors became believers in God. Wherever the wind blew at that time, they bent to that side.

Chapter Sixty-Two: Song Contest "Sing a Song"

The leader of the school ethnographic ensemble prepared Justin and two of his friends to participate in a song contest in our capital. They played folk musical instruments and sang a song based on the poem, "When I Get Tired on My Heart," written by our national poet. They took the first place in the competition, returning home happily from their great victory. The leader of the ethnographic ensemble congratulated them, being very happy that the students that he trained performed very well.

The school paid no attention to their win. No one praised them or even mentioned them. The director did not recognize them for their win. Even though these were talented students, the head of the school probably didn't like them because they stood out from the other students. Justin and his friends wrote poems, sang songs, and played musical instruments.

Frustrated by the lack of recognition, Justin wrote a poem.

Three

There were only three of them.
they wanted to build their own little world
by covering up their despair

Well, let us need the Sun
Need a word
Love and truth
We need life.

Flowers are given to them offstage
That found the key to his heart.
Better to be king for a day

Than a beggar for a lifetime.

The principal invited me to come into his office. He started talking about my son's bad behavior. He said that Justin had started fights with other students. I was surprised that the director of the school, being a friend and classmate of Peter, didn't talk to Peter first. That was probably because Peter would have told him to talk to his mother. Peter was never interested in Justin's grades or his activities or behavior at school.

The next day the deputy principal invited me to his office. "Sit down, Christina," he says. "I want to talk to you about your son. Don't worry about the principal's accusations. Justin is the soul of the school. We're proud that he took first place in the song contest with his two friends and appreciate his playing in a bagpipe orchestra, thus glorifying the name of our school."

"Thank you for your understanding," I said. I left his room relieved, calm, and grateful.

We made friends with the parents of one of Justin's classmates, a good friend who was part of the song trio. His father, Albert, was an engineer, and his mother was a teacher at this school. They lived very modestly. Many years before, the engineer liked to get drunk and chase his family around the house. If he caught them, he would beat them.

He changed his life when he bought a house in the village, giving up alcohol. Their house was about four kilometers away and held two huge greenhouses. We became good friends, visiting each other's homes to chat and celebrate holidays together.

One spring, Albert invited my mother and me to help plant cucumber and tomato plants in the greenhouses. For several days we worked in the large greenhouses. After planting, we came to visit them regularly on Saturdays. One time, Albert answered the door with bad-looking ripped pants and his zipper unzipped. I figured that he worked a lot and hadn't taken the time to take care of his appearance. He seemed very tired.

They had a well-trained German shepherd dog. When visitors came, the dog greeted them in a friendly manner. However, when they wanted to leave the house, the dog growled and showed its teeth until the owner gave the command to let them out.

When they visited us, Peter wouldn't show any anger. They had a very good opinion of him. I knew that he was a hypocrite and would change after they left.

We planted vegetables for two years and Albert sold them successfully. Then he got in touch with a relative of his, a Polish man, who offered them an opportunity to start a new business selling copper in Poland. After successfully selling vegetables and receiving a substantial amount of money they decided to start a new business with him. Albert bought copper from Russia and sent it to his relative in Poland.

This business went quite well. With their additional money, they expanded their house and opened food shops in the town center. Our friendship drifted away as they then associated with the rich circle of town society.

They hired many employees as their businesses expanded, and it seemed that there was no end to their success – until one day when they didn't receive any copper shipments from Russia. After waiting a few days, Albert called the Russian companies to ask them when more copper would be delivered. He found out that the financier officer he had hired had made an arrangement to send the copper shipments to a different address in Poland. Realizing he'd been double-crossed by the director and the Polish relative, he fired the financier officer.

Albert had a lot of money saved from the copper trade that he used to build a slaughterhouse in the village. At first, his meat business went well, but after a year the business collapsed. It was probably due to the extortion money he had to pay.

In a newspaper article, Albert's wife complained that she would have to manage her house herself, even carrying firewood to heat, cook, and do home and lawn maintenance. It reminded me of the story "Goldfish".

Chapter Sixty-Three: More Troubles with Peter

One summer day, I invited Mother and Peter to get in my car for a trip to the nearby forest to pick mushrooms. During our hike, Peter talked and joked with my mother. After a couple of hours of unsuccessful mushroom hunting, but a lovely nature walk, we returned to the car to discover it wouldn't start. The car had gears and would start when pushed so mother and Peter got out and pushed. It still wouldn't start.

I checked under the hood and flipped some switches. Back behind the wheel, I asked Peter and mother to try pushing the car again. Peter became very angry. He grabbed a stone and threw it behind the car.

"What a stupid car you have that won't start!" he screamed.

He began walking back down the road and leaving us behind. He'd only gone a dozen yards when I turned the key and this time the car started.

I drove up to Peter and told him to get in the car.

"Don't bother me," he shouted. Bending down, he scraped up a pile of stones and made to throw them at the car.

"Look," I said to my mother. "He's so childish, he's going to throw rocks at our windows."

After glaring at me for a minute, he dropped the rocks.

My mother said, "Really, Christina, I can't imagine how hard it must be to live with such an immature ill-tempered man."

A few weeks later, Peter decided he wanted to invite friends for dinner. "Christina, could you make a dinner?"

"I could if you give me money for it," I answered.

I made the dinner table by putting my beautiful plates and eating utensils next to them. Evening came and our guests arrived. We discussed our art, then we sat by the table. I served lemon liqueur and wine I had made as we laughed and told stories.

When I began bringing dinner dishes, Peter started criticizing me, calling me by my diminutive name.

"Chrissie, my dear, the eating utensils you placed on the table are not properly arranged. You also did not put the plates the right way. And the food is only lukewarm. You should have heated it more."

I told him I was sorry and that I'd take it back to the kitchen.

"Well, since you're warming up the food, you should heat the coffee too."

While I was back in the kitchen reheating the food and coffee, I could hear Peter talking loudly and telling jokes.

"I am so glad you came to visit, it's a pleasant surprise. You understand, I have a lot of orders now, I'm very busy and successful." Next, he talked about his great work, and how much he earned.

After the meal, the guests thanked us for the wonderful dinner and left. I carried the eating utensils and the dishes to the kitchen to be washed. When I finished washing Peter stood at the door of the kitchen.

"Listen, Peter. At this party I felt like a dirty little house-flannel that had been thrown to the corner. I only had time to follow your commands with no time to talk to the guests. All I could do was work in the kitchen and fulfill your wishes."

I threw down my washcloth. "Peter, do not put me down before guests. If I do something wrong, keep quiet or do it yourself."

"Shut up," he yelled, picking up a wooden chair and throwing it at me.

I managed to close the kitchen door just in time, as the chair broke after hitting the closed kitchen door. That left only a single one of the chairs he had made remaining at the table in the kitchen.

This same type of interaction occurred twice more when we had guests. I decided I would no longer make dinners or host guests.

I started to despair, developing an inferiority complex. I felt stupid and incapable of doing anything right. I didn't confide in anyone, fearful that people would think that Peter could do nothing wrong, and I couldn't do anything right. I worried that people would laugh at me. Besides my mother, I didn't have any friends to share my thoughts with. I knew she would never betray me, and I could talk to her about my successes and failures. We trusted each other. I often felt severe loneliness when I was with my husband.

Every summer I took my vacation with my mother to keep her company and to relieve the stress of my life. I would bring my children, dog, and cat with me. The animals were good friends and sat together on the back seat of my car. At my mother's home, we'd go fishing, eat ice cream in cafés, play basketball and badminton, or throw a ball in the yard.

I decided to leave Peter and go back to the student dormitory where I used to live peacefully. I figured if I had a part-time job there, I could look for a full-time position in a community college. Sadly, when I discussed my desires with the community college director, he told me there was no longer a position available for me. I went back home without hope.

Chapter Sixty-Four: Dinner at Alma's House

Our whole family was invited to visit my classmate Alma who lived with her family far away. We arrived with my son Gabriel, age three, and Justin who was thirteen at the time. My son Gabriel was quite active, which was normal for his age. He explored every room and pulled things from tables.

Alma set various dishes on the table and invited everyone to eat. We all sat, with Gabriel on my lap. After a few minutes, he wanted to get down and play. Peter told Justin to go look after him. The rest of us ate and chatted.

After a while, Justin came back leaving Gabriel alone in another room. He sat down at the table and started to eat.

Peter exclaimed sternly, "I told you to watch Gabriel. Now go."

Justin left and went to watch Gabriel. I apologized to Alma, and also got up from the table and went to the room where my children were. After a while, all three of us returned to the table. When we returned, we found out that the warm dishes were all consumed. Alma told me that Peter liked the food so much he ate it all. She brought some leftovers she had in the refrigerator, apologizing that was all she had to give us.

After dinner, we talked and drank wine. We thanked them for the wonderful time we had and for the good food and then we left.

On the way home, Justin complained of being hungry. I told him that it was his father's fault because he was such a pig to eat all the food.

"Shut up," Peter said.

Chapter Sixty-Five: Justin has a Spell

One afternoon when he was about fourteen, Justin returned home from school very late.

"Mother I am not feeling well. I don't know what's wrong with me. I have a headache and feel fearful."

I woke Peter up and we drove Justin to the hospital. There, the nurse had him change into a hospital gown and administered a strong dose of sedating medicine.

When in bed, Justin said, "Mother, I feel very weak."

I tried to console him. "Everything will pass. Just calm down."

"I want to go to the toilet," he said.

I helped him up and found he couldn't walk to the toilet by himself. He had to hold on to the wall, swaying in all directions. I asked Peter who was staying next to me to help him walk to the toilet. He did so. When we returned to the ward, I put Justin down on a bed. I told Peter that I was not going home until Justin felt better.

Slowly Justin calmed down and smiled, saying, "Mother, I am going to sleep." I kissed him and Peter and I went home.

When I arrived in the morning, Justin looked much better. I spoke to his doctor and told him about the abuse Justin had suffered at the hands of his stepfather for such a long time. After hearing all this and doing tests, the doctor did not find any reason for keeping him in a hospital. He advised me to consult a psychologist.

I could see that Justin's health was in danger. My sense of well-being had reached the bottom, too. I felt that we were standing at the bottom of a pit and couldn't get out. I believed that the doctor's suggestion to see a psychologist was valid. Perhaps he could advise us on how to make our lives better.

The anxiety of the unknown, living in an unsafe environment for many years, and experiencing frequent fears, humiliation, insults, bullying, and violence had created mental effects. After all this harmful stress and family disagreements, I still hoped to learn how to strengthen my mental health and prevent further deterioration.

Once we came to the psychologist's office, I explained to him the current state of Justin's well-being. It appeared to me that Justin was too sensitive to bear the tension at home any longer, mostly due to the cruelty of his stepfather. The psychologist suggested Justin attend weekly sessions, to help him relieve his stress. Here's one of the poems Justin wrote at that time.

The World

I stand and stare into the darkness
I ask to be or not to be?
Such a quiet evening today
To me the waves bring this word gold.

I did not believe that there is a name reality
Happiness in the world but I need it
I'm walking down the street shouting
Through its pain and despair.

Here is one day and night again
And I go again, stand again and ask you
Why?
That waves bring me the word gold.

From its light I walk through the forest
Through the forest floor
And here I am again at the city chimneys
I stand and look at them.

This is how I will go through the world
Standing in your arms
I will ask to be or not to be?
To me the waves bring this word gold.

After finishing his sessions and not finding love and respect from his stepfather, he began to rebel against society. He grew long hair like the English singers "Beatles". He tied a band across his forehead to look like an American Indian. He walked barefoot. He wanted his small world to be more loving and caring. During this time Justin wrote this poem.

Bare Feet

Born from a lotus flower
Flower children spread around the world with long hair
Occupying occasionally city parks
They will give you flowers with turbulent faces.

And bare feet are splashing on the marshes
They speak the language of Beatles rock and roll
And bare feet are splashing on the marshes
They speak the language of Beatles rock and roll.

And the voices of day and night
An old hippie wrote on the jeans
I love you now and forever
John Lennon once sang that.

As he approached high school graduation, he stopped caring about studies and his grades declined. He graduated with average grades. Here's another of Justin's poems from that time.

The Roof

The roof went off sharply
The sky smiled so pale
I look for inch nails in my pocket
I want to nail the roof and I cannot find them.

It is raining on my head
And I'm having fun
Maybe offer it a cigarette
Her smoke is like menthol mint.

I'd rather play the guitar
And I will sing a song
After my cheerful song
The mind of the roof will come back.

But the roof is lazy, it is smart
It does not like my verse
You know, the roof, I will invite Rita
To hit you with a brick.

Justin sought refuge in religion. He wrote this poem and played the guitar and sang it.

To our Lord

They nailed his hands and feet to the cross
Only my heart is left
I am alone but not alone
I'll get up right away and go.

Oh God, God darken the day
The church curtain please tear in half
Oh, heaven, heaven oh Eloi
Why did you abandon me?

Lift your heart up to the sky
And smash it to pieces
My gentle hands will touch them
And will hand them over

And again the day God is behind the mountain
And again the light is a hot light
Oh people, they tricked you
I'm alive here, I'm alive here.

Touch my hands and feet
A stone has already been knocked over from the crypt
You people have been tricked by
Dark Shepherd, Dark Shepherd.

Eloi Eloi Eloi Eloi Eloi Lama Sabachthani
Eloi Eloi Eloi Eloi Lama Sabachthani.
My God my God why you hast Thou forsaken me.
Eloi. (A metaphor for any population or group of persons being domesticated or dumbed down.)

My God, my God, why have you forsaken me? Why are you so far from my salvation, where you have saved me in my silent dreams and moans until now?

Chapter Sixty-Six: A Visit to Peter's Artist Friend

Our relationship continued to deteriorate. Whenever we went to neighbors' houses for gatherings, he wanted to stay much later than I did, and I would walk home alone. Or, if we left together, he would purposely stride as fast as he could so he would leave me behind. I felt like a sheep lost in the fields.

Several times I swore to myself that I would never go anywhere with him again, but events came up that I had to attend with him.

One afternoon a friend of Peter's who was a sculptor invited Peter and me to visit him and his wife. Although by this time, knowing how Peter acted, I was reluctant to go, but Peter insisted I'd love the man's artwork, so I agreed.

As always, I drove and Peter sat in the back seat as if he were rich and I was just a chauffeur. When we arrived at his friend's house, I was impressed at how gorgeous the house looked, even from the entrance to the driveway which was decorated with a stone sculpture of a human.

The artist invited us in and introduced his wife. The interior was densely decorated with beautiful and interesting sculptures, both in wood and stone.

"Are any of these by your wife?" I asked.

"No, just by me. I enjoy carving large sculptures."

"What a talented man you are," I said.

He continued the tour, showing pieces in every room, including two large animals carved from wood by the fireplace.

The artist took me to the dining room where the four of us enjoyed wine and snacks. After an hour or two, we thanked our hosts for the hospitality and left.

When I was driving home, I came to a stop light at an intersection and didn't remember which way to turn. I said to Peter,

"Even though you never drive, you know this area. Could you tell me which direction I should turn?"

"Either right or left," he said.

The light turned green and cars behind me wanted to go. I turned to look at Peter who was sitting up in the back seat with his eyes closed. "Peter, please tell me which direction I should turn."

Without opening his eyes, he said, "It is your car, you must know where to turn."

The cars behind me honked, and I had to make a decision, so I turned left according to my intuition. Fortunately, it was correct and for the rest of the trip we traveled in silence. Once again, I determined that Peter was not ever capable of helping me.

Chapter Sixty-Seven: Smashing Plates

One afternoon Peter came into the kitchen while I was cooking lunch. He asked, "Christina, what are you cooking? It smells so good."

"It's beetroot soup You want some?"

"Yes, I would like to try it."

I ladled some into two bowls and we both sat down and started eating. In a few minutes, he sees a big potato in the soup and gets angry.

"Why did you not cut the potatoes into small pieces in the soup? You know I do not like big chunks."

"Peter," I explained, "you never eat with us. I cooked this soup not for you but for myself and the children. You asked me to have some, so I gave it to you."

He stood up and dropped the plate on the floor, it shattered, scattered the soup.

I did not want to give up after seeing this. "Okay," I said. "We will see who wins by breaking the most plates."

I grabbed a plate from the shelf and slammed it on the floor. He followed me by picking up another plate and throwing it on the floor. He then picked up another one and broke it, too.

"Peter if you want to break all the plates, we'll have nothing to eat on, because I'm not going to buy any more." He stared at me a moment, and then left the room shaking his fists.

Chapter Sixty-Eight: Growing Tulips

It is very difficult to be a woman. You have to think like a man, act like a lady, look like a young woman, and work like a horse.

Hillary Clinton, American politician.

One day my mother and I were talking about how I needed to earn more money. I told her that weaving baskets took a lot of effort and was hurting my back by bending over for so long. She came up with the idea of my growing tulips in my basement.

"When they bloom in the winter, you can take them to the market. They'll sell well during the holidays. I'll teach you how to grow them. You have to find an electrician to install electricity. You need to know how often to water them and maintain them. You'll buy tulip bulbs and put them in dirt in wooden beds. I suggest you grow 500 bulbs in the beginning, and if you're lucky you can grow more next year."

My mother gave me a bit of money to get started. I hired an electrician who put in the wiring and the lights, and I bought the soil, baskets, and tulip bulbs.

To get the soil into the basement, I had to pour it through a hole I made in the first floor, and then put a ladder down so I could shovel the fresh soil into the baskets. I planted the tulip bulbs and every morning turned on the lights and every night turned them off again.

I placed a bathtub in the basement to hold water. To get water, I had to carry it in a bucket from the house through the yard and pour it into the bathtub. Sometimes, Justin helped me to carry the water. Near the end of December, just in time for the holidays, the tulips bloomed.

For the first year, I grew 500 tulips. When they were ready, I put a rubber band on each one and wrapped them in packages of ten in newspaper. Then I placed the wrapped bundles in cardboard boxes.

When I was ready to take the tulips to the market, the yard had filled with snow. I got up at four in the morning and started the car. I loaded the tulip boxes in the back seat. While the car was warming up, I shoveled the snow away from the garage all the way to the main street. Even so, as I backed out, the car was sliding.

Peter had placed three long iron posts near the exit of the garage that made it impossible for me to turn my car. I took a hammer, and, with a lot of effort, I pulled the poles out. I had to drive through the forest to the highway in the dark. It was very scary.

I had left in the early morning to get a good spot in the market. When I arrived, I found a perfect spot near the gate. It was such a cold morning, it took several hours before the customers started coming. I enjoyed my hot tea to warm up. Standing all day and selling tulips I did not have time to eat. I knew I would have to throw out any of the tulips that did not sell that day. However, I sold them all and went home happy.

When I returned home and entered my front door, Peter grabbed me and shoved me against the wall.

He put his fist under my chin and screamed, "Don't you dare pull out any more of my poles by the driveway. Did you hear me?"

I pushed him away. "No! Listen, Peter. I had to go to the market in the morning and the poles hindered me."

Peter said, "I planted roses near the shed and you cannot drive over them."

"Well then, if you want to have your roses protected, you can get up and shovel the snow off the driveway and then help me get out to the main road in the dark."

"Whistle on the dog's ass," he told me. "I won't get up, and you don't pull my poles out," he answered.

That year 500 tulips were not difficult to sell. With my first earned money, I bought myself Levi blue jeans for my birthday and still had enough money to pay back my mother and a bit more for living expenses.

The next year, I purchased 1000 tulip bulbs. I had to do the same routine, but there was more work because the tulip number increased. I had to take the soil out of the basement and replenish it with new soil.

When it was time to sell them, I arose at four o'clock again and shoveled the snow off the driveway. Even though it was a cold morning, with all my labors sweat ran down my face. I loaded up the boxes of tulips and drove through the dark forest onto the main highway. The road was slippery and suddenly my car slid. I released the gas pedal, and the car spun out of control, stopping right at the edge of a ditch.

I got out and stood by the side of the road waiting for someone to drive by and help me push my car out of the snowbank.

Soon I saw car lights. The driver stopped and asked if he could help. He took a shovel from the car and shoveled snow from under the wheels. I got into the car and started the motor while he pushed the car into the road. I thanked him and he drove away.

At the market I found a nice location to sell tulips, however this time I didn't sell all of them. The next weekend I brought Justin, and we sold all the tulips we'd brought.

I planted another batch so I'd have tulips ready for March eighth, which was Women's Day. I knew it was a big tulip-selling day.

I called my mother and she agreed to help me. She suggested I bring them three days early so we'd have time to prepare the bundles.

So, on March 4th I prepared for the trip. When I went to my car, it wouldn't start. The company towed my car to the mechanic for repairs. After inspection, the mechanic informed me that he had to order a special part and it would take at least a week.

I walked over to a neighbor's house who was a basket weaver and told him my situation. He kindly offered to help me. Together we loaded up all the tulip boxes into his trunk and drove the four hours to my mother's house. When we arrived, Mother served us lunch. We moved all the boxes to my mother's basement and the neighbor went back home.

Beginning two days before the holiday, we set up in the yard near my mother's house. Each one of us brought four boxes of tulips and found spots close to each other. In the market there were a large number of sellers – our competitors. I was a little embarrassed because I wasn't from the area, but Mother said, "You brought the tulips here. Don't look at the buyers but rather look at the nice tulips."

Buyers were buying them without even considering their beauty and stability. On the holiday day, we sold the last of our tulips. All the tulips were sold out, not only by us but also by other traders. I kissed my mother for helping me. With the money I made, I bought a small color television.

Chapter Sixty-Nine: A House on the Bank of a Stream

For five hundred dollars I purchased a one-acre farm in a nice place in the countryside about four kilometers from where we lived. The land was on a hill by a stream, near the forest, with a small house and a dilapidated barn. The house had only a small kitchen and one larger room. Both buildings required a lot of restoration. Close to my farmhouse lived one neighbor and across the stream a second one.

My son Justin, 16-years-old, was delighted with the farm.

"Mother, I will bring all my antiques from my grandmother's house and establish a small ethnographic museum here. With the ensemble, we will perform in the evenings where we will play and sing." He brought in his antiques and arranged them in the room and kitchen.

I planted potatoes in the garden and had a successful harvest in the fall. For the winter, I also made a barrel of sauerkraut, froze various berries, made compotes, jams, and collected mushrooms that I preserved with salt and stored in a wooden barrel. I felt confident we'd have enough food to last the winter.

The house's yard needed to be leveled. I found a man who had a tractor, and on the day he arrived, he paused when he came to the small bridge that ran to our property. After he inspected the bridge, he decided it would be strong enough to withstand the weight of this tractor. He drove slowly onto the bridge and got halfway across when the bridge broke and the tractor fell into the stream. Fortunately, the driver wasn't hurt, although he had a scared white face when he climbed up on the riverbank.

He told me that I'd need to find another powerful tractor to pull his tractor out of the stream.

I got into my car and drove around to a few farms, and fortunately found another farmer with a big tractor within an hour who agreed to come help. After arriving and putting on chains, he started to pull the tractor out of the stream, but one of the chains broke and had to be replaced with two stronger ones. It took several hours, but finally he succeeded in pulling out the half-submerged tractor. After a lot of effort, the stuck tractor was pulled out of the stream.

So, after all this effort, I ended up paying both tractor drivers and had to pay to have the bridge rebuilt, and never did get my land leveled.

I returned home and told Peter the story of what happened.

"Peter, my situation is extreme. Because I have to rebuild the bridge. I am asking for your help."

"Okay," he said. "I will help but you pay for the materials."

I agreed.

Next, I had to find the building materials. I drove out to a busy road and flagged down some trucks, asking them if they could get me gravel. Eventually, I found two who would sell and deliver gravel. Soon two big trucks arrived filled with gravel. I paid them for the loads and went to the store to buy the cement. Next, I had to find somebody with a cement mixer. Peter found someone and soon that machine was delivered to the stream by the ruined bridge.

The next Saturday morning, Justin, Peter, and I arrived by the bridge. Peter separated the good lumber pieces from the broken ones. Together, Peter and Justin began working on the rebuilding.

While sitting on the bridge, Justin fell into a log pile and severely injured his leg. I put him in the car and drove him to the hospital. There, a doctor cleaned and bandaged the wound. I then drove Justin back to the house and placed him in his bed. Then I went back to the bridge.

Peter and I worked all day but didn't finish the job by sunset. When we returned home, I began to worry about having left the cement mixer at the site.

"Peter, what if someone steals the cement mixer? Maybe you could go guard it?"

"I'm too tired. I think it'll be safe enough."

"No, someone needs to guard it."

He shook his head. "You worry too much and I'm too tired. If you're determined to guard it, go yourself or ask Justin."

I went upstairs to talk with Justin. I was surprised to find him up and dressed.

"Where are you going?" I asked.

"This is Saturday night. I'm going to the school dance."

"Dance? I thought your leg hurts," I said. "How could you dance?"

He walked a bit around the room, and I could see he was limping a little.

"Well, maybe I won't do any dancing, but I'd like to meet up with my friends."

I realized he wasn't going to help me guard the mixer, so I decided to go by myself with my German shepherd dog. The dog was happy to go with me. When I opened the car door, the dog jumped in. When we arrived, we parked right next to the cement mixer.

I left the dog inside the car and waded across the stream to my house. Behind the stream, there was a forest where my neighbor Bethan had her farmhouse. After resting a bit, I decided to visit her. She was happy to see me and, though it was late, we had a bit of conversation.

When I was leaving, Bethan said, "Christina, please come visit me often. I'm lonely here."

I told her I would and returned to my car. The dog was waiting and wagging his tail.

I got back into the car, locked the doors, and pulled my seat as far back as possible so I could sleep. I also pulled my dog's seat back who was sitting in the passenger seat. As the night wore on, the full moon rose above, illuminating the forest, the neighbor's farmhouse, and us. I began thinking about werewolves coming out of the forest under the full moon like I'd seen in a movie.

I usually fell asleep by 9 p.m., but tonight I was too anxious. Once in a while, I looked out at the forest and the full moon. The dog lay quietly next to me.

In the distance, I heard a bell ring, and it reminded me of a book I read where lepers put bells on their necks to warn people to stay away. I shook off that thought, knowing that leprosy was extinct in this area. But I kept wondering where the ringing was coming from. It was getting louder.

The dog raised his head and growled. After a bit, the ringing moved away until the sound disappeared.

The moon continued to illuminate the forest and us. I lay down, and my dog was calm. I stroked the dog's hair and told him to sleep. I thought after midnight the werewolves and devils would start to show their power. It was scary.

The night was strangely silent. Occasionally I heard a cow mooing or a horse trotting.

I had just dozed off when I awoke to the bell ringing again. This time the sound was closer and getting stronger. I thought it would be the end of my life. I thought it was such a strange destiny to die in the dark like this. I was afraid to raise my head, but the dog jumped up and pawed the door, wanting to get out. I looked out the window and didn't see anything. The dog showed his teeth and barked.

Then, the sound of the bell faded away.

I told my dog, "Oh, what a good boy. You are my protector. Calm down now and sleep. He looked at me and lay down. Once again it became very quiet. I decided the ringing of the bell wouldn't be heard again, and we could sleep peacefully until the morning. We dozed off.

Half an hour passed, and the bell started ringing again. In the beginning, the sound of the bell was mild, but soon got louder and clearly was coming toward us. Soon, I heard the sound almost next to us. I sat up and saw a person coming straight at us. The dog pressed his nose against the window and barked, foam falling from his jaws.

I shouted, "Bethan, is that you?"

She answered, "Yes, it's me."

"Where does that bell come from?"

"My dog has a bell around his neck," she said, "and we go around our farmhouse like this, scaring the wild boars. Boars come at night and dig the ground and search for potatoes. What are you doing here at night, Christina?"

"I'm guarding the cement mixer with my dog."

"Now you can sleep easy," Bethan said.

"Thank you. You should also go home and rest."

"Fine. I will not walk with my dog here again tonight."

I closed the car window. I was glad that I hadn't let the dog out of the car. It was hard to guess what would have happened. I petted my dog again and praised him for being a good guard. Both of us settled down peacefully. How good that everything was resolved and there would be no more ringing of the bell.

About forty-five minutes after Bethan left, I heard footsteps coming. The dog stood up and jumped back and forth from the front to the back of the car, looking forward and backward, barking, and scratching at the doors. In the darkness, I saw a man walking forward from the forest straight at our car. The dog jumped on the back seat and barked incessantly. Saliva oozed from his jaws.

I yelled, "Peter! Peter, get up. Get up." The shout was intended to scare the man coming toward my car. Suddenly the dog fell silent.

The man called out, "Mother, it's me, Justin, I came after the dance to help you guard the mixer."

I got out of the car, and we hugged each other.

"Thank you, son, for caring about me."

"If you're okay, I'll go sleep in the house," he said.

I sighed with relief. "Knowing you're nearby, I won't be afraid to stay with my dog in my car."

He went to sleep in our house, and I slept in the car until morning came.

When we returned home the next morning, I told Peter about our night's adventures.

He did not show any interest in it. I showered, changed clothes, and ate breakfast. Then we both got into the car and drove back to the bridge. By late afternoon we had finished reconstructing it.

Chapter Seventy: Singing and Dancing

A few months later, my niece Melody came for a visit. Justin had gone out with his group of ethnographic singers to sing by the river on our farmland. In the evening Melody, the dog, and I took a walk down the road that led into the forest. We'd gone in about a mile when a car came towards us and stopped a hundred meters away. This frightened us and we ran into the woods for a good ten minutes. When we stopped, we couldn't hear anyone chasing us.

We made our way through the woods and onto my farm, following the sound of Justin's group.

Melody asked if I'd been bothered by cars like this before.

"No," I said, "but the local people told tales about ghosts in the forest."

The head of the ethnographic ensemble established a private school, and I sent Gabriel to be placed in the first grade. The director not only taught music but also taught his students dance. Gabriel willingly joined the national dance group.

A few months later, the school dance group and ethnographic ensemble were invited to the Estonian capital, Tallinn, to perform at their private school. The director invited me to ride the train with them. After getting to Tallinn, we toured the sites of this city, and the students performed at the concert hall. Justin sang in the ethnographic ensemble, and Gabriel danced national dances.

The teachers at the Estonia school were impressed with the talents of the ethnographic students. They asked the head of the ensemble, "Where did you get these talented students from? Leave them with us."

The head of the ensemble smiled.

Gabriel was often restless and unable to concentrate on his lessons. Peter would try to help him, but he had little patience and often ended up yelling at the boy and sometimes smacking him on the back of the head. When that happened, Gabriel would break down in tears and be completely unable to work.

I got angry at Peter after seeing this way of parenting.

"Is this how you raise a child? Do you want to show your power by fighting with him? He will grow up hating you and not learn anything good from you. Is this your parenting?"

The music teacher prepared Gabriel to sing a song about sailors to perform during a class meeting of students and parents. Peter came to the meeting and the teacher told him that Gabriel had a very good voice.

When Gabriel saw his father in the audience, he said, "Mother, I am too scared to sing."

"Please sing," I told him. You sing beautifully." I held him close to me. "Lose your fear and look at me as you sing. I will encourage you."

My young son is very sensitive and shy. He sang the song. Everyone in the audience applauded him. After the concert, he ran up to me and hugged me.

"Mother I love you, I'm happy."

From the outside, it looked like our family was beautiful, talented, and in peaceful harmony. But it was just an image, an exterior, as in a well-staged play.

Chapter Seventy-One: Tatar Aunt

My aunt worked as a brewery engineer in the city center. She lived in a large house on the second floor. Her salary was small for such an area, so, having insufficient income, she decided to build a chicken coop in her backyard. She asked Justin and me to come help her build it during our summer vacation.

When we entered her house, we were struck with the unpleasant smell of manure, discovering that she was keeping the chickens in a small room by her kitchen. The three of us stepped out back where she had piled the materials for the coop. Walking by the boards, I stepped on a nail that pierced my foot. When I pulled the nail out, blood flowed from the hole.

We went to a nearby hospital where the doctor gave me a tetanus shot and bandaged my foot.

We went back to my aunt's house and built her chicken coop. Afterward, my aunt made us dinner. While it was cooking, she placed a hen on the kitchen table to show off how pretty it was. The bird pooped in the middle of the table, and my aunt wiped it off, although leaving a smear of manure on the table. Then she brought out the food and placed it on the same table.

I could not swallow a bite, for I could still see the manure on the table. I wanted to throw up.

I asked her, "Could we please go to another room to eat?"

We ate in the living room instead, and we thanked her for the meal.

During our trip back home, Justin and I laughed at the events of our day. After two weeks my foot healed.

Later that summer, my aunt decided she wanted to learn how to drive a car and get a driver's license. Soon after getting her permit, she came to visit me. While turning into our driveway, she missed our gate and drove straight into the wooden fence and knocked it down.

My aunt got out of the car and said, "Oh look at what I've done! I'm so sorry."

"Don't worry, Aunt. When people learn to drive, they have accidents. We'll fix it."

Chapter Seventy-Two: Selling Tulips Again

For my third year of growing tulips, I decided to grow 3000. This large amount naturally required more investment and work. I planted my tulip buds late in autumn knowing they'd bloom in February and March. After the tulips bloomed, I packed them and put them in boxes in our cold basement.

To prepare for the big Prussian holiday on February 23rd, I decided to ask Peter's friend Frank for help. I drove to his house and parked in front, walking up the long sidewalk to his door. His wife answered and glared at me. When Frank came out, his wife slipped past us carrying a baseball bat.

While Frank and I talked, she went down to my car, circled it, popping the bat in her hand a few times, and then came back.

She asked, "Are you two lovers?"

Frank laughed. "No, she's just here asking if I could help her sell her tulips on the holiday sale in four days. Why? Were you going to break her car windows?"

She nodded, saying sheepishly, "I was going to, but I'm glad I changed my mind."

One day before the Prussian holiday, I woke Justin up at 2 a.m. and together we loaded about half the tulips into my car. We drove to the city market, arriving at 6 a.m. to find sellers already selling flowers. We took out two tables and placed them in separate locations. As soon as we put the tulips on the tables, buyers lined up.

Speaking in Russian, Justin said, "These are very fresh tulips, I picked them this morning. How many do you need please?"

I sold mine in silence.

Around noon, a man in a heavy gray coat came to my table and said, "You have to give me the tulips for free. If you do not, you will not leave the market alive."

I gave him as much as he asked for. Then he said, "If another man asks you to give him tulips for free, tell him that Volodia was already here and he will go away."

This made me anxious, but I decided to stay there and continue selling my flowers. No one else came to me or Justin and asked for free tulips.

I saw girls coming to Justin and buying from him. They were joking and talking with each other. He was young, tall, and handsome, so girls wanted to flirt with him. This is how we stood all day and sold. We ate and drank at the market from the food basket we had brought from home. Standing in the cold and half-starved, we sold almost all the tulips we brought. At eight o'clock in the evening, we packed up our tables and the remaining tulips and bought a bit of food to bring home.

When I drove back home, I kept looking in the rearview mirror to see if anybody was following us, but fortunately we returned home without incident.

Our house was quite cold, although Peter was there, sitting in his big chair watching TV.

"We've been out in the market all day selling tulips and now we're cold. Why didn't you turn on the house heat?"

"If you're cold, turn on the heat," he said.

Justin brought firewood into the kitchen and lit the furnace. I made hot tea. We drank, ate, warmed up, and then went to bed.

When we got up in the morning, Justin and I opened the suitcase full of money and spread it on the sofa. We threw the bills up in the air, laughing and shouting, "We're rich, we're rich!"

We hugged and danced and laughed and laughed. It was too bad that I didn't have a camera, it would have been a nice memorable photo.

"Let's go to the market, Justin, and buy whatever we want."

He agreed, and off we went.

When we came back from the market, Peter was carving something on the second floor. We'd just walked in when Peter's cousin called and said he'd like to come visit Peter. I told the cousin that I'd let Peter know he was coming.

I knocked on Peter's workshop door and stepped in.

"Peter, your cousin called and is coming to see you."

He snarled at me and yelled, "Can't you see I'm working? Close the door and don't bother me."

"Well, I was just letting you know …" I started to say but had to duck because he threw a box of nails at me. I managed to close the door and heard the nails hit the door and scatter.

Half an hour later his cousin came, and I directed him upstairs. When he saw the nails on the floor, I heard him ask what happened.

"I accidentally scattered them," Peter said. "Please sit down and be comfortable. I will make you a cup of coffee."

Peter climbed down the stairs to the kitchen, made the coffee, and carried it back up. Soon they were laughing among the scattered nails.

It was common for Peter to have tantrums and throw things at me. Probably he was mad because I made so much money at the market and hadn't offered to share with him.

The next morning Frank was waiting for me when I arrived at his house. The morning was cold and windy. In the middle of the trip, my car broke down. Frank got out of the car and determined that the oil was leaking. Around us there were only open fields without any other cars around. The cold winter wind continued to blow.

Frank suggested he should drive, and going very slowly we arrived at the market and found a spot to sell flowers. He left me there and asked where he could find a mechanic. Somebody gave him a mechanic's address and he took the car there while I sold tulips. In a few hours, he returned and helped me sell.

This time we had a lot of tulips left. As we were driving back from the market, Frank told me a story about Peter.

"Christina, you probably don't know that Peter found a substantial amount of money."

"No, he didn't tell me."

"It seems that a couple of years ago Peter hid five thousand rubles in a piece of your artwork hanging on a wall in Justin's bedroom. He had forgotten about it until last week, and though he was happy to find it, in the meantime the rubles have become outdated and worthless."

We both laughed.

"You know, Frank, I already told you that our money is handled separately."

"I know," he answered. "Don't tell Peter I told you this story."

"We returned home in good moods. I told him that I was very grateful for what he did for me in this difficult time and paid him for his help. I thanked him for our friendship and told him I'd always remember it."

A few weeks later I took the unsold tulips to my local market and sold them for the Woman's Day holiday.

Chapter Seventy-Three: Summer Holidays

In the following summer vacation, I took my two sons and dog to my mother's house. We always had a good time, including fishing in a rowboat, eating delicious ice cream in a cafe, and visiting parks and museums. This year, we took my mother on a trip to the seaside. At Luna park, we rode the merry-go-round and enjoyed the other vendors and attractions.

During the summer I helped my mother with whatever work she had at that time. I always swept the street, which was a large area. No one else from the house would do this. For me, it was a pleasure. I put on my shorts and swept to keep myself in good shape.

Peter came unannounced to visit us during our vacation. He invited me to go rowing on the lake with him. He suggested I could fish while he rowed.

The morning was sunny and warm. He rowed across the river and near the count's palace in the northern part of the lake. We entered into a labyrinth of reeds where I fished. I was lucky and caught several. Peter took his clothes off and sunbathed and napped.

After a few hours, clouds moved in, and I told Peter we should head back home. He didn't react, so I took the reed and swiped it across his nose. Again, he didn't respond, so I swiped it again. Peter still didn't say anything, but jumped up and dove into the water, swimming to the shore, leaving his clothes in the boat. Dark clouds gathered overhead, thunder rumbled, and a great storm of rain set in. Thunder and lightning accompanied rain falling in buckets.

I rowed the boat to the shore and tied it down. I left the boat and started running and shouting Peter's name, but he didn't answer. I ran to the count's palace where some people were sheltering from the storm. Peter wasn't there.

I hid under the roof and waited for the rain to pass. After it stopped, I returned to the boat to find it half-filled with water. As I rowed back towards home, my legs were half immersed in water. Fortunately, because the boat is made of wood, it doesn't sink.

When I reached our home, I saw my mother standing by the shore. She asked, "Where's Peter?"

I told her what happened, that Peter had jumped from the boat, swum to shore, and I hadn't seen him since.

Mother said she became frightened when the storm arrived. She had checked with the yacht club, and they told her there weren't any boats still on the water.

"I calmed down when I saw you rowing in the river. Christina, I am so happy to see you."

I tied the boat, and we went home. When we came in, we saw Peter.

"Peter. why did you leave Christina alone in a storm?" my mother asked.

"I got mad when Christina swiped my nose with the reed. I jumped out of the boat, swam to the shore, and during the storm I crossed the lake bridge in my bathing suit."

Mother said, "What kind of husband are you to leave your wife during a storm? You're pathetic."

I said, "Peter, you asked me to go fishing with you and to have a good time together. You ruined everything with your unpredictable behavior. Why did you even come here? To show your rudeness?"

He said he was sorry and left the next day.

After he left, I invited my mother, nieces, and kids to go to our resort by the Baltic Sea. We went to the parks, ate at restaurants, and swam in the sea. After a week together, we went home tired but happy. After a fun summer vacation, we packed up and returned home.

Chapter Seventy-Four: Dealing with Unhappiness

I learned little by little to distance myself from the anger and hatred that I received from Peter. It took a lot of effort to avoid this anger.

I learned how to make a drink of alcohol I could tolerate. The recipe required two bottles of cognac and ten washed lemons. I removed the seeds and ground them with the peel. Adding one kg of honey, I poured all the ingredients into a jar and mixed everything well. I let it stand for ten days in a glass container.

When I felt sad, I drank one shot of my drink and played very loud music. This was a way for me to relax and exit my sadness. When I listened to music it calmed me down. Sometimes, when there was a bigger family disagreement, I would get into the car, put the music on full volume and just drive. Music distracted me from my problems, and driving a car made me concentrate on the road. I returned home relaxed and looking forward to another day.

Chapter Seventy-Five: Melody's Wedding

After graduating from music college, my niece became engaged to her boyfriend and soon they planned a marriage ceremony. Melody's mother, Agatha, asked me to be the matron of honor at their wedding. I gladly agreed. I read many books and seriously prepared for this important event. After all, I had to appear to know all the wedding customs. I knew that the role of the matron of honor was to entertain the guests and participate in the wedding feast. A large two-story house by the river was rented for the wedding.

Together with my mother, we baked a big honey cake. We decorated it with white sugar flowers that we made. I had the handyman make a small table on which I placed the cake. The groomsmen of the wedding party would bring my cake to this table at a certain time specified in the ceremonies.

My husband Peter and his daughter Amelia came to the wedding. She was invited to be a bridesmaid, and my son Justin was the best man. His daughter wore a very beautiful dress she made. Amelia inherited her father's character which was not the best. I pretended to always agree with her even when I didn't, and otherwise kept quiet around her or made simple conversation and this way kept my relationship with Amelia pleasant. She lived with her mother in a village not far from where we lived.

For guests who came from far away, there were beds made with linen on the second floor. The guests could rest there after the wedding ball.

I sewed my clothes for the wedding. On the first day, I wore a long pink dress, and on the second day, I wore a wide beige pants I copied from the German magazine "Burda". I put on a white blouse and black high-heeled shoes.

When the wedding feast began, I didn't see Peter. I found him lying on a bed on the second floor.

"Are you sick?" I asked.

"No, I am not sick."

"Then you need to come down and spend time with the guests and watch the wedding party that I lead."

He said he would come. An hour passed and still he didn't show up. I asked my mother to go and get him to come down. Peter obeyed her, at least long enough to eat, and then he went back upstairs again.

The ball was spectacular. Neighbors and guests liked the scenario I conducted.

"Christina, you entertained us very well tonight," guests said. "You were well prepared and put a lot of love and soul into this event. All the wedding customs were perfect."

After the wedding ball on the second day, at noon, as the guests prepared to leave, Agatha gave them leftover cake, cookies, or a bottle of wine. After giving them these gifts and saying goodbye to them, she turned to me with an angry look.

She said to me. "Why did you come here? To show off?"

I did not answer. I turned and walked away. She ruined my good mood. I had put a lot of effort, money, and time into preparing for this wedding. I think that she did not like my truthful statement when I said at the wedding ceremony that my parents raised the bride.

When driving home, Peter sat in the car in a soul mood and wouldn't talk to anyone. I asked him, "Are you sick or feeling bad?"

He didn't answer.

During the drive, Justin, Amelia, and I shared wedding impressions. She left for her home in the evening. I said, "Have a good trip home."

After getting married, Melody lived with her husband's parents in a village and eventually gave birth to a son. She rarely returned to visit her parents. In this village, it was peaceful and pleasant for her to live. She had good and kind relatives. She felt happy, safe, and cheerful there. Melody fell in love with his parents, and everybody loved her.

Chapter Seventy-Six: Corresponding to the West

Promise me you will always remember: You are braver than you believe, stronger than you seem, and smarter than you think.
- *English Writer A.A. Milne*

When my country received its independence in 1990, an advertisement appeared in a newspaper; "Whoever wants to correspond with foreigners, you have to write to an address in Dublin, Ireland." I decided it would be a great joy for me to visit a capitalist country. I wrote a letter to the given address. I wrote about myself and attached my photo.

I wanted to feel the adventure of travel and looked for a country that could give me a better life for myself and my children. I dreamed of being a free bird. I wanted to escape Peter's tyranny, constant humiliation, and disrespect. To my surprise, I received many letters from all over the world. It was hard to answer them all. It took a lot of time and effort to respond to each one. All the letters were written in English. I always wanted to learn this language, and this was a good opportunity to do so. I used English-Lithuanian, and Lithuanian-English dictionaries, writing while everybody else was sleeping. Papers and letters accumulated on the floor and bed. In the morning, after a few hours of sleep, I jumped out of bed, took a shower, and went to work. When I got to my school, I asked my English teacher to correct my mistakes in the letters.

One night my mother got up and found me sitting at the table writing.

"How long can you sit and suffer here? Get some rest."

"Mother, I will write until I manage to get the first invitation and can leave the country. You always taught me, 'If you start you have to finish it.' I will only be happy when I reach my dream of many years. Please, Mother, go to sleep and rejoice in my determination."

"Have you had any success?"

I thumbed through my stack of correspondence. "I am reading two letters that came from Australia. I started to correspond with two women and their families. After several months of correspondence, I asked them for an invitation document. Explaining that I do not need anything other than an invitation to visit Australia. Both families answered me with their apologies stating that they have families and could not invite me."

Another letter came from Switzerland. I thought I would have an opportunity to visit that beautiful country and corresponded with him. However, he said that currently it was difficult to get a visa to his country. I put the letter aside. Soon I received another letter from Switzerland. The family was interested in my country and asked if it was safe to visit here. I wrote that it was safe.

One letter came from America from an author who lived in Colorado. He was interested in visiting me. I encouraged him to come, but a few weeks later he called and told me that he had become too busy to travel and was delaying his visit.

A week later, I received another letter from America. This was written by Belle, a woman living in Iowa. She wrote that she was a musician who played saxophone in an orchestra and organ at church. Her husband was a farmer, and she had a son and a daughter. I corresponded with her for two long years. After our long correspondence, I asked her for an invitation to come to America. I wrote her saying that I do not need anything besides an invitation. Belle's friend sent an invitation in the next letter.

Chapter Seventy-Seven: Justin's Poem in German High School

After graduating from high school, Justin entered a university with the ambition of becoming an Orthodox priest. After studying there for one year, he decided that this was not his calling. He wanted to attend a certain high school in Germany where he knew some friends. I flew to Germany, found the high school, and talked to the head of the school to get Justin admitted there. The principal of the school admitted Justin to start school as a student in the last grade of high school. In July, Justin left for Germany.

Here's a poem he wrote at this time.

Nobody

Messy hair of
homeless child
I opened the door without windows
and there are only graves, the remains of the gods
and the snake rides out of love.

Pearl whites outside the cold door
I collected the necklace for you
come one mermaid young
bring a crown of silks.

Thunder houses swarms of ticks
waiting for you in the doorway
come with friends to play dice
if you do not have your own home.

I have a house

not only have a roof
it tilts from the orbit of the wind
straw falls when the storm blows
and the slave weeps without child.

The lever quivering in the wind returns
my Libra constellation
a stone at the bottom of the swamp starts crying
and the voice of their music is pure.

Gone are the home wicket paths
I roll a bunch of dice
threshold angles
House of Thunder
friends mock
but nothing of the sort.

Chapter Seventy-Eight: Renee's Wedding

In the middle of June, my second niece prepared for her wedding. The wedding ceremony was in the same place as her sister Melody's wedding. Renee's parents did not ask me to be matron of honor, instead asking her friend to lead the wedding ceremony. For the groom, Sven, it was his second marriage, and the priest did not want him to get married in the church. Sven bribed the priest so they could get married in church.

During the wedding, while the guests and my mother were sitting at the table, the bride's mother, Agatha, approached my mother with a pitcher of beer and threw the beer directly in my mother's face. My mother didn't say anything but went home and changed her clothes.

After the wedding, Renee and Sven moved to his mother's house in the same town where Renee graduated from high school. Her parents remained living close to them. Sven's mother's house had a kitchen, living room, and bedroom. The newlyweds settled in the bedroom of his mother while his mother slept on the couch in the living room. A year later, they had a son.

The grandmother was excited to have her first grandchild and eager to hold him. However, Renee refused to allow her to even approach the child's bed. She was very rude to her mother-in-law, refusing even to show her the baby. Despite being rebuffed, the grandmother made pancakes for Renee, who came to the table, ate without thanking or even talking to the old woman, and went back to her bedroom shutting the door.

My mother called me and said we should go see Renee's new child. We purchased flowers and a gift, and when we arrived Renee opened the door and invited us in. Sven was at home and the two invited us to sit on a sofa in their bedroom. The baby slept in a crib.

We congratulated the couple and gave them our presents. They offered us drinks and cookies.

While we were sitting, the phone rang. Sven answered, talked a bit, and hung up. After he finished his conversation his wife asked him, "Who is calling? Again, some woman?"

Their conversation became loud and angry, and we got up, said thank you and left. On the way home, we discussed how this seemed to portend a lot of trouble. Living in a marriage of distrust and infidelity would never work.

Not long after our visit, Renee's mother-in-law came to Renee's parents' house. She pleaded with Agatha to come to her house immediately because Renee and Sven were fighting like cats and dogs.

Agatha and Simon went and brought Renee and their grandson back to their house. A few days later, Sven went and apologized to Renee and her parents. He promised to be a serious father. She forgave him and went back to his mother's home.

A month later, Renee and her husband were invited to his friend's birthday party. Having long blonde hair, blue eyes, and a comely figure, Renee was quite attractive. She wore a lovely dress and high heels.

At the party, everyone was dancing except Sven.

In the evening, Agatha and Simon received a call from the hospital reporting that Renee had been injured. There they found their daughter lying with bruises on her eyes and a swollen face. The doctor said that she'd been badly beaten with bruised ribs and a facial fracture.

After the doctor left, Renee told them the story. She said everyone at the party was dancing except Sven, so Renee danced with the host, Sven's friend. In the middle of the party, Sven dragged Renee out the door and to the hotel room that they'd rented for the night. There he screamed at her for dancing with his friend, threw her against the wall, and beat her up. Then he walked out the door, leaving her crying and bleeding on the floor. The next-door tenant had heard the commotion and when she came and saw Renee so hurt, she called for an ambulance.

After hearing about this unforgivable incident, Agatha insisted Renee divorce him.

"His behavior is unpredictable. The next time he might kill you."

Renee shook her head. "I love Sven. I'm sure he'll apologize and promise that it will not happen again.

Agatha stomped her foot. "How can you love someone who abuses you so cruelly? You should hate him and break all contact with him."

"No, no," Renee insisted. "I'll forgive him, and we will continue to live together."

Renee had to stay in the hospital for a week. Afterward, she went to her parents' house to recuperate. A few days later, Sven showed up with a bouquet of flowers.

Agatha told him to go away and never come back, but, instead, Renee forgave him and returned to live with him again.

Two weeks later, Sven had another tantrum. He ordered Renee to take their son and get in the car. He drove to the cemetery and told her to kneel down.

He pointed his gun at her head and said, "I am going to shoot you and our son."

Renee, sobbing hysterically, managed to say, "Why are you punishing us like this? I love you."

His anger suddenly passed. He got in his car and drove off. Renee took her son and walked back to her parents' house.

After this event, Agatha called me and asked me to help her. She wanted me to write a letter to her daughter urging her to divorce Sven as soon as possible.

I wrote and sent the letter, but never found out if she even read it, for she never responded. In any case, Renee did eventually get divorced and moved in with her parents.

A year or so later, Justin went to visit Renee on her birthday, bringing flowers. He found her lying in bed drunk, with a neighbor in the kitchen cooking scrambled eggs. As Renee was too drunk to talk, Justin talked with the neighbor. He gave him the flowers and asked him to give the flowers to Renee when she felt better. Eventually, he found out that Renee and the neighbor were in a relationship.

Chapter Seventy-Nine: Foreign Travel

About a month after Justin started his senior year at the German high school, I bought a ticket to visit him there.

I looked at Justin. "You look and act differently. You had long hair tied across your forehead with an Indian ribbon. Now I see that look is gone and replaced by short, very nicely combed hair, perfectly suited for your deep blue eyes, dark hair, and beautiful features. This is a surprise to me."

He was very polite and cheerful, which I missed when he lived with us. Now he was full of youthful joy and the fullness of life. We were both very happy to see each other.

"Mother, remember my difficult adolescence days when I grew up and experienced a lot of pain at the hands of my stepfather? Now I can sing and play the guitar again. Thank you for always fighting for me, and for your love of me. My friends are planning a visit to Paris. I always wanted to see that town."

I told him that I had received an invitation from my American friend and would soon be going to the American Embassy and get my visa.

He was very happy for me, saying, "Mother it is your dream finally coming true."

Justin gave me an envelope containing a poem he wrote while studying in Germany. He said, "Mother, when you are flying to America and you are high above the clouds, open this envelope and read it." He gave me a small brown plush hedgehog that I still have.

I spoke to the school principal who praised Justin as a good student with a bright personality. These words made me happy.

I spent two days with Justin. Afterward, we embraced, and I left with tears of joy.

When I got back from Germany, I went to the American Embassy to get my visa. Finally, my dream to see America would come true. I wanted to observe the American Indian culture, their museums, and their way of life. When I was in high school, I read Fenimore Cooper's books about American Indians, their lives, their dignity, and their tribes. I wanted to see it all with my own eyes. Jania, a teacher who lived in the same town as me, went with me to the American Embassy. She also hoped to get an entry visa.

At that time, to visit America, you needed to have an invitation and then go to the embassy for approval. When you got there, you needed to have many documents. These documents should show where you worked, how much you earned, and when you planned to return. I had to get confirmation from the director that I was being laid off for a year and that I would return to the same job afterward. In the morning, we got on the train and left for the embassy.

After an hour or two standing in line, I got to the consul who examined my documents. She asked, "How long will you stay in America?"

"Three months."

"Are you going to work?"

"No," I replied. "I'm going to visit my pen pal."

She stamped my passport with a visa. With this permit, I could go back and forth between America and my country for a year.

Jania also received a visa. She had relatives in Ohio and wanted to visit them. The consul told her she'd have to leave her husband and son behind.

Riding on the train back we talked of our plans. We decided that we would fly to the United States together in the fall. I asked her if she knew anyone in Chicago who could help me when I arrived, but she didn't.

I remembered that my mother mentioned once that she had a friend who lived there. When I asked her, she told me that the friend had moved there after the war and that she had an address but no phone number. I asked other friends and received three phone numbers of acquaintances living in Chicago.

Jania and I bought tickets in September to fly to the United States. She had already been to America and worked there. She advised me not to put anything nice in my suitcase, to take work gloves and work clothes.

"You will not believe this until you see it, Christina. Unlike European women, who want to look beautiful not only in front of ourselves but also in front of others, American women don't care how they dress."

I told her I didn't believe her. I bought a German magazine, "Burda", where I found designs I liked. I took clippings to fit my size and sewed myself burgundy shorts from woolen material. I added long suede over-the-knee-length Italian burgundy boots. I also sewed a short green jacket from woolen material with burgundy appliqué the same color as my shorts. In addition, I had a burgundy knee-length coat with a cape. I painted one part of the cape in batik style and embroidered its upper part with a sewing machine.

One of my favorite items was a black beret I restored from two of my father's berets and put a beak in it. I kept this beret for years afterward, often receiving compliments whenever I wore it.

I packed not only work clothes but also several good-looking outfits. I brought many gifts for my pen pal, including various wicker baskets with interesting designs. I also had a gift for her daughter, a knitted doll of my own creation with clothes knitted on it. I packed everything into one large suitcase.

Before I left, I asked my mother to look after Gabriel until I returned. I sold my car which had broken down and been repaired numerous times. It served me well for many years. I took the money

243

that I saved and the car money that I received and purchased a ticket for the flight to the United States.

At the airport, I embraced my mother and Gabriel. They wished me luck. On the other hand, Peter didn't say a single word. I had known for a long time that I needed to leave him. The visa and my money gave me freedom.

With five dollars in my pocket, I flew to Chicago.

Chapter Eighty: Justin's Poem on Way to America

Rising above the clouds, I took out the poem written by Justin in Germany.

Justin's poem.

Mother it is for you.

You gave birth to me tiny and featherless,
when the face of the Sun burned in fire,
You prayed life to give me wings
minted in a gold forge.

And you heard his shouts of joy,
when your delicate body was burning in the fire
thus your hands carried him to life
like pubescence of sow-thistle in space.

And here he goes, says the first word, laughs,
he is already 19 years old
not far away, unborn babies are still calling him in his
lifetime.
He is tall and thin and moves around among the girls.

The highest Love crosses life
he goes cheerful and quiet through the forest path
to his free gaze his youth speaks,
and he goes to look for her, to dream her dreams.

And the world did not sink him cheaply because he is,
but it is not new

And when you look often Mother
through the empty window and the open field to the new rye

Remember me, my smile, poems and many things, quarrels
I thank you that I am human today.
That love carried to my heart as well
wherever, remember me again.

Read when you are sad and happy. Let my "hedgehog" wink at you often.

OM SAI. RAM. (Sai Reiki Mahamantra). Hindi Sai Mantra.
Be WITH Mother.

On the left side of the envelope there is a brown cross and a shining open book under it.
Inscription in the middle.
See you later.
Clouds Separate Us.
FOR MOTHER
His sign Your "Light".
September.

I was deeply touched after reading it, and it helped me calm down.

Chapter Eighty-One: Arriving in America

I realized that I was flying into the unknown, where no one was waiting to meet me. A huge crowd of strangers would be at Chicago O'Hare International Airport. My flight mate decided that she wouldn't fly from Chicago to Ohio since there were more jobs in Chicago.

Belle had written to me from Iowa and told me that she wouldn't be able to find a job for me with a tourist visa. Like my friend, I decided my best plan was to stay in Chicago. Before the plane landed, the flight attendant handed out forms. One question, "Are you female or male?" in the questionnaire, I didn't understand because I didn't know what these two words meant in English.

I turned to the man behind me. "Excuse me, could you please help me answer this question?"

"Oh, of course."

I showed them the question and asked. Please tell me am I male or female?"

They laughed, saying, "I don't know, but I think you are a female."

"Thank you," and then I laughed at myself also.

The plane landed successfully, and we applauded and thanked the pilot for a great and smooth landing. We left the plane and passed through a long corridor until we were met by immigration officials. American citizens stood in one line, tourists in the other. When I reached the official, I showed him my passport and visa.

He asked, "How long you will stay?"

"Three months."

He stamped my passport for six months. I thanked him and waited for Jania. After passing through customs, we both went to get our bags. We found them, took them, and approached another official who checked our bags. This one asked me whether I was bringing sausages or hams. My answer was no.

We left with our suitcases and came to a huge room where many travelers were waiting. Some stood with flowers for their loved ones, others watched the TV screens that showed when the planes would arrive. Nobody was waiting for us.

We stepped to one side and wondered what we should do next. It is evening. I never thought that this airport could be so big.

My co-passenger was worried. "Where are we going to stay?" she asked. "Probably the police will kick us out if we don't leave. We should take a taxi and leave the airport."

"Calm down," I said. "Let's try calling those three phone numbers. I predict one of them will respond and take us in."

I dropped a quarter into a phone and tried to call one of the numbers. The operator spoke so quickly I couldn't understand what she said.

I hung up and asked a man standing next to me, "Excuse me, sir, could you help me make a telephone call?"

"With pleasure."

I gave him the three phone numbers, but after trying them he told me that none of them answered.

I thanked him.

Night had fallen. We decided to take a taxi to my mother's classmate's address who lived in an area called Marquet Park area. Jania had more money than me. Outside, we found a taxi driven by an African American. We gave him the address and an hour later we arrived at my mother's friend's house. I saw a light in the window and rang the doorbell. Nobody came to open the door.

I rang again one more time. Still silence.

I later found out that in this neighborhood if you don't call in advance, nobody would let you in. In the beginning, that area was settled mainly by immigrants from Europe. At the time of our visit, the residents were mostly African American.

We informed the taxi driver that we still had three phone numbers and asked if he would be so kind as to take us to a phone booth and help us make the phone calls.

When he stopped by the phone booth, he said, "Don't get out of the car, this area is dangerous."

I gave him the three phone numbers, and he called. When he returned, he told us that no one answered at any of the numbers.

"Don't be afraid of me, I have a family. I'll take you to my house and you can sleep over for one night."

My companion and I discussed it and decided we should try the phone numbers one more time. At the booth, we tried again, and to my surprise, a young man answered.

"Hello," I said. "My friend and I just arrived from Lithuania and your phone number was given to us by a friend who lives there. Could you please accept us to stay for one night, or perhaps more until we find a room to rent?"

The fellow replied, "My mother is not at home, but you could come, and I will let you in. Can you write down my address?"

I passed the phone to our taxi driver who got the address and drove us to the location. The young man let us into his house and showed us where to put our luggage. Then he called his mother, telling her what was happening.

After talking with her, he said to us, "I have to go to a birthday party and I can't leave you here, I will take you to a restaurant nearby and you can stay there until I come back. After the party, I will pick you up and bring you back here."

We got into his car after leaving our things at the house and he took us to the restaurant.

The restaurant was dimly lit, with many customers sitting at tables or by the bar. The ones at the bar were mostly men wearing baseball hats. The bar was decorated for Christmas even though it was only September. We sat at a table in the back.

I whispered to Jania, "So this is what America is like? Everyone in this restaurant speaks English or Lithuanian."

A waitress approached and greeted us in Lithuanian. "Would you like to order something?"

We hardly had any money left, so all we could afford was hot tea. My chair was against a wall, and it was 11 o'clock in the evening. I leaned against the wall and fell asleep. Jania pinched me, saying it'd be rude to sleep in the restaurant.

When the waitress returned with our tea, she asked where we were from, how did we get there, and where were we staying.

We told her the story, admitting that we didn't have anywhere to stay.

"You look like decent women, nicely dressed and speaking well. If you need a place to stay, you may stay at my place. I will accommodate you."

We told her that we had left our bags with a woman who we didn't know, and that her son brought us here. We told her where she lived and she said she knew this woman, it was her friend.

We drank our tea and soon we were sitting in her car as she drove us to her house. When we got there, she placed a mattress in the living room floor for us and made our bed.

As soon as we lay down on the bed, we fell asleep.

In the morning our hostess made us breakfast. After eating she offered to drive us to the employment agency. We dressed in work clothes, and it took only a few minutes at the business before the agent offered us each jobs.

She explained that both jobs would be to take care of elderly women who were sick. Both jobs required living in the home or seven days a week.

"If you agree to take these jobs you have to pay me one week's salary," the agent explained.

We agreed to the terms and the agent drove us to our potential employers. While she was driving, Jania told the agent that she wanted to take the first job that the agent had offered. Our hostess followed behind in her car.

When we arrived at the first house, the agent would only let Jania go with her inside. After meeting the elderly lady, Jania accepted the position. She was hired and stayed in this house with the elderly lady.

The agent then took me to the second job offering. When we went into the house the owner told us that the position of this job had been taken. I went into the hostess' car and we drove back to her house.

After a few days, the hostess offered me a babysitter's job.

"Yes," I said. "It would be happy to have a job like that. I hope they will hire me."

"If they hire you, Christina, you will have to pay to me one week's salary after one week of work."

I agreed, and she advised me to bring clothes in case they hired me. We met with her client, the environment seemed nice, and they hired me. The job was five days a week, living in the home.

It was a big two-story mansion in the western suburbs of Chicago. There were two girls in the family, one eight years old and the other five. Each morning the girls were picked up by school buses. While the girls were at school, I had to clean the house, make the beds, and clean the showers, and toilets. I made lunch for the girls when they came back from school. In the evening, I cooked dinner for the whole family.

About the third day I was there, I put some meat in the microwave to reheat it. I must have put it on for too long, for a bit later when I was upstairs cleaning, I smelled smoke. I ran back to the kitchen and found it full of smoke. I cleaned out the meat and opened the windows to ventilate.

When the owner returned from work, he asked, "What is that smell?"

"I'm so sorry. I left the meat in the microwave and overcooked it. I think I broke your microwave." I offered to buy him a new one. "You can take its cost out of my salary for however long it takes."

"Don't worry, Christina," He answered. "It was an accident. We'll throw it away and I will buy a new one tomorrow."

There was enough work in that big house to keep me busy the whole day. I needed to be nimble. Finally, after cooking and serving and cleaning up, I put the dishes in the dishwasher and was done for the day. I went to my room which was on the second floor and had free time until morning. My room had a wide bed, TV, a shower, toilet, and closet. At six o'clock each morning I walked downstairs and prepared breakfast. After five days, I received my first salary. I liked this job. The family was very friendly and always kept me on the move. On the weekend I returned home by train.

I got off the train at the main station in Chicago. Walking by the stairs, an African American grabbed my arm and asked for money.

I said, "I don't have any money."

He replied, "Then may God help you."

I had to take two busses to get to my hostess' house. There I paid her my first week's salary, as per our agreement.

Chapter Eighty-Two: Life in America

Six weeks after my arrival, Belle, my friend in Muscatine, Iowa, who gave me an invitation to come to America, invited me to visit her at Christmas. I was eager to see another part of the country. Once I bought a bus ticket, I wrote her stating the date and time of my arrival.

About this time, I asked my hostess to help me find an apartment. Very quickly she found a room in a house to rent close to where she lived. The owner was Lithuanian. I told the owner that I would have a roommate on an occasional weekend. We agreed on a rental price and my hostess helped me move my luggage.

I paid the hostess the last rent due and thanked her for her generous help. I said, "Without you it would have been very difficult for me to find a job and an apartment."

"Christina, do not forget me," she replied.

"We will be in touch," I promised.

In my rented room, there were two mattresses placed on top of each other, a chest of drawers, and one window with two heavy fabric curtains, the latter attached to metal holders. There was a shared kitchen. What a blessing to have this small room and be free from quarrels, arguments, poverty, abuse, and violence. I felt that this little corner of America was paradise.

It didn't matter that the bed was without bedding or pillow. I lay down and started to dream of how happy I was to be able to have my own room and free of all conflicts.

After a few minutes, I got up and put away my few autumn sweaters, clothes, and work gloves into the chest of drawers. I took off my white sweater and wrapped it to make a pillow. I took the curtain off the metal brackets, and it became my blanket. I slept with my clothes on. During the night, a metal bracket of a curtain stabbed me in the leg. I knocked the curtain to the floor.

The following Saturday, Jania visited and together we went to our first hostess and asked if she could refer us to a good dentist. She supplied the phone number of her dentist and that afternoon I called and made an appointment.

On the appointment day, I took the bus to the dentist office. He examined my teeth and put a temporary filling on my aching tooth. He also told me that other teeth need to be fixed. He told me that Eastern Europeans all have problems with their teeth. He warned me that repairing teeth costs a lot of money if you don't have insurance. I told the dentist that I want the front teeth fixed. I continued going to him until he fixed all my bad teeth.

I received a letter from my mother. She wrote,

"All is well with Gabriel. I am writing about an unpleasant incident which happened one evening. We were preparing Gabriel's homework. Peter came into the room and Gabriel asked Peter to help him solve some math problems. It seems that Gabriel can't concentrate on math. Peter, not having patience and probably not being able to do the problem himself, hit Gabriel on the back of his head.

"This was not the first time it happened. When I saw this, I tried to stop it. I told Peter that this is not the way to raise children. You should be a good father. After these words of mine, Peter grabbed my shoulder and pushed me from the chair to the floor.

"Gabriel shouted 'Dad, Dad what are you doing?'

"Peter left without saying anything. Gabriel came to me and helped me to get up. He asked me, 'Grandma, are you alright?' I said to him 'Yes,' and hugged him.

"The next morning Peter came into the kitchen and told me that he was very sorry. What could I say? I thought what a tyrant he is! Christina, I understand now what you had to go through when you lived with him."

Living here we met Arturus, a Lithuanian neighbor who lived very close to my rental apartment. Jania and I introduced ourselves. He offered to take us to a Lithuanian club where we could enjoy dancing, listening to music, and dining. Delighted with such an offer we met him at his house. He seemed to be a very nice person. He arrived in America after the Second World War and was active in the Lithuanian community.

After talking with Arturus at his home he took us to the "Lithuanian Club Hall". The hall looked like a scene from an old movie. There were many large round tables in the dimly lit spacious room, each covered with a white tablecloth. Portraits of Lithuanian former leaders hung on the walls, reminding people of the days gone by.

We sat down at an empty table. After a bit, I got up and walked around the room, studying the portraits. While I was up, the music started, the musician playing an accordion and his wife beating a drum. Couples danced waltz, polka, tango, and other slow dances.

I noticed several women scowling at us, and I guessed they were jealous of our youth and good looks, perhaps worried we were going to try to seduce their husbands. A heard one call us "Barracudas".

Soon a man came to our table and invited me to dance. I accepted and we danced a tango. He took me back to the table and he said he hoped that both of us would come back to the hall. The next song I danced with Arturus.

In the middle of the evening, a lottery was announced. We bought some tickets and two of them were lucky. We won a plush toy that was already owned by someone else and another toy. We showed our lottery prizes to the guests sitting by the table with us. We were all having fun, laughing, and enjoying our prizes, and showing them to each other. It seemed that the lottery prizes were typically unnecessary and sometimes used items that people donated. Sometimes they donated a bottle of wine.

This was how they collected money to maintain the hall and pay taxes. There was a bar in the corner of the hall where one could order drinks. It was a nice and unusual party. After the lottery, we started dancing again and eventually Arturus took us home. We thanked him for the pleasant evening.

On Sunday morning, Arturus offered to take us to the shopping mall. As we drove, he told interesting stories about his life. He appeared to be a brave, friendly, and humorous person. His wife was deceased, and he had two daughters who lived on their own.

At the mall I bought sheets for my bed. After that he also offered to take us to his place for a meal. He spoiled us with delicious food he cooked, and we drank some wine. He then turned on some music. It was a pleasant evening.

On Monday morning we had to go back to work. We went to the bus stop and waited. When we got in, the driver greeted us with a smile that showed perfectly white teeth. His pleasant smile lifted our moods.

The bus took us to the Chicago train station where Jania and I boarded trains going in opposite directions. We said goodbye and looked forward to our next meeting. After talking with her, I decided that she had a much harder job than I do. I believed my work was more interesting compared to hers.

The next weekend, I decided to go visit my mother's childhood friend, the one that didn't open the door for us when we arrived. She lived close to me. This time when I came, she was gardening in her front yard. I introduced myself, and she welcomed me kindly and I told her how my mother was doing.

She offered me a bedding set as a gift. When I entered one of her rooms, I saw an entire display case decorated with amber. She was an artist and made wreaths out of straw. During holidays she decorated and sold them.

Having learned how to get to the shopping mall by bus, I visited it in my spare time. I bought various clothes, sweets, and other things for my son and mother, and packed them in a large box. Arturus drove me to the parcel dispatch point where I sent my Christmas gifts.

As Christmas approached, I had been working as a babysitter with that family for three and half months. Although the work was pleasant and easy, I wasn't receiving enough money to live on. I found another woman to replace me. Christmas was coming and I had to prepare for my Christmas visit to my friend in Iowa.

Chapter Eighty-Three: Iowa City

Just before leaving for Iowa, I received a postcard from Justin.

Dear Mother,
Christmas and New Year are coming. I want you to stay strong and remember how much we love each other. Be aware that all that was painful now lies in the past. When spring comes bringing many beautiful spring flowers remember how life is beautiful, too.
I miss you so much.
Stay healthy and happy.
Now let's listen to Christmas bells together.
Justin.

At the bus station I presented my ticket and boarded a Greyhound bus for Davenport. I dressed in the same warm clothes I had on when I came to America. I felt very confident. Sitting on the bus, I watched the landscape, so different from Lithuania.

We arrived at Davenport in the evening. The driver announced that the bus was broken, and we couldn't continue until it was repaired. I didn't have a telephone to call Belle and inform her that my arrival would be late. The driver apologized to everyone for the inconvenience and offered free pizza to all the passengers.

When he asked what kind of pizza I wanted, I told him vegetarian pizza with mushrooms and a coca cola to drink. Soon he brought a huge pizza and the drink. The pizza was very tasty. After eating, the passengers talked with each other, and someone asked where I came from. I told them Europe. They surprised me by saying that was cool.

I settled back on my chair and tried to sleep. With the thoughts racing through my head and the excitement of being in a new place, I found sleep difficult. After an uncomfortable and mostly sleepless night, in the morning the driver announced that the bus was fixed and ready to roll. Within two hours the bus arrived at my destination village. The driver told me that it was my stop. I thanked him and wished him and all the passengers, "Happy holidays."

The bus left me alone in a small building surrounded by fields and no one around. I started to get scared, wondering what to do next. Behind me I spotted a small house with a sign stating, "The Grocery Store". There, I asked the saleswoman if I might use her phone.

I dialed Belle's number, and she answered right away.

"Christina where are you?"

"I am by the bus stop outside the store. Did you get my letter that I am coming?"

"No, I did not," she answered. "Wait for me. I will be there in ten minutes."

I thanked the saleswoman and went outside to wait. Standing on the platform I shivered in the cold blustery wind.

When Belle arrived, we hugged.

"Christina, it is very nice to meet you."

"Me too," I answered. "Thank you for coming to pick me up and especially thank you for the invitation."

She drove us to her house, a small cottage placed close to a much larger house where Belle's husband's aunt lived. We entered the room, and she introduced me to her husband. Her husband was a farmer and a photographer. Their cottage had two floors and a swimming pool in the backyard. The walls were decorated with paintings by Belle and photographs by her husband.

She showed me photos of her son and daughter who were going to be there for Christmas. In the evening Belle's husband cooked steaks and potatoes and corn-on-the-cob with pumpkin pie for dessert, a wonderful farm fare treat. After dinner, they showed me to the room where I would sleep. Before going to sleep, I presented them with gifts I had brought.

The next morning, after getting up and eating, they offered to take me to a local store. They bought me a camera. This was the first American gift I ever received, and I was very thankful. In the evening, she invited me to go to the Methodist church where my she played the organ.

Her daughter was a zootechnician, as was her husband. They arrived the next evening. I gave her my creation doll. Then she brought into the house two small puppies and said these were their children. After getting married and living for a long time without children, she had twin sons a few years later. Neither son married.

I was very excited to celebrate Christmas with an American family in the middle of Iowan fields. It was so strange as to be interesting.

The table for the Christmas holiday was decorated very artistically. We had a great feast, with a huge turkey, beans, and a type of potato that was orange and sweet. Belle served both cake and pie for dessert.

On Christmas evening, their relatives, neighbors, and friends came to celebrate. I introduced myself to all the guests. Everyone welcomed me and gave me interesting and memorable gifts. I was prepared and gave all the guests gifts that I had bought in Chicago. Although initially I felt shy and uncomfortable, they were all so welcoming that by evening's end I felt I had known them for many years.

In the morning, they offered to take me to the farm of their friends who raised cows and sheep. I asked Belle if they needed a worker to help look after the livestock. She said they didn't, so I knew I had to return to Chicago. After one more day, Belle took me to the bus station. I thanked her for the wonderful holiday, and I returned to Chicago in good spirits.

Living abroad was about looking for my future. My first impression was fascination, finding friendly people, speaking a different language, and studying a new culture. It seemed that this wonderful new world was just what I had been looking for. Those first months, everything was impressive, exotic, and delightful. But then, after a few months, I began to get bored with my job. The doldrums of the same household and everyday life became tiresome. It was a normal life, only in a different environment.

Chapter Eighty-Four: Dating

A life spent making many mistakes is more honorable than a life spent doing nothing.

- *Irish-British critic George Bernard Shaw.*

It is difficult and unpleasant to live alone without a close friend by your side. According to the zodiac I am in the constellation of Virgo. I needed closeness, love, romantic touches, and cuddly nights.

I received letters from my friends in Lithuania asking what I did with my free time. They said probably going to theatres and concerts. They imagined that money was falling from the sky. I explained that I had no free time and little spending money. After working long hours during the week, on the weekend I liked to go to a place where I could talk with people and dance.

As I didn't have a car, I depended on my acquaintances to take me to the dance clubs and restaurants. Sitting at the table, we listened to music and watched people dance. For us, everything was new, especially how American ladies danced and how they dressed. We noticed that their movements were free, without restraint. We were much more modest in our dance. Sometimes when we talked or danced, people told us to relax and not be so tense.

A person dancing with me said, "You look so constrained and unhappy."

"No, I am just tired," I answered.

In reality, I didn't know what to say. After a few weekends, we loosened up and danced more freely. Someone asked where we were from. When I told him that all of us were from Lithuania, he asked me where Lithuania was. I discovered that most Americans do not know geography.

I started looking for ads in newspapers, magazines, and dating agencies. I corresponded with the pen pals. I rented a mailbox at the post office so I could receive my letters confidentially. I found dating agencies in Canada, North America, and Hawaii, describing myself to them and describing the kind of man I wanted to meet. I said he should be honest, have a good sense of humor, love travel, and financially stable.

Soon I received many responses. A letter came from Canada from a man who claimed to be a hockey coach and a University professor. Another said he was an engineer. I also received letters from a Hawaiian aviation officer, a Virginian military officer, and a Texan biology professor. I replied to all letters.

I received a second letter from the Canadian professor. He informed me that he would be in Chicago for a convention and could meet me. Two weeks later, I put on my best dress, and we met him at the Chicago train station. We went to a nearby restaurant where he treated me to dinner and to a very interesting conversation. Before we parted, he invited me to fly to Canada, but I explained I couldn't because I only had a tourist visa.

Over the next year we maintained our long-distance friendship, with him coming to visit every other month or so. He said he loved me, and it seemed perhaps we might marry. But then, one day he wrote that his daughter was very ill, and he wouldn't be visiting again for quite a while. After that, he didn't answer any more of my letters.

I continued to answer all the other the letters I received, however none of the other correspondents impressed me.

One of my acquaintances introduced me to Adam, a computer specialist. He had lived in London for a year and taught computer science. Sometimes when he came to visit us, he brought food from a fast-food restaurant called McDonalds. He sat down at the table, unwrapped the paper from the hamburger, and ate it himself. It seemed strange that he never thought of buying more hamburgers to share with us.

We knew each other for about six months, during which time Adam would invite me to go to the park or some other interesting place. In all that time we never kissed or touched, it was purely a friendly platonic relationship.

One day when on his way out, he leaned in to kiss me.

I told him, "Look at me, but don't touch."

"Is that your religion?"

I answered, "Yes."

He nodded, smiled, and said goodbye.

I decided not to see Adam anymore because I could tell he wasn't the person I was looking for. I needed deeper feelings in a relationship. I began to wonder if anywhere in this world for me was a man who loved me and in return, I would love him? I began to doubt if it were so.

Many of my girlfriends married American citizens and received a green card that provided a path to citizenship. Some of them won a green card in a government lottery, although I never did.

Young maids dream of the good fairy. Princesses dream of a fairytale prince. Queens do not dream, they act. The handmaidens believe that queens create miracles and are magical themselves. Great deeds and amazing successes make a Queen.

Chapter Eighty-Five: Woman with a Broken Leg

Returning from Iowa, I had no money and no job. With the New Year just around the corner, I needed money. I called the Polish employment agency, and the agent asked me if I spoke good English and if I had a driver's license.

When I told him yes to all, she offered me a job in a village called Dwight. It will be a live-in position, seven days a week with accommodation. After two weeks of work, I would get two paid days off. The woman had a broken leg and needed help to get around. I would have to cook, wash clothes, set the table, and keep her company. The salary was much higher than I had before.

"Be prepared to go for an interview tomorrow," the agent said. "Take some clothes and if she accepts you, you will stay there and work."

The next morning the agent drove me to the village. When we entered the house, she introduced me to the lady with the broken leg. The woman said it would be nice if I kept her company until she healed. I told the lady that she had a very nice house, and I would enjoy working for her. She accepted me for the position, and I paid the agent one week's salary. The agent said goodbye and left.

The lady showed me the room where I would sleep. The bedroom had a separate toilet and shower. Throughout the house, the rooms were clean and neat and tastefully arranged. She had a cat which always sat on a chair at the table right next to her and slept with her at night.

The lady's sister had a farm and brought us fresh cheese and milk, and soon I got to know their family. The lady's son, having been in Japan, learned how to grow Japanese trees and owned a Japanese tree business. He brought a small Japanese table as a gift to his mother which she was very proud of.

The work was easy and interesting. The company was nice, but after a few days became boring. After all the housework was done there was nothing else to do. I wondered what they paid me for. Looking through one window I could see a school in the distance, looking through the other, the neighbors' houses and the fields. When it snowed, I went outside to shovel the snow in the yard. When I came back, the lady forbade me to do it again, saying I shouldn't do that work. I told her that I was happy doing it, breathing fresh air and exercising at the same time.

After two weeks of my work, the son came to look after his mother when I went home for the weekend. I went to the train station, bought a ticket, and after two hours I was in the Chicago train station. From there I got on the bus and went to my rented room.

I relaxed during this weekend, and Sunday evening with full energy I returned to Dwight village.

The next day, my lady decided to go to the bank. One of the reasons they hired me was because I could drive.

I asked her, "Does your car have manual transmission?"

"No, it's automatic."

Before we went to the garage, she started her car from the kitchen. This was news to me. The vehicle rumbled and warmed up. We entered the garage, and she sat in the passenger seat, and I sat in the driver's. I never drove an automatic car. After sitting in it, I looked at the window full of buttons, wondering what they were all for, deciding that they were probably for opening windows.

I asked her, "How do I get out of the garage? How do I put this car in reverse? What happens next?" I pressed on the brake.

I told the lady that I did not have a car like this. My car has a manual transmission. I asked her, "Please show me how to drive out of this garage. What do I have to do?"

She showed me what to press and how to get into the reverse gear. Happily, we successfully left the garage. I drove slowly. She told me where to turn and we successfully reached the bank where I drove up to the bank window. The teller opened the box for the check to go in. I wanted to open the car window. I pressed all the buttons near the window until my window opened. I did not turn off the car's engine. I was too far from the window and couldn't reach the opened box with my hand. I had to back up the car. I opened the vehicle door. I kept one foot outside and the other one on the brake. I put the check in the box without pressing the button. The wind blew the check away from the box. The car, being in drive, slowly started rolling forward. I quickly jumped back into the car and hit the brakes. The car stopped. I then put it into the reverse gear. I approached the window again, driving backward, and stopped. The lady told me that I had to switch the car to the parking position which was letter P. The car stopped and I got out and found the check lying by a bush. I took the check to the teller's box and apologized. She said it wasn't a problem and paid the money. I got in the car, and we successfully returned home.

After this ride, all driving problems became a joke. The ice was broken. My lady was extremely tolerant and had a sense of humor. When we were driving home, she complimented me.

"Christina, you drove perfectly." We both were laughing.

After this episode, we became good friends. The lady advised me saying, "Christina when you earn your money, put it in the bank."

I said, "Can I do that?"

"I will take care of this next time we go to the bank," she said. The next time we went to the bank I showed them my passport and opened a bank account.

While talking on the phone to her friends, she praised me and told them that I am working very hard by washing our bedding and our clothes.

I laughed when I heard her. Washing clothes with a washing machine, and putting them in the dryer was a simple task, taking them out, folding them, putting them in the closet, is it hard work? She did not know that I had to do much more difficult jobs in my country.

I did not stay in this job for long. The lady's leg healed nicely. After three months the doctor removed the cast from her leg. She did not need my services, so I lost my good job. I said goodbye to her, and her son wrote a very good reference. I then left to go back to Chicago. Once again, I didn't have a job.

Chapter Eighty-Six: A Nice Elderly Man

I needed to look for work again, so I called the same agency. The agent offered me a new job with an elderly man who walked and was able to do most things for himself. His wife was in a hospital, and he needed an assistant and a companion. I would have to work two weeks straight without going out and then have two days off.

The agent said, "Christina, put on a white shirt and black pants. Take some more clothes. If he accepts you, I will leave you there."

I picked up my things and she drove me to a town called Munster. When I entered the room, I saw an elderly man sitting on a recliner chair. At the first glance, he seemed unsympathetic to me. When we sat down the agent saw my unhappy face and tapped me on my side.

"Christina," she whispered, "if you want to get this job, smile."

I forced a smile, although I felt I didn't want this job.

The elderly man asked me if I had any references and I showed him the letter the son of the lady had written. He liked what he read and then started to tell me about my job routine.

"Make me breakfast, lunch, and dinner, and clean my rooms. You can go for a walk whenever you want."

I told the agent that I was staying. I paid her for getting me the job and she left.

He told me my room was on the second floor, and when I went there, I found a room with a bed, a wardrobe, and a few decorations. I had to go down to the first floor to use the toilet and washroom. But it was a clean and warm place. I was happy with the situation, realizing that in my free time I could read books, write letters to my correspondents, and rest.

I spent most of the day on the first floor making meals. He didn't need any help in the evenings. Much of the daytime was spent watching TV programs with him. While sitting in front of the TV, he told me about his son who lived in Indianapolis and was a professor at a university. He told me that on the scheduled weekend, he would come to replace me.

Each morning, I made breakfast for him. He came to the kitchen with a walker. He would always greet me with "Good morning, Christina. How early you wake up."

I usually prepared oatmeal porridge with milk and banana slices. We'd sit together and he'd drink coffee and I had tea. For lunch he liked a meat and cheese sandwich with a soda to drink. Although when I first arrived, he had been shy, perhaps scared of a stranger, soon we became good friends. I found out that he liked to socialize and had a good sense of humor. After breakfast, he used his walker to go to the living room and watch TV. He usually invited me to watch TV with him, but he also encouraged me to walk around the town.

"In our town there is a Jesuit monastery with a beautiful park next to it," he said. "Follow the central street and you will reach it."

Walking down the street, I saw a man planting flowers near his house, and a woman holding a child in her arms and talking to her neighbor. As I continued to walk, I saw another man who was planting flowers around the trees. I think, this is a good life for women.

When I came to the monastery, I walked around the entire complex. I enjoyed the sculptures there and in the park. It is a beautiful place, but I did not meet a single person walking. Then I entered the monastery, I saw a man dressed in white clothes painting the walls. He introduced himself and told me that he was from Poland and was working at the monastery. I told him that I was working here in the city.

I inquired, "Where are the monks?"

"They're in their rooms."

When it was time for me to go back, the man invited me to return so we could talk some more.

I liked the park. I sat on a bench, meditating while the birds were chirping overhead. Being at that home and having monotonous days, it was good to get out of the house. When I returned to the house, I told my charge what I had seen, and he smiled. Over lunch I asked him if he'd like me to make him a European dinner.

I took the meat out of the refrigerator and told him that the refrigerator was almost empty, that we lacked potatoes, tomatoes, salads, and fruit. I told him that I have an international driver's license and could go and buy food. He gave me his insurance card and told me to drive carefully. I got into his car and successfully drove to the market. I purchased the needed products and drove back to the house. He praised me for a job well done. I made a dinner which he enjoyed a lot. He told me it was delicious.

Two weeks later, his son arrived and greeted me with a handshake. He told me that my handshake was as firm as a businessman's. He paid me my salary and took me to the bus stop.

"Christina, be careful with this money. I know you don't live in the best area."

"I will. See you on Sunday night."

We hugged and said goodbye.

After working for one month, my employer announced that his wife was returning home from the hospital. He was very excited and happy saying that he missed her very much.

During my free time, I went back to the monastery and met the painter again. I told him that I had three hours of free time. He said he had important things to do in Chicago and offered to drive me to my apartment to check my mail. He promised he could finish his work and bring me back in time.

We got into his car, and he dropped me off at my rental, promising to come back to me in an hour. He did not show up on time, and I started to worry. After two and a half hours, he arrived, and apologized. I was not happy since I had to be there on time to give food and medicine. I had no telephone to call and tell him why I was late.

When I returned, I saw a police car by the house.

My employer asked, "Christina what happened to you? I was really worried about you. After it got dark, I called the police to look for you."

I said, "I am very sorry to say that I walked too far, and it took me longer than I expected to come back."

The policeman told me to go outside and speak to him. I told him the whole truth and apologized. He told me to be careful and not to walk at night. I promised that there will not be any more misunderstandings.

When I returned to the living room, I hugged my sweet man and said, "Thank you for going through all this for me."

He said, "Christina, you are like a daughter to us, and I was really scared."

I asked if he had eaten and taken his medicine. He answered yes. After discussing all this we each went to our rooms.

The day his wife came back from the hospital, I bought her a bouquet of flowers and put it on the living room table. Soon the ambulance arrived, and she came through the door with a walker. When she entered the house, she saw me and asked her husband, "Who is this lady?"

Her husband explained that my name was Christina and that he had hired me to help him get through the lonely days without her. He explained that I made tasty food and cleaned the rooms.

The wife kindly greeted me and kissed her husband. She said that she had missed him very much. She sat down on the sofa to rest, and I asked her if she wanted something to drink. She shook her head no.

After sitting for a while, she took the walker and went to the other room. When she came back, she was upset and told her husband, "Do you know that our son spends money unnecessarily? Our son pays Christina a high salary."

The husband answered, "I know it seems like a lot, but we need help."

She said, "We do not need any care. When my son comes to visit us, I will tell him that we can take care of ourselves and that he is wasting our money."

I began to think that I was about to lose this job. The woman was basically good-natured but clearly domineering. After calming down, she showed me a white wooden cabinet covered with ceramics.

I asked, "Did you create these?"

"Yes, these are all my creations."

"I admire your talent."

"Thank you, Christina. I will give you this white ceramic vase as a present." She handed me a beautifully decorated vase.

She said that she attended ceramics classes and learned how to make vases, pots, and other small works.

"It's really beautiful," I said in praise again.

Although my work was easy, it was boring, the same talks and routine every day. No creativity. In the evening, I watched two spouses sitting on their rocking chairs and watching TV. Seeing this made me want to run away to the fields and scream. I wondered if this would be the rest of my life. I wasn't satisfied, but I couldn't get any other job at this time. My only choices were childcare, elderly care, or house cleaning.

When the son and his wife arrived, his mother asked, "What did you think when you hired a caretaker here? We do not need any help. We can both take care of ourselves."

He answered, "Mother, you are not right, you need care as well as help with the cooking and cleaning."

"No," she said. "I do not want to waste our money unnecessarily."

The son looked at me and said, "I am sorry, Christina. I don't agree with my mother's decision, but I have to let you go. They want you to be here for two more weeks until my mother recovers. After two weeks I will come again and take you to the bus station."

I thought it was a pity that I had to leave a nice home and lose my job.

The son told me that his father was very happy with me. "Thank you, for taking good care of my father."

I said, "It was my pleasure. It was really nice to meet you and your parents. Could you please write a reference for me?"

The son agreed, and after our conversation he and his wife left. I went to the kitchen and made dinner for us. After the meal, they invited me to come and watch TV with them. I thanked them, but told them no, and went to my room.

I heard the man say to his wife, "Let's go to the bedroom. I miss you."

The lady warned him not to speak loudly because Christina would hear. I smiled after hearing their conversation. They both took their walkers and, slowly leaning on them, went into the bedroom and then closed the door. Both were sweet and needed each other. They needed warmth, intimate closeness, and kisses.

The two weeks went by quickly. I said goodbye to everyone, and we hugged. The man said, "Christina, don't forget us. Please write or call."

As the years went by, I always sent them greeting cards and we remained friends. I returned to Chicago without having a job.

At any age, we want to be hugged, loved, and comforted. Without love, a person dries up like a tree without roots.

Chapter Eighty-Seven: Letters from Justin

After returning home from work one of the weekends, I found a letter addressed to me from Germany in the mailbox. I opened it with the greatest joy. My son Justin wrote to congratulate me on the upcoming Mother's Day holiday, adding a poem written by his own creation.

Mother

Spread your wings on a gloomy day
Lift up, come down again
I write you letters on the moon
Let me congratulate you with Mother's Day
I still wish for endless patience
I am preparing for joyous meetings
And the warmth of a cozy home.
This short letter is coming to you,
And I am staying.
Your son
Justin

I had a pen pal in West Germany who had two daughters and a son. I had given Justin their address, and when he had free time, he visited them. The family liked to celebrate holidays and Justin was their favorite guest.

In Lithuania, education was paid through high school, and after I began earning money in America, I sent some to Justin every month for his education and for his living expenses. Living in Germany and being a student, he visited many European countries, becoming acquainted with their cultures. He loved to read history books, however, his favorite books in high school were philosophical. He liked to read books by Immanuel Kant and always wanted to study psychology.

His last high school year in Germany passed quickly. He improved his German by studying in the high school and soon spoke it fluently.

When I came back home at the end of the employment, I found another letter from Justin. While studying in Germany, Justin had fallen in love with a girl named Juta who was also a student there. He composed a poem with music for her and played a guitar and sang the lyrics below.

Juta

Spring will come as many have come
Winter will come and so will thousands of others
Those meadow flowers will bloom again
Bloom on the banks of the river Nemunas.

I will cry quietly quietly quietly
That we could not be together for so long
And don't tell me that I have and you have cheated on me
We are separated by thousands of kilometers.

I will laugh quietly quietly quietly
How the plane will lift the trap
I will fly home with it again
I will fly back to my space

And tell me heaven
And you are a small person
Why stations and planes

takes away many dear people

As a necessity or an accident
For others, it is a new joy
For others, it is a loss. Really.

I will cry quietly quietly quietly
A hot kiss from your lips
Left like a seagull in the sea
Flying over the waves.

I will laugh quietly quietly quietly
And my gaze will rise to space
And the plane will land in Lithuania again
I will wait again, maybe not for you.

So, you fly with your wind
Maybe remember me or maybe not
And blood and blood later
It freezes in the veins like a cold.

My heart rejoices in you
May our paths
Meet again.
The pouring rain brings us together.

I will be happy quietly quietly quietly
I will rejoice with you
And do not tell me that you cheated on me
Whether it is God or fate do not say

I will be happy quietly quietly quietly

Or maybe I will cry at the same time
You are crying, leaving in tears
It is already morning,
and I am so worried about you.

The sound of a plane taking off.
You leave in tears
The plane is taking off in the morning.
And I am so worried.

A month later, Justin sent a postcard from Italy. He wrote, "I just recently walked with my high school friends on this bridge in Rome in Castel Saint Angelo. It is a Roman construction of the first century that leads to Saint Angelo Castle. Now it is +16 C in Rome and is still cold in Lithuania. It was snowing here in San Marino and raining in Venice. My friends and I still want to go to Paris. Anyway, I live quite well with my worries, joys, and pains. Summer is approaching, the end of studies and then exams. I love you very much. Hold each other tight. Love one another.
   Health and happiness
   Son, grandson, brother.
   Have good luck.
   Justin

Chapter Eighty-Eight: More Work

I received a job offer to work on the south side of Chicago. The patient lived in his own house suffering from Alzheimer's disease. I went to the house where the man's son was waiting for me. I showed him my references from previous jobs. The man's son hired me. The man was sitting at the table, looking calm and not say anything. The son told me that work would be for five days with a live-in position. The son showed me the room where I would sleep. The man would sleep one room away. The house had a bar with all kinds of drinks, and the son said the man drinks beer fairly often.

As with any Alzheimer's patient, the job was very difficult, requiring close attention to the patient.

When I went to sleep, I pushed the chair by the door so that the Alzheimer's patient couldn't enter my bedroom. One night, I heard a soft whisper and a rumble at the door. I saw a black hand squeezing its way through the door, trying to push it open. When it was open enough, a man looking like a monster came through the door. He was wearing black clothes with a huge hat on his head. I screamed and jumped out of bed. I kept on screaming and turned the light on.

I saw my man and asked him, "Why are you scaring me, dressed up with these strange clothes?"

I told him strictly to go back to bed and sleep. I accompanied him to his bedroom. In the morning, I went to his room and found out that all the clothes from his closet were thrown on the floor. He laid naked on the clothes. I told him to get up. He could not do it on his own. After a lot of effort, and with his help I got him up. I then handed him his robe and put all the clothes back in the closet.

I decided this job was too much for me. I told the son to get someone else who will work with his father seven days a week. The son could not find anybody, so I found a man and the son hired him. It was a great day when I left this job.

I started to search for a new job. I called the same agency, but the agent informed me that at this time she didn't have any jobs. It was May. Since I had to fly back to Lithuania the end of June when my visa expires, there wasn't much time left for me.

I had a friend who worked as a waitress on weekends in the banquet hall of the Lemont Lithuanian Center. She offered to get me a job there. She said I had to dress in a short black skirt, white blouse, white gloves, and black high-heeled shoes. I got the job. There, I had to work very quickly. I had to bring dishes and drinks to the guests. I got a salary and received tips for my work.

At the same time, I found a job as a salesperson in a European food store operated by Lithuanian immigrants. The store had a bakery and sold meat products. I was paid a small salary. On weekends I worked at the banquet hall and on weekdays in the bakery. They taught me how to use their cash register.

The owner said that my work included not only behind the counter but also if there were no customers to work in the kitchen. As soon as a customer came in, I had to clean my hands and go serve the customer. She said I could eat whatever I wanted. There was no time for eating. If I managed to gobble down a bun like a dog, it was my lunch. There were no chairs in this store, so when I needed to sit down, I'd find a box.

Seeing this, the owner warned me, "Christina, if you want to earn money, you need to work."

I said, "I am working all the time. I need to sit down and rest for a while."

The owner also did not like my walk. I answered her that was the way I walked. I always returned home very tired. I worked there until it was time for me to fly back to my country. I felt that the shop was exploitive at the highest level.

Chapter Eighty-Nine: Return from America

One day you will wake up and there will not be any more
time to do the things you have always wanted to do. Do them now.
-        *Brazilian novelist Paulo Coelho*

I asked my mother's childhood friend to write invitations for my mother and son to visit America. She agreed and wrote a nice letter. It was June and I was preparing to fly back to Lithuania.

Before departing I went back to the dentist and he inspected my teeth and stated I have to come back for my tooth implant. He gave me a note saying what had to be done.

I left two boxes packed with my things inside, telling my landlady that if I didn't come back, please mail me the boxes. I left her money for shipping. She asked me to take two huge suitcases on the plane and deliver them to her parents in Lithuania. She had helped me a lot and I agreed. This meant that I had to take three huge suitcases back to Lithuania. She drove me to the airport and helped drag the suitcases to the airline counter.

The woman at the counter told me that my flight had been cancelled. She recommended that I could take another flight that required me to transfer from one New York airport to another. I agreed and she changed my ticket. I flew to New York.

When I got to the first airport, I picked up the three bags and took them to the shuttle bus going to the second airport. When I got to the second airport, I had to check them in. I felt lucky that I did not have to pull the suitcases.

After waiting two hours for my flight, I flew to Amsterdam. In Amsterdam I took a shuttle bus to my hotel without the luggage. I had 24 hours before my next flight. The price of the hotel and food was included in the ticket price. The hotel was very close to the center of the town. Once I checked in, I asked the person at the desk what I should see in Amsterdam. He gave me some good ideas and I toured the city center. One street in the center was full of artists and musicians, as well as tourists. I enjoyed being there. People rode on bicycles and walked through this area. In the end I sat down and listened to music and watched people passing by.

The next day my plane landed at Vilnius airport. Everything was so strange here. This city looked smaller than I remembered. I picked up my three suitcases and went through customs. My friend's parents were there to greet me. I met them and turned over the two suitcases to them. The train took me to my former hometown. At the train station, I saw my mother and son standing with a bouquet of flowers. My son ran up to me and grabbed me in a bug hug. My mother came to me with a smile while tears of joy ran down her cheeks. It had been nine months since we had seen each other.

Gabriel asked, "Mother will you be leaving again? I want you to be with me. I miss you very much."

I hugged him harder. "You both will come visit me in America in a month."

When I entered through the gate, I saw Peter working on something in the yard. I said hello. He raised his head and looked. He said hello and turned back to his work. In all the nine months I was gone, he had never written or called to ask how I was doing, or what I was doing.

The three of us went into the house. Nothing had changed. My mother put a meal on a table and asked me to invite Peter. I went outside and asked him to come and have dinner with us. He didn't come until the middle of our dinner when he came in and sat down. We ate in silence.

The next morning, I rose early and went down to the kitchen where I heated a cup of tea. After drinking it, I entered the corridor and saw Peter.

He asked, "Was it difficult in America for you?"

"Well, it wasn't easy."

Then he told me that he was filing for divorce the next day. I told him that it was in the cards. That ended our conversation.

I thought about my wasted youth with him, the terrors he caused and the insults I had taken. It was time that this Satan left on his own accord.

Jania had given me some money to take to her husband, so a few days after arriving I went to visit him. He invited me into his house, and I sat down by the table. I handed him the money and we talked a bit about his wife and how hard she was working.

When I stood up to leave, he grabbed me and pressed me against the wall. He put his hand on my breast and said, saying, "Christina, I love you."

He grabbed my chest with his hand and said that "I haven't had a woman for a long time. My male part is swollen."

I pushed him away and told him to go out on the street and find a prostitute. I slammed the door and left.

I was having ambivalence about returning to America and so I asked my mother what I should do.

She said, "Go back and as soon as possible. You see there is no life for you here. You are young and beautiful. Hurry up and don't waste any time. Open a new page of your life."

Then I told my mother that I had to be back within a month. "You and Gabriel have to go to the American embassy with me to seek a visa. I have invitations for both of you from your friend."

A few days later the three of us went to the embassy. I told my mother that if they want to see Gabriel's parents, tell them I am outside.

They both received visas easily. Probably it was due to the grass-snake's influence, thanking Gabriel for lifting him out from the hole.

I bought the tickets for them to visit United States, arriving the next month which was July. I advised them not to tell anyone that they are flying to America, including relatives and especially not his father. My son kept his word even though they were together for one week. After returning from the sea resort, Gabriel asked his father to let him go to his grandmother's house for vacation.

My children were very important to me. While I was in America, I sent parcels to both of them and to my mother. While these parcels gave a sense of my caring, they only gave temporary happiness. While living in America those nine months, my thoughts were always with them.

I raised two wonderful children with the help of my parents. I considered raising my children as both a responsibility and a wonderful privilege. I wanted them to feel my presence, my support at all stages of their lives. I fought for myself and for them. I gave them my love, warmth, support, and communication.

In my family, I focused on the value of kindness as was taught to me by my parents. I think that children brought up in this way will understand the downtrodden, will be able to care for others, even while their own problems will be hidden behind their smiles.

Chapter Ninety: Returning to America.

My mission in life is not merely to survive, but to thrive; and to do so with some passion, compassion, humor, and style.
-         *American poet Maya Angelou*

When I returned to the Chicago airport, I was asked by a customs officer why I had come back so quickly. I told him that I had to fix my teeth, and that there were no such facilities in Lithuania. The doctor was already waiting for me here. I showed him the note he gave me. The customs officer read the dentist's note and put a stamp on my passport. The passport was valid for half a year. I caught my breath. I was free!

I took a taxi to the house where I used to live and found Jania at home. She told me there was a unit with two bedrooms available for rent. I called the landlady and she came, providing the papers for me to sign. I moved the boxes I'd stored with Jania into my new place.

I sat down on the boxes in the empty room and made plans. I decided my first purchase would be for a car, and then the necessary furniture, bedding, and other household items. I had to prepare for my family members coming the next month.

Without a car it was hard to get around in Chicago. Jania suggested a Lithuanian American who sold automobiles. When we got to his showplace, he showed me a white, five-seater Ford Taurus. Saying it was in excellent condition, he offered to sell it to me for $3,000 dollars. We took a test drive in it, and I could tell it ran smoothly and quietly.

I didn't have a mechanic that could check this car, and definitely needed one, so I agreed to buy the car. The next day I came back with Jania and paid him. We both got in our cars, and I followed her home.

I was happy that my new car had automatic transmission. When the residents of the house saw my car, they started to ask me to drive them around. I told them I would have to practice driving and familiarize myself with the driving regulations and directions of the state.

The first few times I drove, I got lost. After taking Jania to the airport, on the way back I took the wrong exit on the highway. I saw only African Americans standing on the streets. The street names were completely unknown to me. Here I was, a single white woman in a car on the east side of Chicago and was getting uncomfortable. Eventually I saw three policemen standing by their police cars.

I approached them and told them I was lost, asking if they could help me get to Western Avenue.

"Get in your car and follow me," one of the policemen said. After several blocks and turns, he opened the window and pointed. "Go straight and do not turn anywhere until you reach the desired street."

I thanked him and drove home. After that, I bought a large map of Chicago and its suburbs.

Next, I searched for furniture. At Balfa, a charity organization, I found bedding and some household appliances. The bedding included a beautiful pink bedspread with crowns and a pink flower on the base with two pillows of the same pink color. I took the bedding and went to the laundromat to wash it.

From my friends I received two wooden beds and a chest of drawers. My mother's childhood friend provided me with a sofa and armchairs, the set beautifully red with ornaments and red fringes at the bottom. A Lithuanian doctor who lived next door gave me a table which I placed in the kitchen, with few chairs. I found another lady that gave me her paintings. These had a few defects which I repaired. When all was set up the room felt welcoming and cozy.

The day my mother and child arrived the car ran perfectly. As if God was watching over me, there were no traffic jams and the radio played comforting music. The plane arrived on time, and I gave my mother a bouquet of roses. We hugged and cried, so happy we were to be together again.

On the ride home, they stared out the window, fascinated to see a big city where everything was new and different. When we got to my apartment, I provided food I'd prepared, and then they went to the two beds and quickly fell asleep.

A few days after they arrived, I had a party, inviting my friends to come meet my family. I thanked them for their support, saying it's thanks to you that my apartment looks so nice. Then I turned the music on, and we danced.

Chapter Ninety-One: Life in Chicago

After the Second World War, so many Lithuanians settled in Chicago that they created the largest Lithuanian colony outside of Lithuania itself. A beautiful Lithuanian church was built next to a private Catholic school. During the summer, Gabriel mowed the grass of our yard and the neighbors' with a gasoline-powered machine, earning money that he saved.

Soon after my family arrived, I took them to a sports store. I asked Gabriel, "Would you be happy if I buy you rollerblades? Do you like my idea?"

He said, "I've never tried them, but they look like fun."

I bought rollerblades for him and for myself. We took them out to Lake Michigan and skated on its sidewalk. He joined the Lithuanian Sea Scouts, delighting in their rafting trips where he learned how to control sailboats. He also started to attend private swimming lessons.

The beginning of September I needed to register my son in school. I decided to enroll him in the nearby American Catholic school that had fees at $ 200 dollars a month. He'd completed three years in Lithuania and was admitted to the fourth grade. After attending for a week, he told me he was surprised that there were no physical education classes. He liked sports, dancing groups, and singing, things not taught in his school. He learned English quickly by communicating with the neighbors' children and in the school.

Gabriel enjoyed the school and participated with the Sea Scout group. He participated in swimming competitions at school where he took first place. The local newspaper published his picture holding a medal he'd won.

One afternoon our next-door neighbor brought over a model of the Eiffel Tower and asked if Gabriel would like to put it together.

It had hundreds of pieces and took him several weeks to finish. Once complete it stood about a meter tall. He was very proud of his work, and when he gave the completed model back to the neighbor, she rewarded him with some candy.

Six months after arrival, I had to renew my visa. I filled out the necessary documents and sent them to the Immigration Service. Soon I received a letter stating that my visa has been extended for another six months.

A Swiss friend who I had been in contact with since Lithuania gained independence asked me if he could come visit me in Chicago. He arrived in Chicago during the winter, and I met him at the airport and drove him home.

When he entered the house, I introduced him to my mother and son. He gave Gabriel a gift from Switzerland, a long Swiss dark chocolate brick Toblerone with honey and almond. My mother had made zeppelins, a traditional Lithuanian meal made with potatoes and meat inside.

He tasted it, and said, "It is delicious. Thank you, I never had a meal like this before."

When I got up in the morning, I suggested we go to Indiana dunes. When we got there, we found that they were covered with snow. We took some photographs and after a few hours returned home. The next day, I took him to Chicago's downtown city center. We visited an art museum, and, in the evening, I took him to see the John Hancock building. On the highest floor, the 96th, was an observatory. We sat at the bar enjoying the panorama of the city at night. After visiting us for a week, he returned home.

After a week my mother became ill with bladder pain. I took her to Cook County Hospital which offered free medical care. As we walked into the hospital the sole of my mother's shoe came off. A nurse ran up to her, pointed to her shoe, and told her to sit down.

She said, "I saw your sole come off your shoe as you walked through the door. Please sit down and wait. I will get a bandage and help." She came back with a bandage and wrapped it around the sole of her shoe. Mother was surprised that the nurse was so kind to her.

After arriving at the registration table, she received a number. It took her six hours to see a doctor. The doctor checked on her and prescribed medication. After taking the medication she was fine.

My mother Greta joined the activities of the Lithuanian community and became an active member of their board. She joined the church choir. Mother enjoyed the parishioners' activities and organized several Lithuanian parties for which she cooked traditional Lithuanian food. She became known as an excellent hostess and was respected by all the parishioners, distinguished by her diligence and tolerance.

My mother loved to dance, never missing a Sunday at the Lithuanian dance club. We'd have lunch there, dance, and occasionally organize a lottery. We'd leave by seven o'clock. On weekends and on nice days during this first summer she would walk around Lake Michigan, enjoying the city and its skyscrapers.

In the fall I received a letter from my aunt, the one who raised chickens at her home. Unable to make a living as an engineer, she wanted to come to the United States. She wrote to me and asked me to get an invitation. I asked Dr. Mekas, a Lithuanian doctor living next door, who knew my aunt, and wrote an invitation. He also agreed to meet her at the airport.

My aunt was able to get her visa and a month later, Dr. Mekas retrieved her from the airport. I put her in Gabriel's room and found her a job taking care of an elderly woman. She asked me to drive her to work. I felt I had no choice and agreed, driving her both ways every day.

One morning when I had to be at work early, I woke up my aunt and asked her to hurry up saying, "Aunt, we have to hurry up. It's a long way to drive to your job, and I have to be on time for my job."

She replied, "Christina, I have to drink my coffee."

"Please Aunt. Take your coffee with you and drink it in the car."

She did everything very slowly and we left the house late. When I approached the traffic light, I saw a sign that prohibited right turns from 7am to 7pm when the light was red. I saw a police car standing on the other side of the intersection. Being under stress, I turned to the right even though the light was red. The policeman flashed his lights and I stopped, opening the car window. When he came, he asked for my car insurance card and driving license.

The driving license was international but in English. He examined the license and asked why I had such a license. I said it is a international driver's license. He took the driving license and said they will send it back by mail. He gave me a ticket with a fine and a document that I could drive with until I got my license back.

He said if I paid the fine, I wouldn't be put into a computer. He walked around my car, and I got out from my car and followed him. He turned to me and said angrily, "Stop following me."

After going around it, he went back to his car and drove off. I got into my car and said to my relative, "Well, if we had left on time, nothing would have happened. Everything is in a hurry now." We drove off.

A month later, I received my license in the mailbox.

After paying the fine, I went to the driving license issuing department to see if I was entered into the computer. The answer was yes, I was. After six years, the fine record would be removed from the computer.

I decided that I should take the exam to get an American driving license. I bought a driving book and, after learning all the theory questions, I took the test. I passed my theory and driving tests the first try. After a few months the aunt who'd been living with me moved out.

Because I had a car, over the next few months I found many different jobs, including working as a painter, a driver, a designer, a baker, a bartender, and a waitress. One of my girlfriends offered me a job working with a man who needed help organizing the interior of his three-bedroom apartment.

The girlfriend said, "Christina, you have a very neat and nice-looking interior in your apartment. I recommended you to my acquaintance to organize and make an interior design for him."

The man worked as a fireman. I called him and received his address. When I arrived, he gave me a tour of his apartment. In one bedroom I saw various playboy magazines, a style of magazine I'd never seen before. He made lunch and explained to me what I should do. He stated there was no hurry and that I could start whenever I wanted. The job intrigued me and since I didn't have another job at this time, I accepted. I informed him that I would start in two days.

He introduced me to a woman who baked various cakes who offered me a job. Every morning, I started baking at four a.m., and after baking for eight hours, I went to the fireman's apartment and worked on his interior.

After two weeks the fireman came to visit me in my apartment. After the first visit, he came every week or so, often bringing me flowers. We enjoyed each other's company. He never proposed to me and appeared to be indifferent to me. Of course, I did not show him any of my feelings either. He was a good friend and my employer. After finishing the interior design of his apartment, we remained good friends.

One weekend evening I went with some friends to a rocker party. When we arrived, I saw a lot of rockers and different classes of people. The men at the party were all Americans, the majority of the women were Lithuanians. Not long after our arrival one of my friends, an actress, became intoxicated and climbed onto a platform in the yard and danced and performed. All of us applauded her grand show. Afterward, she sat down next to me.

"Christina, you don't know how hard it is for me right now. I have a job taking care of an elderly person and I am very unhappy with my situation. I want to shout that I should be on a stage. I want people to hear that I am an actress. I've travelled around the world with performances, and now I have to sit with an elderly woman and take care of her. I really cannot stand it."

She paused to finish off her drink, which contained vodka. "Christina, I was invited by a man to come to America and marry him. I met him in Lithuania at my theatre. He liked everything about me and proposed to me. He wrote an invitation for me to come to America. He met me at the airport and took me to an apartment. There he left me, saying, "I cannot marry you right now.

"Very soon he married another woman and left me with nothing. When I earn enough money, I will go back to my country and start all over."

I said to her, "Don't worry. You just have to believe that a better time will come, and your grief will leave you."

In the middle of the evening, I asked a rocker to give me a ride on his Harley-Davidson motorcycle. I had never ridden one before.

"Of course," he said. "Sit on the back and I will give you a ride."

His motorcycle was black and shiny like glass. I settled onto his steel horse. His motorcycle was much more powerful than the one I rode for a year while working in the countryside in Lithuania. I felt like I was riding on a unicorn that could bring me happiness. It was one of the most exciting and fun evenings I spent in Chicago.

Chapter Ninety-Two: Mother's Vacation

An upcoming vacation gives us something to eagerly anticipate.
    -Jaime Kurtz, American author

When my mother and I left for United States, I asked Simon to look after the first floor of the house we lived in, but he refused. I would have thought that if he didn't take care of that level, surely the one he lived on, the second floor, would eventually be destroyed. It turned out that it was Simon's intention to get the first floor for a much lower price by neglecting it, and his strategy worked. Greta sold him the first floor for a very low price, and I lost my inheritance.

In another instance, without telling my mother or me, Simon sold my grandmother's reclaimed land in Joniskis district and used the money to buy an apartment by the Baltic Sea. He promised before the sale to give me half the money he received, but never did.

A few months later, Greta decided to fly to Lithuania for vacation. Simon invited her to go with him to see the apartment by the sea. During the visit, Mother inspected the apartment and the resort town and praised his purchase. Simon had to leave for two days to go to the city where he lived, leaving Greta with his wife.

After Simon left, Agatha said, "I don't want you here. Why didn't you go with him?"

After a few more days by the sea, all of them returned to Simon's home in the city. That evening Agatha got angry with her husband and hit him in the mouth, knocking out one of his front teeth.

My mother cried, "Agatha what have you done to my son?"

Agatha turned to her and yelled, "It's all your fault for giving birth to an alcoholic son!"

Greta left the room without answering.

After visiting Simon, Mother took the bus to visit her sister who lived in Vilnius with her daughter. Together, they went to the Vilnius TV Tower with its observation deck in a restaurant called "Bird trail". The restaurant was located on the one hundredth floor with a high-speed elevator that covered the distance in forty-five seconds. They had a very happy reunion, talking and later touring a beautiful garden. Staying with them for a few days, she visited the old town of Vilnius. She thanked them for a nice time and happily returned to the United States.

Chapter Ninety-Three: Updates and Poetry from Justin

After graduating from high school in Germany, Justin returned to Lithuania. He applied to Vilnius University and was accepted for a degree program in psychology.

Dear Mother,

I am writing to you as I am sitting at home and thinking about the twists and turns of my life.

Today I will open a part of my heart to you.

It's good for me to live, it's good to study. When I get tired, I fall into bed. I believe that the day will come when I will taste the fruits of my studies.

I live well, I have something to eat, and some money in my pocket. I have a roof over my head, as well as girls all around me in the University. What is a student without beer and debt? I am sitting in your house. I have a home, and I love it. When I'm in it, I escape from people and all the world. I feel the goodness of the house. The coziness and the lovely works of art that you created, Mother. Your art is surrounding me and reminds me of sweet memories. The warmth of goodness floods my whole body.

I think about my future and what I want to be. I also think about my birthplace, the lake there, and the fish we used to catch together. I think about you, grandma, and my brother very often. No matter if I sometimes made you angry, we were always close. I love you all very much. I miss you by my side. Life does not stand it moves on. Just as rain falls outside the window, it is then absorbed by the earth and taken up by the plants. We created the world, and it is still good to me to live in it and enjoy it, to feel my being. From one's birth, the time starts melting away. You look out the window, and the sprouts are already there. That's how the Earth breathes, you just need to listen to its breathing.

When you feel alone it hurts you, then you look for someone with whom you feel attachment, maybe sometimes a person, or a thing, or a place, or maybe even some sincere words. Then it's good for me to feel my roots, I'm still a descendant of my grandparents, I have their blood. Blood is life, followed by nation - it's good for me to understand and be understood.

"What you sow is what you reap. Sow a seed or plant a flower - take care - it will grow. Sow a rotten seed - nothing will grow".

Be strong, hold each other, live. Life is for you.

Time will pass, we will meet maybe in winter or next summer.

Mother, grandmother, brother. Be healthy and happy.

I am with you and for you.

I have to pass my psychology exam tomorrow. It's already evening and I'm going to prepare.

As you know, I ride with a Zaporozhets (Zap) car. And I wrote a poem about it and created a blues music.

My Zap

I had a blue Zap
and I loved his blue eyes
but one day
the engine broke

My Zap is lying in the ditch

and I rest under the pine tree
I feel cold
terribly cold I swear.

And the policeman came and said
return the license
you do not know how to drive
so buy a bicycle

I will not give the license
How about after that
I will go home
I will ride a motorcycle.

He went
I rest under the pine tree
I feel cold
it's terribly cold I swear

I was a student then
I ate bacon bread
vitamins
And all kinds of pigments

My image ZAS 966 B
it suits me very well
let them laugh
who do not like it.

But my Zap is lying in the ditch
And I rest under the pine tree
I am cold very cold

I swear.

Be happy!
I am Justin
P.S. I am so far away from you across seas across oceans.

As I dream, I create another poem

Trojan horse

Harnessing the Trojan horse
Behind elaborate feather
Picking up a sharp feather
I ride on the hump of the poor horse.

And the pencil is broken
A few rows are enough.
They won't help me write
You cannot howl like a dog.

And I feel sorry for the Trojan horse
And his wheels are dirty.
Holy groves
And beautiful goddesses.

He went to the duel
That horse is powerful
The last was a wish
Iron Age.

Well, it will be enough to write poems
You're not Homer.

Wash your feet, go to bed
Cloud hangings.

During his freshman year at the university, he became involved with the Catholic Federation. There he met a professor priest who offered him a job as a guide at the Lithuanian camp in Michigan State during the summer. He accepted the offer and with a tourist visa came to the United States.

At the camp, he organized the camp's programs and participated in the camp's activities. After two months, the campers returned home, and he bought a ticket on a Greyhound bus and came to Chicago to visit us. While in Chicago, he desired to find a job for one month to earn money. He found a job that required carrying bricks to the masons.

This is the poem he wrote about visiting Chicago for the first time.

Chicago

When the city wakes up
on the railway tracks
And the sun is shining
on the helpless bridges

Walls of skyscrapers
flooded with cars
And countless souls
We don't know where they are going.

Lamps cut out
remaining light
Between the garbage and the streets

the homeless are looking for them.

Walls of skyscrapers
flooded with cars
And countless souls
We don't know where they are going.

On the weekend I took him to downtown Chicago. His first impression of the city was that it was impressive and unique, especially seen from the 96th floor of a skyscraper. There we sat and sipped beer and watched the endless reflections of lights. In the evening when thunder and lightning struck the sky, it seemed that the earth was on fire. We could see Lake Michigan through the window and the traffic of cars passing through Lake Shore drive. It was an extraordinary sight.

While living there in the summer and working on construction, Justin created a poem and music about America, playing it with the guitar and singing it for us.

America

America America America
This word is sweet on the lips of a compatriot.
And when I go to America
Here you will see what will happen to you.

America America America
I am loading bricks on the edge of downtown
an old man passes by waving his hand
forget, forget, forget stupid. (forget, forget, forget)

America America America

I pass the blocks of Marquette Park
Lithuanians have lived there since ancient times
But the area is changing; Lithuanians will disappear there
soon.

America America America
There is no mail in the mailbox
maybe I got into a fight with the postman
Maybe he cannot find the way anymore - it's not nice.

America America America
The plane rises and the thought with it
faster faster to Lithuania
Faster, faster home.

And so it goes down fantastically
Someone is carrying beer and flowers
And the beauty of the old town of Vilnius is revealed
You do not need to look at green frogs.

America America America
This word is sweet on the lips of a compatriot.
And when I go to America
Here you will see what will happen to you.

At the end of the summer, Justin returned to Lithuania to
finish his studies. Soon after he got there, he purchased a leather
rocker jacket and a few other minor things he needed. One night,
thieves broke into his house and stole all the things he brought from
America, including the album of silver coins we collected together
and his clarinet.

Chapter Ninety-Four: Life Continues in Chicago

One evening, my usual parking spot was taken, and I had to park at the corner. In the middle of the night, I woke up to a terrible noise in the street. I ran outside and saw a car had hit a tree right next to our window. The police pulled two Afro-American men out of the wreckage and handcuffed them. The police had been chasing them, the driver was speeding, and before hitting the tree they hit the rear fender of my car, knocked out the taillights and dented in the side of the car. These people did not have car insurance.

After the accident, the car required a lot of expensive repairs. It was towed to a mechanic and repaired. I drove it for a few months and sold it for a small price. I replaced it with a bigger car, one with eight cylinders. The car ran well, and I was happy with it. My friends asked me, "How do you like this car? Is it difficult to park in small parking spaces?"

"I like it because it is big," I answered.

Besides the rent of my two-bedroom apartment and normal living expenses, I have Gabriel's school and my new car to pay for. I decided to rent one room of my apartment. Lily agreed to pay rent for a single room and live with us. Not having a car, she often went to buy food. The food store was not far from my apartment.

One time when she was returning with groceries, a police car stopped by her. An African American policeman opened the door and asked her to sit in police car. He told her, "Do you know that it is dangerous for you to walk here?"

He drove her back home. Soon they became close friends. He visited her often and they spent time together in her bedroom. He was tall, not thin, slightly hunched, similar to a bear. We called him Bear.

Lily's mother came from Lithuania on a visit and Lily introduced her to Bear. The mother asked me to dissuade Lily from being friends with Bear.

She said, "Christina, I do not like their friendship."

"I will try," I answered.

On the occasion of Lily's mother's arrival, we prepared a dinner with music and dancing. We invited Bear to come to our party. He was the only man at our party. When he came, we talked, ate, and turned on the music. I asked my mother Greta to go and dance with Bear. I took a picture of them dancing. It made a good addition to my album. We spent a pleasant evening having fun with laughter and dancing.

After a while Lily met a Persian man in a single dance club. He worked as an engineer. They started to date. Her friendship with the Bear was not lost, though. In the evenings, the Persian entered through one door and Bear exited through another.

Being illegal, she wanted to meet a serious man and marry him.

I suggested she contact a dating agency located in Chicago. After filling out the application and paying the dues she received offers from men. After a short time, she met an educated professional man and they got married.

After their marriage they went to Las Vegas for their honeymoon.

One day, a woman I knew offered me a job in a European bar near where I lived. They hired me. It took me a couple of days to learn the names of the prepared cocktails.

One night while I was working in the bar, a couple of drunken American men got into an argument and started fighting. The owner called the police, it made me nervous.

In another evening, as I finished cleaning up, a man came up to me and gave me a $50 dollar tip. I gasped.

"How much do I have to give you back?"

"Nothing," he said. "I sat here by the bar and watched you work all evening. You do everything very quickly, you serve cocktails, you are very cultured and polite. You are a nice-looking lady and people who come here sometimes are not in the best mood. You should find a better place to work."

I thanked him for the tip and his advice. At the time, it was scary to walk to the car after leaving the bar at night, even though the car is parked nearby. After working for three weeks, I quit that job because it didn't feel safe.

My next job was as a waitress in a Polish restaurant. This restaurant required memorizing the entire menu. The job was to bring and serve breakfast, lunch, and dinner as ordered by customers. Many businessmen came to eat lunch at this restaurant. I felt intimidated, as the men were so nicely dressed as to cause me to blush. My face turned red after asking for their orders. Blushing was an issue left over from my school days and it kept popping up sometimes. I had to serve, I had to smile, I had to do everything that was part of my duties.

One time during lunch, I ordered dishes for the guests but forgot one guest to serve. He sat patiently, waiting for me to approach him. When I got close to him, he called me and asked, "I'm sorry, have you forgotten me?"

I told him that I was really sorry, I'd only started working recently. I took his order and brought his lunch as soon as possible. I apologized to him again.

After two months, I was working well. Many of the same guests who had eaten in this restaurant came to eat again and asked to be seated at my tables. They always left a good tip.

One day the owner invited me to his office. "Christina, do you have legal documents?"

"Yes," I answered. "I do have a visa."

"Now they are starting to check documents for work permits. When you get the proper documents, come back any time."

One winter weekend, I joined Gabriel and some friends on a ski trip to Wisconsin. There were no big mountains in Lithuania, so I'd never learned the slalom method of going downhill. To prepare for the Wisconsin trip, I practiced slaloming in the west suburbs of Chicago going down smaller hills. I fell down a lot of times.

When we arrived at the ski resort in Wisconsin, I was uncomfortable going down from the big mountains. After a little practice, my fear disappeared, and I went down the blue and black marked mountains with Gabriel. After skiing, we took off our skis, and left them outside and went to eat and warm up by the fireplace inside the lodge. After warming up, we skied until the evening.

Every year I filled out an application for a green card, but I never won it. I continued to renew my visa. Some of my friends and relatives asked me to fill out the forms for them for a green card lottery. I helped some of them to fil out the applications, and some of them won the lottery.

One Saturday night, me and three of my girlfriends and I decided to go to a nightclub. After parking, we had to cross a main street. When we were in the middle of the street, I saw a fast car approaching. I grabbed my girlfriend's hand who was closest to me and told her to stop. The other two girls started to run holding hands. I shouted, "Stop!" but it was too late. The car hit them both.

They both lay motionless on the street. I ran into the nightclub and yelled for somebody to call 911. Back outside, I saw one of the girlfriends slowly getting up, while the other friend was bleeding from the back of her head and remained motionless. I bent by her and asked if she could move.

The ambulance arrived quickly, taking both women to the hospital. My other friend and I followed them to the hospital where we waited for a long time. We didn't get to see them but were told they'd been admitted. While one recovered with minor injuries, the one with the head injury took a long time and required several operations.

After this, and based on the crime of the neighborhood, we decided that it was time for us to move to a safer area.

Chapter Ninety-Five: Justin Coming Back to America

After graduating with a bachelor's degree, Justin drove his motorcycle to Peter's house and told him about his accomplishments. Justin told Peter that he graduated college and received a bachelor's degree. He talked about his poetry book and his singing and playing in a folk band at the University. Peter told him that he'd accomplished great achievements and that he felt guilty that he'd done nothing to help. After this discussion both parties agreed that there was irreparable harm to their relationship.

Peter said, "You have grown into a polite, virtuous, and talented person. You are a personality. Come visit me more often."

Justin never visited him again.

After graduation, Justin obtained a green card and decided to come to the United States to earn some money. His plans were to take the money he earned and return to Lithuania to start a construction business.

Soon after his arrival, he joined the Catholic church choir. It was nearing Christmas, and he created a melody to the poem he had written, "To Our Lord," which is in this book about page 209. He sang so beautifully that women in the gallery were wiping at their tears.

He explained to me that his long hair and ponytail showed his lifestyle.

"I am a biker. Without a motorcycle or music, my life would not be exciting. Bikers ride steel horses. My friends from student years nicknamed me Light. When I was very young, my grandparents bought me a bicycle, and then a moped. It was replaced by the motorcycle. I like my steel horse. I spend a lot of time on him in my native country and now after coming to the United States."

Here's one of Justin's poems.

Motorcycle

My motorcycle is parked by the road
Honey, I am a biker
The free path of the road smiles at me
And I have a long road ahead of me.

I was born free to fly with the wind
Honey, I am a tramp
The maple green leaf smiles at me
And its reflection fell on the asphalt.

Don't say that I
That you let me down
And don't say Honey
I'm leaving

And the enchanted motorcycles will spin
Like the darkness of the black night
All the cycles of the year are behind them
Like leaves lost under the wheels.

Justin rode his motorcycle the thousand miles from Chicago to the biker convention at Sturgis, South Dakota. This legendary rally was said to be the biggest motorcycle event in the world, with attendance reaching around 700,000 participants. He reported having great pleasure meeting so many people who shared his interest in motorcycles, feeling he'd become part of a large happy family. On the way there he explored several of the United States' natural parks, but on the way back he had to endure thunderstorms.

Biker

Long sideburns and hair
Feeling of Motorcycles their long ways
May the moon protect your mother
Those who travel do not stop.

Brother, give me your hand
If you are tired
In the long way to go
Or you are broken

I press the starter
And leather rustles
Burning blind time
And the rolls cheer up.

And if you go out like you always do
To the world empty it will not be a problem
Crossed hammers this emblem
The moon protects like your mother.

If you have Ural
Or maybe Java too
Or you ride Harley
But you do not show off

I press the starter
And leather rustles
Burning blind time
And the rolls cheer up.

Chapter Ninety-Six: Agatha Comes to America

What a person cannot do, neither can the state. The state can only punish, and a person can repent.
  - Lithuanian philosopher Juozas Girnius

My sister-in-law Agatha called me and asked me to send an invitation to come to America. I explained to her that an invitation can only be written by an American citizen, so I can't do it. I explained the situation to my friend Dr. Mekas, and he agreed to invite her and to meet at the airport. She got her visa and arrived in Chicago as scheduled. However, Dr. Mekas didn't show up to meet her.

No one responded to a loudspeaker announcement for the person who was supposed to pick up Agatha. Immigration took her to a special room and informed her that if she couldn't be picked up, they'd have to place her on a plane back to Lithuania.

When she called me and told me that nobody met her, she was crying. They'd put her up at the Hilton Hotel before sending her back in the morning.

"Christina, do you realize what you've done? They're sending me back home tomorrow. I spent all my money on the ticket. How will I live now?"

Dr. Mekas later told me he had an emergency patient and couldn't contact me. I felt that I had to help Agatha financially and sent her $500 for the price of the ticket she paid and my apologies for the mix-up.

The $500 was more appreciated than the apology, I suppose. They'd often complained to us how their life was difficult because they were always short of money. For at least two years before this event, and for the following two years, we sent them parcels.

Two years later, Agatha asked me to fill out the application for a green card for her and her husband and the family of their daughter Melody.

I told her that she could fill out it herself while in Lithuania.

"No, I am asking you to help us. Probably you will have better luck."

I agreed to do that against my will only because my mother told me she wanted it for her son Simon. I filled out the applications and sent them for their approval. They approved the forms, returned them to me, and I mailed them to the office. To my surprise, they were all approved to apply for a green card.

After arranging all the necessary documents in Lithuania, they asked me to send them the necessary papers for entry to the United States. A difficult task awaited me. I had to get the documents certified by a notary public, find them a living place, and fully support them.

Fulfilling these demands was very complicated. Financially, I could barely afford my own apartment. Further, because I wasn't a citizen, I couldn't write any documents in my name.

I asked Greta if she had some legal friends who could write the necessary documents. It took a while, but eventually Mother found a woman through the church who agreed to do it.

Once everything was done, we sent the documents to Agatha who took them to the American Embassy where she got a visa to come to the United States.

We next looked for an apartment for them to rent. By good fortune, my mother found out that one of her friends in the church choir was moving to Florida and leaving some furniture in her apartment, one that wasn't too far from ours. We rented it, and added bedding sets, some furniture, dishes, and eating utensils from the Lithuanian charity organization. Mother and I purchased some decorative items as well, setting up fresh flowers in vases on the tables. All and all, it was a lovely little place, clean, cozy, and private.

When all was done, I looked around the place we set up and felt proud. I remembered that when I came to this country no one welcomed me, I had no place to live, no one to talk to, and nowhere to sleep. They would have all of this.

I met them at the airport and took them all to my mother and our rented apartment. My mother was waiting for us to come with a prepared meal. She was happy to be with Simon and his family again. After the meal, we took them to their new apartment.

It all seemed so nice that I hoped our families would finally come together in peace. It would be a new beginning for both families. Yet, based on my past experiences with Agatha, I feared it was just a dream.

My mother found jobs in a meat factory for Agatha and her daughter Melody and a job in construction for Simon and for Melody's husband. Melody's son was seven and she enrolled him in the public school. Since both parents were working, the boy stayed with my mother after school until picked up by his parents in the evening. It soon became apparent that my dream of happy relationships with my relations was not to be, as Simon and Agatha completely ignored us.

Chapter Ninety-Seven: Peter Comes to America

Shortly after the arrival of Simon and Agatha's families, Peter called me and told me that he was coming to visit the United States. He promised to find work and share the money from our Lithuanian property.

"That would be nice of you," I said. "I certainly could use the money. Let me know when you are coming. I will find a place for you to stay."

Simon and Agatha agreed to accommodate Peter in their apartment. Peter agreed to pay rent to them once he got a job, and they gave him one room. The day after his arrival, Peter met with my mother and gave her a present of a CD with songs that he and another four men sang in ensemble.

He asked me to help him find a job, so I referred him to an individual who had evicted houses that needed to be cleaned. These houses were left very dirty, often full of cockroaches. Every morning I got up at 5 a.m. and drove him to work. In the evening, he was brought back by a fellow worker. He wasn't used to such work as this, requiring heavy lifting in a filthy environment, and complained every day.

A few weeks after his arrival, while driving him home from work, he surprised me with these words.

"I want to say a friendly word, a peaceful word to you, Christina. I was afraid to say these words before as I did not want to show my weakness. When you left, I realized that my life was empty without you. I never thought you would leave me. You were always so calm and proud. I came to America to tell you this, thinking that we could be together again."

I pulled the car to the curb and shook my finger at him. "Peter, I don't love you anymore. If you had gotten over your pride and shown me love earlier on, I wouldn't have left you. It's too late now. That fireplace has gone out and will never be lighted again."

I was so angry, I had to count to a hundred before continuing. "Look. You want to start a new life? Okay. First off, earn money here and give me what you promised to pay me. You can start by paying for your son's private school. It costs $200 a month. I know you just got paid. Tell me what you got on your mind and give me the money now."

His face turned red with anger. "$200 is almost all I earned! Okay, here!"

He threw money at my face. I grabbed it and stuffed it in my purse.

We drove the rest of the way to Simon's house in silence. Just before he got out, I said, "If you want to make a new life, work hard and save your money. Then you can find a place on your own and maybe find someone else to love. But it won't be me."

He got out of the car in a huff. He never paid me again for Gabriel's school fees.

About a month after Peter arrived, Gabriel went on his rollerblades to visit his father. My son wasn't wearing the arm and leg protectors we'd bought him, and when riding back he took a tumble, hurting his arm. As soon as he got home, I took him to the hospital where an x-ray showed he'd broken both of his wrist bones. Late at night, the doctor on duty took Gabriel to the operating room, fixed his arm, bandaged it, and sent him home.

A few days later, we followed up with a specialist doctor who took another x-ray. He showed us on the computer that the bones were not placed straight, and Gabriel would need another operation for them to mend properly.

After this second operation, they admitted Gabriel to the ward and invited me to stay with him. Gabriel, recovering from anesthesia, asked me to stay by his side.

"Of course, my son, I will stay tonight and all day tomorrow if needed." I settled into a reclining chair next to my son.

In the middle of the night, Gabriel moaned. "Mother, I'm in a lot of pain."

I asked the nurse to come, and she brought him a shot for his pain. I stroked his hair, kissed and comforted him. I told him the pain would go away.

"The hand will heal, and you will be able to play sports again. Calm down and try to sleep. I will sing a lullaby, the same which I sang to you at home."

He made a small smile and soon fell asleep.

He was released from the hospital the next morning. After one week we returned to the specialist who took another x-ray.

He said, "You can see the bones in your son's arm are healing very well. I inserted a steel plate because both bones were badly split. Now when the hand is healed it will be as strong as it was before.

We returned home happy. Many more months passed before the hand became as strong as it had been.

Gabriel needed his hand, for he was especially interested in drawing. His work included precise pencil on paper sketches with very small details. One drawing he did of downtown Chicago along Michigan Avenue with its skyscrapers won first place from his school. When Gabriel received the award, he was surprised.

He was a polite, well-liked young man who always greeted everyone with a smile. He loved sports, including the sea scouts, golf, and basketball. At school, he took extra courses so that he could more easily enter the university after graduating.

After two months, Peter decided work in America was too hard. He returned to Lithuanian without giving me another cent. Before leaving, he told me that he had a woman waiting for him in Lithuania. I wished him good luck.

Three years after the divorce, he clapped his hands in joy that all his wealth now belonged to him alone. Because he wouldn't give me any money, I flew back to Lithuania and filled out court documents demanding child support for Gabriel.

On arrival, I called Jania who at this time had returned to live with her husband. She invited me to her house, and we had a pleasant conversation about our time together in Chicago. She invited me to spend the night but said I couldn't stay longer than that. Her husband was friends with Peter and hosting me would have caused difficulties.

Over the next two days I conferred with a lawyer who filed the necessary documents, and I returned to America. Once Peter found out that child support was being deducted from his salary, he wrote an angry letter to me. It was hardly worth it, considering the very small amount I received, and it all had to be put in my bank account in Lithuania.

Chapter Ninety-Eight: My niece Renee Comes to America

Agatha and Simon's second daughter, Renee, applied for several years to get a green card to come to America. After about two years she won the lottery.

Once she had the green card, she told her boyfriend she was going away.

"Renee," he asked, "Are you deserting me?"

"Do you want to come and be with me?"

"Yes, of course."

"I will miss you very much," she said." It will be very hard for both of us, and as soon as I settle down, I will definitely invite you to come. We have to be strong, and I will wait for your arrival."

"Renee, you know that I love you."

"I love you, too," Renee answered.

Before leaving Lithuania, Renee divorced her husband, kissed her sweetheart goodbye, and brought her son to America. Her sister Melody met her at the airport.

When Agatha heard that her daughter was coming, she asked my mother to find a new house that would be big enough for their whole family. Greta knew a lot of people and was able to find a three-bedroom apartment with a living room and kitchen.

Renee got a job at the same meat factory where Agatha and Melody already worked. As employees, they bought meat at a reduced price, but never let Greta or me have the discount.

Some months after Renee arrived, she met Joseph, a Lithuanian man, at a nightclub. When she returned home, she told her parents, "I have found a suitable life partner for me. Mother, how beautiful he looks. He is an athlete. I danced all evening with him, and we agreed to meet again. I gave my phone number and our address. You will see, you will really like him."

"And what about the sweetheart you left behind in Lithuania? Didn't you promise that you would send him an invitation?" Agatha asked.

Renee shrugged. "He asked me to send him $350 dollars to play the green card lottery and I decided not to send it. I don't love him anymore."

Joseph visited several times over the following two weeks, each time bringing a bouquet of flowers. However, after the first meeting or two, they realized that they had major differences in opinions and attitudes and had loud arguments.

After the guest left, Agatha said, "Renee, I do not like your friendship and your quarrels. You are not married yet. Why are you in a hurry? After all, there are so many interesting and good men. Wait, you are beautiful, take your time, find a companion in your life who will really love you. You came here recently. After all, you have one very painful life lesson living with your first husband. Your friend who is waiting for your invitation in Lithuania is a very serious guy. You should wait for him. Meanwhile, keep going to dances or parties and you will have more acquaintances."

Renee scoffed. "I like this one."

A week later, Joseph proposed to her and she accepted. Within a month they married. He moved into the house with Agatha, Simon, Melody, and Renee. The newlyweds quarreled loudly every day and night.

Agatha asked my mother to find an apartment for her and Simon. They wanted to live peacefully. Greta offered them an apartment next to her own house. They moved in, and Agatha ignored Greta, never stopping by to say hello or check on her. The only time either one came to visit was on Mother's Day when Simon came by himself with a bouquet of flowers. Melody with her family moved to another apartment close by.

After a year, Renee had a second child, a son. My mother asked me to go with her to visit and congratulate Renee. We purchased flowers and a gift for the child. When we came to the house, her husband was not home. Renee put the flowers in a vase and placed it on the floor. Soon Joseph returned from work. He looked tired and said, "Hello."

We congratulated him on his first-born son. As he walked towards us, he knocked the flower vase to the side. Water spilled all over the carpet.

Renee screamed at him. "Don't you see where you are going? What a fool you are."

He apologized to us for accidentally knocking over the flower vase. My mother and I looked at each other in silence. I picked up the vase with flowers and placed it on the table. We told them it was nice to visit you and to see your little boy and then we left.

The next year, Renee's boyfriend won the green card and came to the United States. Of course, by then Renee was already married and as far she was concerned the relationship with him had ended.

Eventually she had two more sons. This meant that the family had four boys to take care of. Joseph worked as a truck driver all week and returned home only on the weekends. They both liked to drink and smoke.

One evening Melody called Greta asking her to come immediately to Renee's house. When she arrived, she saw that Renee was intoxicated and arguing with Joseph. His truck was parked by the curb, and he was carrying bags from the house and throwing them in the back of the truck.

Joseph told us that he was leaving Renee. "I can't live like this anymore. My wife is always unhappy, always fighting and calling me all kinds of obscene names." He went back into the house and brought more things to his truck.

Renee ran out the door and climbed into the truck, shouting, "Help me Help me."

Joseph asked her to get out. She refused, continuing to shout, "Help me." He grabbed her arms and pulled her out of the truck, setting her gently on the ground.

Greta scolded Melody for not helping with the situation. Just standing and watching. Greta turned to Renee and told her to be quiet and go into the house and take care of her children. With her head hung, Renee returned inside, along with Melody and Greta.

The house was a mess, a broken mirror had left shattered glass on the floor.

"Renee, why are you repeating your old life?" Greta asked.

"My husband is leaving and will not come back," Renee said between tears. "How will I live without him?"

Greta shook her finger at her. "It's your own fault, drinking and fighting all the time. Get hold of yourself. Go and get some rest now."

Joseph drove his truck to his mother's house and stayed there. The next day Renee called him and apologized and asked him to come home. He agreed and returned.

Within a year, they bought a house in the suburbs. After not being invited for two years in their house, my mother wanted to see the house and her grandkids. When we arrived for the first time, Greta and I met the whole family. I saw her youngest son, three-years-old, for the first time. He was very cute, his hat on his head reminded me of a pilot.

I asked him, "Are you are going to be a pilot when you grow up like your grandfather?"

He asked me, "What's a pilot?"

"A person who flies an airplane."

He tilted his head and put on a mischievous smile.

All of us went out into the yard and played basketball and other games for several hours and had a nice picnic lunch.

Mother and I returned home content, thinking all was well. Then, a week later, we found out that their house was being foreclosed on by the bank. They hadn't been paying their mortgage.

Agatha purchased a house under her name for them, and Renee's family moved in while Agatha and Simon stayed in their apartment.

A few months later, during a cold winter night, Joseph brought a friend home, both of them drunk. They continued drinking and talking loudly, and Renee, who had been asleep, stumbled out to the living room and asked them to be quiet, so as not to wake the children.

Joseph yelled at her and soon all three were screaming at each other.

Renee called the police and when they arrived, everyone calmed down. However, after the police left, the three took up the fight again, Renee smashing their wedding picture on the floor. She roused the children, got them dressed, and told her husband to go to sleep. She and his friend left together, he helping to take the kids to Melody's house for the night.

Joseph, being drunk, looked at the broken wedding photo and decided that Renee is being unfaithful to him. He went to the gas station and brought back two tanks of gasoline that he poured on the beds and the floor. He repeated the trip, and when he opened the door this time, the fuel exploded, breaking not only their windows but those of the next-door neighbor's house as well. The fire burnt everything down except the garage and one brick wall. The police arrived, found him standing in the yard, and took him away.

He was sentenced to three years in prison. After that, since he only had a green card and being not a citizen, he was deported back to Lithuania. Renee had discouraged him from getting his citizenship, worried that if he had it, he might leave her.

I never understood why my brother's family didn't like us. In all the time they lived in America, I saw them few times. I invited Renee to come and visit us with her kids many times. She always found excuses of why she could not come and visit us or invite us. It was very sad for Greta and me. In time we completely drifted apart.

Agatha visited me only once with her husband Simon. When they were leaving, she told me she thought it would be better off if they never came back again. This saying had various meanings to me such as jealousy and how far I advanced over them, or perhaps our problems in Lithuania were still around.

When the fire occurred, I was 900 miles away, enjoying a warm break from the Chicago winter. Justin called to tell me of the fire, and I immediately ended my vacation and headed north. When I entered Illinois, the weather turned freezing with snow. Suddenly, the car hit a patch of ice and spun at high speed. The car crossed the oncoming traffic lane on the highway, went through a ditch, and slammed into a tree. The airbags went off and smoke poured from the motor. My door was jammed shut so I slid over to the passenger door and climbed out.

Soon, police, ambulance, and fire engines arrived. Blood was running down my arm and face. The paramedic bandaged my wounds. A policeman invited me to sit in his vehicle while he inspected my car, then issued me a ticket for driving too fast for the road condition.

A truck towed my car to a repair shop in a nearby town. The mechanic there told me that the car was a total loss. The doors were folded, the bags were out, and the radiator was broken. He offered me a reasonable price for the engine which I accepted. I called a friend who came and brought me back home.

I found a lawyer in the county where the accident happened who agreed to take my case. I stressed to him that I did not want to have a mark on my driving record since it was an accident. He told me he would fix everything. Two months later, he called and said that he had settled my case and I didn't need to come to court and it wouldn't be on the record. However, when it came time to pay my insurance next time, I found out the accident showed on my driving record.

Once I get back home my mother asked me, "Christina what happened with your face?"

"I had an accident – nothing special, don't worry. Did you know that Renee's house was destroyed?"

"Yes."

After I healed, I rented a car and we drove to the hotel where Renee's family was living. We brought clothes, shoes, and money. After talking with Renee about her difficult time, I decided to call the Lithuanian newspapers in Chicago, and I placed an ad stating, "Call for help". I described what had happened to the family and that they needed help, asking for donations of clothes and supplies. I noted a bank account that would accept monetary donations. I gave Melody's address in the newspapers. I never found out if Renee received any help from my ads, though I believe she probably did.

After time passed, the insurance allowed them to rent another house because the family was big. Insurance paid for everything. A few months later, Mother and I visited Renee in her new house and brought fruit and clothes. They lived there until the insurance paid for a new house to be built in the same place where their old house stood.

On a Sunday morning, a year later, Greta went to church to sing in the choir as usual. The priest approached Greta and asked her, "Why are you not at the baptism?"

"What baptism?"

327

"Your three grandchildren are being christened this morning," he explained.

Greta was devastated that she hadn't been invited to her grandchildren's baptism. "I can't understand why they are so rude to me," she told the priest. "I served them all my life even though I've never received a single kind word from them."

The priest laid his hand on her shoulder. "We don't do good deeds for the reward of gratitude. We find happiness in what we do for others. Helping others is a kind of success for the one who helps. As they say, God sees us and will reward us sooner or later for our good deeds and punish us for our bad ones."

Chapter Ninety-Nine: Bella Comes to America

On my return to Lithuania, I visited a childhood friend, Bella. After the Lithuanians gained independence in 1990 and with the formation of a new government, the land and houses confiscated during the Soviet years were returned to their original owners. One of these houses was Bela's parents' old house with Bela's intention of opening a restaurant there. I met Bella at this house during my visit. She lived in a four-story sixteenth-century brick building that she inherited from her parents. The first floor had a large restaurant and below that a basement that served as a bar. The kitchen sat on the second floor, a banquet hall on the third, and a small hotel on the fourth floor.

I met her at her restaurant, and she treated me to a delicious meal. Bella asked me to tell how it was living in the United States. I told her about my life, how work was hard but there were many more opportunities than in Lithuania.

"The restaurant is a lot of work," she said. "My income from it is very small. I have a second job teaching music at school. I am very tired from all of it."

We sipped our tea in companionship, and I commented, "It seems you have a very hard life. You should consider taking a break from this hard work and come visit me in the United States."

A few years later Bella received an invitation to visit the United States, and when she arrived, she stayed in my mother's house. We agreed the first two weeks would be free, and after that she would have to pay rent. She found a babysitting job for five days a week with accommodation.

After she'd made some money, she decided to obtain a driver's license. Bella asked me if she could use my car to pass the exam.

After my accident, I bought another car that also had eight cylinders. I told her, "Fine, but my car is automatic, has eight cylinders, and is very long."

When she saw the car, she expressed delight in how beautiful it was. The car was heavy as a ship, wide and long. I showed her how to turn on the gears, how to stop, and how to drive in reverse. She had driven a car in Lithuania, so quickly learned the entire system of this one.

During the next two weekends we practiced driving my car in a park and from there to small streets. She drove slowly through various intersections including dealing with the traffic lights.

I gave her a traffic rule book with the questions and answers. Although she hardly knew how to read English, she memorized all the questions and answers. When she was ready, I took her to the driver's exam.

Upon entering the building, she submitted her documents, and an officer directed her where to sit to take the theory exam. She answered all the questions quickly and glanced at me. I signaled her to stay seated until others had finished so she wouldn't be the first to turn hers in. After a few others finished and turned theirs in, she did hers too, and received a passing grade.

The next step was an eye exam, which she passed, and then waited outside for the driving test. Bella sat in my car and soon the officer came and walked around the car inspecting it. He asked her to turn on the lights and to press the brakes. Everything worked. He sat next to her, and they drove off. She returned shortly and the instructor told her that she passed the exam.

Bella was joyful. We went back into the building, paid the fee, and had her picture taken. She received her driver's license.

Two weeks later, she asked me to introduce her to a man who was an American citizen and would want to marry her.

"Bella," I said. "You know this is a difficult task. I will think about it. I know that you are limited with your English, but I will try."

I remembered my old computer friend, Adam, who I had dated for half a year and called him. "This is Christina. Do you remember me?"

"Of course, I remember you," he said. "How are you? We haven't talked in a long time." He told me he was still working and still not married.

"I have a good partner for you," I said. "She recently arrived from Lithuania where she had a restaurant. Her name is Bella and she's thin and beautiful like me. Also, she's a musician."

"Okay, I'm interested. Please come and introduce me to her." He gave me the name of a restaurant we should meet at.

When we arrived at the restaurant, Adam was waiting. From the first glance they liked each other and soon started to date. After one month of dating, he proposed to her and a week later they got married. He sold his house in Illinois, and they moved to Kentucky to a house in the countryside near a forest. Bella took a job in an Illinois casino an hour away as a waitress.

When they settled down, Bella invited me to visit her. My mother and I traveled together and found her lovely home surrounded by flowers standing on a hill. Inside, the walls were decorated with her artwork, much of it woven fiber. We sat in her living room and complimented her and her husband on their lovely home.

Adam said, "I'm lucky to have a wife with such good taste."

He cooked dinner, serving us grilled fish fresh, vegetables, and a fruit plate. After dinner we thanked him for the delicious meal. After dinner we walked to a nearby lake, where, the next day, her husband took us fishing. I love fishing. We took our fishing equipment and worms, and I caught several fish that he cooked for us for dinner.

After dinner, Bella entertained us by playing piano and singing. In our conversation Adam said that he liked to joke and sometimes screamed. Bella agreed with him, and said, "Yes, we like to eat ice scream in the evening." We laughed at her joke.

Bella was very much in love with her husband. Sundays they attended church where she gathered a group of people from the church and organized and conducted the choir. She used her knowledge that she received studying music in college in Lithuania.

One day, after mass, Bella saw her husband talking to one of the women in the choir and became jealous. When they got home, she counted her husband's Viagra pills and decided one pill was missing.

When Adam entered the kitchen, she attacked him. "You are missing one Viagra pill. Who are you making love to?"

He was quite surprised. "What pills are you talking about? Bella why can't I talk to a single woman? Everywhere in the church and in shopping centers when I speak to a woman you are attacking me. Why are you so jealous? You know it is common here to talk to people and give compliments and to tell jokes when talking. And you know I love you and am faithful."

A few months later, Bella developed more inappropriate and weird thoughts. She called me on the phone to tell me that her husband tried to push her into a snake's nest while they were biking through the forest, and that at night he placed a snake in her bed. She claimed that one night her husband gave her an electric shock in her leg, even though he was asleep at the time.

Over the next months she developed worse delusions. She claimed that strange people were stalking her, hiding in the yard and would catch her if she stepped out. She thought her husband wanted to drown her.

Adam tried to help her. So that she wouldn't have to drive through the woods at night, he purchased a house in the city. He taught her how to use the computer so she could work at home.

Over the next few years, whenever I passed through Kentucky I stopped to see Bella. Often, she invited me to her restaurant where she worked and treated me to a delicious meal. She showed off the many awards she'd received from the casino. At one of their talent shows, she won first place by playing the accordion and was awarded a guitar signed by a famous guitarist.

One season her city hosted an art exhibit. Bella entered it with her leather goods, coats she'd created in native Indian style with patches, tassels and knitting. She invited me to enter it with my acrylic paintings. I took two of my paintings as well as two pencil drawings made by my son Gabriel.

The week before the exhibit, I was driving to Kentucky on a highway near the town where Bella lives, bringing my entries. I felt that something was wrong with my car and exited the highway, stopping at a store.

A man came up to my car and said, "Smoke is coming from your engine."

"What should I do?" I asked him.

"Your car is overheated. You'll have to wait at least half an hour for the engine to cool down before you can drive again."

After the specified time, I got back on the highway, but after only a few miles, I saw that smoke was coming from my car's hood again. I turned into the first street and waited for the engine to cool down. I tried once again to drive, but after only five minutes I had to stop.

While I was standing on the side of the road, a short Afro-American man with sagging shorts came up to me and offered to help. He said, "I saw you standing by the road. I'm a mechanic and can help."

I looked at him, and although he didn't look reliable, I felt I had no other choice and accepted his offer. He looked at the engine and said that I needed a new hose. He suggested that I leave my car and go with him to a car parts store where he will buy the hose. He said the store was very close.

Before we left for the store, I asked him how much would I have to pay him? He said thirty dollars and I agreed. I locked my car and got into the man's car. At the car parts store and he explained to the salesclerk what he needed. I paid and we drove back to my car.

While driving he talked about his sick father and showed his picture. I said it was a pity.

We approached a gas station. The man said, "I'm very low on gas. I'll stop and you fill it up."

I went inside the gas station and stood in a line. While I waited, my mechanic leaned into the door and yelled. "Hey, buy me a pack of cigarettes."

I yelled back, "Which brand do you want?" He told me. People looked at me and him strangely. I laughed.

I wondered what I had gotten into. I bought him cigarettes and paid for the gas, and we left. We drove back to my car.

When we got there, he told me to make sure my wheels were still there. Fortunately, they were. He opened the hood and cut off a short piece of the hose and took a bigger piece for himself. It was getting dark, so he gave me a flashlight to shine on the motor.

"Don't worry," he said. "It will be fixed soon."

After a short period of time he said, "I am finished. You can now drive without fear."

"How much do I owe you?"

He gave a big smile and said, "Well, I saved your car. You should pay me sixty dollars."

"No, the agreement was thirty. Look, I filled your car with gas and bought you a pack of cigarettes. That's all you deserve." I gave him thirty dollars.

He turned around and quickly disappeared.

I started driving but as soon as I got to the main street, smoke came out of the hood. I stopped and called a towing company. They towed my car to a mechanic that was still working. It took him only half an hour to fix it, a problem with the water pump.

I called Bella and told her I would be late. When I arrived, I apologized for being late, and, sitting by the dinner table and sipping wine, I told my story. The next morning Bella drove me to the art center, and I left our art works. I thanked them for the hospitality and returned home.

I returned for the exhibition's opening. Everything was laid out artistically, including Bella's knitted items and a beautiful leather coat she designed. There were paintings from several artists including mine and my son's. The director of the art museum and the city's mayor gave speeches. It was a wonderful time with an opportunity to meet other area artists.

At the end of the exhibit two weeks later I received a message from the art director that one of my paintings had won first place among more than sixty artists. It was a picture of an Amarillo flower, four feet square. I drove back to Kentucky to pick up the pictures, my award money, and the certificate of first place. After that I entered several other art exhibitions in other states.

A year after the successful art exhibition, Bella received a letter from Lithuania. Her daughter had a serious illness and needed a difficult operation. Bella called me and asked for help, saying she didn't have money to pay for the operation or even enough to fly back to Lithuania.

I placed a "Cry for Help" ad in the Lithuanian Chicago newspapers, and asked the charitable organization called "Daughters of Lithuania Inc." for help. I gave Bella's name and address where people could send money directly to her. Her husband also placed an ad in the church's newspaper and a request was mentioned at a mass.

The appeals were successful, and Bella flew to Lithuania to be with her daughter.

Chapter One Hundred: Alma Comes to Visit

A true friend is always by your side in adversity and trouble,
If you are sad, he is not happy
You do not sleep - he worries,
Without any words really
I will always give you a hand.
So actions are not equal,
A friend or an accomplice.
  -William Shakespeare, English writer

Alma's and my friendship had been broken for many years. When Alma's financial position had improved significantly our friendship vanished. Then, many years later, Alma found me living in the United States. She informed me that for work reasons, she was coming to work on her thesis.

She came to the University of Nebraska and attended a conference. From there, she called and told me she missed me and wanted to see me. She had to fly to Fort Lauderdale, Florida, to meet a Lithuanian professor and asked me to meet her there over the New Year's holiday.

On New Year's Eve, I flew to Florida and checked into a Daytona Beach hotel. I rented a car and drove to Alma's place where she was staying at the professor's house. From there, we drove back to Daytona Beach and walked along the streets. She was surprised at how many people were out partying. The center streets were closed to traffic and all the restaurants and shops were open and music was playing everywhere. Many bikers came to celebrate New Year's Eve. She was surprised how friendly people were.

I heard country music playing on a street with my favorite song, "Boot scootin' Boogie". I invited Alma to dance in the middle of the street. When we started to dance, people joined us. Then they asked me if I was a dance leader, I said, "Yes I am." I took country western dance classes, and I knew the steps of "Boot scootin' Boogie".

I danced with Alma remembering the good old school days. We celebrated the turning of the new year in the street, and then I drove her back to the professor's house. The next day I spent exploring the rich and beautiful Palm Beach city.

Alma called me late that afternoon and told me that she had finished her conversation with the professor, and nothing had come of it. I drove to pick her up.

I took her to the main street of Palm Beach where Alma was very surprised to see the beauty of the city. Standing on the sidewalk, she stomped her feet and yelled at me. "Why did you not bring me here earlier? Tell me, why?"

I answered that she did not want to, she was too busy with her professor. It was more important for you to talk to her. She ignored what I said and kept shouting. I said please don't shout. She calmed down and I took her to a clothing shop. She was very impressed and wandered away, looking at all the lovely items.

"Christina, look at this! Look at that! Oh, what a beautiful purse I found."

I asked her not to shout so loudly, and she calmed down.

The next day we flew to Chicago, and I drove her to my mother's house. She spent several days in Chicago, and I took her to see some museums and more interesting tourist places. One evening we went to the city center, and we sipped cocktails on the 96th floor bar of the John Hancock skyscraper.

Before we left for the airport, she showed me a questionnaire that she planned to give to the airline passengers. The answers would be used for her thesis. She told me that the passengers would be happy to fill it out since they had nothing to do. I told her that the passengers want their privacy, and the airlines weren't going to allow her to do that. I strongly advised her not to do it. She seemed angry with me when I left her at the airport.

A few months after Alma's departure, after returning from work in the evening, my mother and I were watching a Lithuanian news station. It was a courtroom scene where Alma was on trial. We heard an accuser telling the judge that as a teacher at the university, Alma told the students that they could bribe her in euros to get better grades on their exams. They had a witness who caught her in the act of accepting a bribe.

Having never committed a crime before, she apologized to the court and her colleagues. She was sentenced to one year of house arrest. The judge said that if she did not do any more illegal things during that year, the arrest will be lifted. She resigned from the University. We wondered if this was common practice in Lithuania.

Nothing changes a person like a change from worse to better. It took some time for her to get over this situation. She was always a smart person and started to pursue a new carrier. She made ceramic pieces, painted pictures, and wrote poetry. Her artwork was successful, and she published a book of poems and pictures she painted.

Chapter One Hundred and One: My Mother's Friend Matina

My mother had a friend, Matina, who came on a tourist visa, but hoped to move to America permanently. As such, she wanted to find an American citizen to marry. One day, she met a Lithuanian man in the park of Chicago who invited her to come live in his house. He lived alone and he needed a companion.

She took her belongings and moved into his two-story brick house. When she entered, she saw cockroaches climbing the walls and running on the kitchen table.

"How can you live like this?" she demanded.

"They don't do anything bad; they just run around."

She set out poison to kill the cockroaches.

"Why is it so cold in here?" she demanded.

"I only heat one room with an electric stove and that's enough for me."

She brought in space heaters for the other rooms.

"Why is there no hot water in the shower?"

"I like cold showers. If you want hot water, heat some up on the stove."

Even after all this, when he asked her to marry him, she said yes. However, the engagement didn't last long. His family told him not to get married, and he told her she had to move out.

Matina moved into my mother's house and brought a couple of cockroaches in her belongings. Mother put extermination tablets around the house and the bugs disappeared.

That summer I invited Matina to come with Greta and me to pick blueberries in Michigan. At the blueberry farm we picked five gallons from bushes. On the way home Matina asked me how she could meet a professional man. I suggested she could contact a dating agency. She liked my idea and asked me to drive her to this agency.

The agent there explained the dating service rules. She agreed and paid a substantial fee, which bought her a one-year guarantee. Matina filled out questionnaires about her wants and desires and had a professional picture taken.

Matina wanted me to look at her prospects on the computer and communicate with them. I found her three prospects: a priest, a rocker, and an engineer. When I showed these to her, she asked me to write to each of them and report that she was interested. I wrote each one an email, but not one responded.

After three months, Matina asked me to call the agent and find out why she had not been offered a single candidate. When I called the agent, she said Matina had to call herself, and told me not to call again. When I told this to Matina she called the agent immediately, and frequently. Even so, the agency found no one for her.

After a half a year, the agent provided Matina with a phone number from a man from Wisconsin who wasn't even registered with the agency because he didn't want to pay the substantial fee.

During the telephone conversation with the man, he said he'd be interested in meeting her. He invited her to come to his house and stay for two weeks. He said during these two weeks they would decide whether they were compatible or not.

My mother and I joined Matina on the two-hour car trip to meet Matina's Wisconsin friend. The man saw us arrive and came out to greet us. Matina didn't like his appearance and whispered to me, "Christina, I don't want to stay. I don't like him."

"No," I insisted. "You have to stay for a while until you find out what he's like. After the promised two weeks, if you want to come back, I'll come get you."

We all sat in the living room, talked, joked, and had a snack. His home was cozy, clean, and tastefully decorated. In the evening, Mother and I thanked him for his hospitality, said goodbye, and left Matina behind.

A few days later Matina called us from Wisconsin. "Christina, I am so grateful that you left me here. He is an intelligent, sweet, polite person. I like him a lot." In two weeks, I came and brought her back. She packed her belongings and asked me to drive her back to Wisconsin, which I did. After a year of their friendship, they get married.

His unmarried son often came to visit them. He was a former musician who sang in an ensemble and played guitar. He worked as a manager in a food store and had a good sense of humor.

Matina's husband was a Korean War veteran and the two of them attended dances held at the war veterans club on Saturdays. They lived happily for three years until her husband came down with cancer. They put him in the hospital where she visited him every day until he died a month later.

According to his will, all his possessions, including his car and house, went to his son, although as his wife, she received his pension. Matina had to leave the house and find an apartment. She asked her acquaintances if they knew where she could find an apartment. She also called me and asked me to help her find an apartment. I came and drove her around and after a long search we found an apartment which she liked. The area had a lot of greenery and was near the city center, a casino, and the bus station.

She moved into an apartment on the second floor. Once settled, she invited us to come visit her. As a gift, I brought one of my paintings. At her request, I helped her with the interior design.

Her son-in-law visited her with a new big car he bought. He often invited her to fly to Las Vegas and paid for their trip. His condominium was one story with a big fully furnished basement near a small lake and forest. He invited me and my mother to his house to listen to music in the basement where he had a pool table, ping pong, and pinball machines. There we talked and danced as he played music from his large collection of records. We always had a good time with him.

He told Matina he'd never been to Europe and invited her to take him as his guide to Lithuania. There he met Matina's sons, one of whom was a pianist and played in a piano bar. The two musicians immediately found a common language and held a duet concert at the piano bar. Matina's son played piano and her son-in-law guitar. Before they flew back to America, the son-in-law did some paperwork to donate to Matina's son some items when the son-in-law died.

Over the next several years, Matina and her son-in-law continued their friendship with frequent travels. Every year they took a gambling trip to Las Vegas. When COVID came, the son-in-law died, leaving his possessions to Matina.

Chapter One Hundred and Two: Observations on Success

When a person does everything in such a way that success depends only on him/her and not on anyone else, he discovers the best way to live happily. This is a restrained, manly, wise person.
  - Greek philosopher Plato

Success comes to him who hustles while he waits.
  - American inventor, Thomas Alva Edison

This book describes the lives of close family members and some close friends: their successes, failures, lifestyles, and accomplishments. Thus blows the joys of fate. When writing about these individuals, it was difficult for me to determine if my judgement was always accurate. I was usually writing about a person based on my experiences with them. Sometimes the family and friends around me did things that most people would consider horrid, consistent with a bad temper or judgment. Yet, I was still involved with this person. Although I might wish I could have helped them, often I was trapped in their aura because I was related to them or had to share their environment.

During all these years I helped many people. Even when I didn't receive thanks, I felt good about helping. All tasks for me and for people around me I tried to accomplish. Good people often go unappreciated for their kindness and are unable to be bad even when it's expedient.

What is the best path to success? Over time, everyone experiences the best and the worst that fate has to offer. It's important to define the goals one wishes to pursue. On the path to success, don't lose your enthusiasm and go all the way until you see the light at the end of the tunnel.

Success isn't necessarily measured by money or fame. Everyone must establish their own criteria of what it means for them to be successful. Success doesn't come to us; we go to it.

Many successes and failures affected my family and friends. In my life I've emphasized my strongest capabilities that have allowed me to overcome everyday obstacles. I've patiently and cold-bloodedly endured the blows given to me by fate, without fear of failure. I took small steps on the road to success, which I took through large sections of failure.

What is success really? Success is usually associated with a series of purposeful and random events. It happens regardless of our will. Are you happy? One's happiness doesn't depend on what other people consider levels of success, for everyone has their own definition of success.

According to Goddard Neville, there are two worlds. First is God's and the second is Caesar's. We must determine which one we choose.

God's world consists of our spiritual values like love, peace, and happiness. We feel human when we enjoy them.

Caesar's values are material such as power, money, and authority. Sometimes people strive for these at great cost. Material goods are not inherently evil. The more one has, the more one can share. I feel happy helping people. For a long time, I thought that material values were not compatible with spiritual values. But I discovered that the more I have, the more time I can devote to volunteering to help others.

Spiritual success requires repeating from morning to night that one is in love with your life. Perhaps your mind asks, "Am I really in love?" However, there are statements that the mind does not reject. One asks, "Am I talented, safe, and adequately rich?" Wealth is not only material, but also about adequate abundance. The mind recognizes that I am unique, born that way and developed along unique paths.

If we bend the stick in pursuit of well-being only for ourselves, if we don't consider those around us, if lose interest in them. If we don't help others, the law of cause and effect is activated. How we treat the environment is how the environment treats us. It's all about our vision and how we act on it. You need to have a vision of how to live life and many possibilities open up. No one will come and help you if you don't want to achieve your desired goal.

I made it a high priority to come to the United States, writing letters for four years and seeking an invitation. Vision grew confidence, confidence enabled success. Without vision and confidence there will be no success. Have them and firmly pursue your goals, believe in them and success will come. If you don't try, the door closes and opportunities remain untapped.

Success favors those who seek to satisfy their own desires and follow their true vocation, rather than the expectations of others.

Success rarely falls from the sky. Over my life, I collected items and memories that I wanted to write about. These stories of people really happened. There might be some differences in a few details that individuals would disagree with, but I feel these stories are truthful and helpful for the readers to protect against the forces that are against them.

I am always looking for new goals. I am not standing still. I work a lot. Time is precious, it moves quickly throughout our life. I write books at night when it is quiet and the whole family is asleep. I know that if I start something, I have to finish it and meet my expectations. It is never too late to start something new. A new goal is a new beginning.

I always try to meet people who have achieved more than me. These are strong personalities guided by an iron will with unbreakable enthusiasm and tremendous faith, never caring whether others will approve of their decisions. I always try to learn something new. I set high standards for myself. I always aim to satisfy them. My dreams set my goals. I strive for them until I reach them. Sometimes it takes years. I do what I want to do, and I believe in it, and I take inspiration and encouragement from people who have achieved more than me. Comparing myself to such people, I develop the hope that if someone has achieved it, I can achieve it too. If I want to change something in my life, I align myself with stronger people, I observe and analyze the lives of great people, and I realize that an easy life is in sweet dreams and fairy tales.

People rarely consider what price high achievers paid to achieve their success. When we watch high achievers, we always see the bottom line. I consider, "What did he sacrifice to achieve? How much time, effort, and money were needed to make him what he is now." We do not get anything in life for nothing. But to get something, we must sacrifice. Sometimes this feels like lost time in a person's life.

Sometimes I wonder why some people remember the bad things I did for them and not the good things. We get what we deserve, after all.

I have achieved a lot while living in America. I wrote two books in English. The first book "The Therapy of Natural Living" which is rated five stars, has more than 400 pages. Both this one and my second book, "Good Health through Grains", are sold on the Amazon portal.

I am a recognized artist. More than once, my achievements have been published in magazines and newspapers as an artist, designer and as a prize-winner in the creation of landscape and flower compositions.

Chapter One Hundred and Three: Favorite Sayings of a Successful Life from the Author

1.   Communicate!

The more contacts you have, the more likely you are to succeed. It is not necessary to be friends with everyone, it is enough to have a sincere relationship so that you can turn to them in case of need. Be willing to help your friends when they need you. No one became poor by helping others.

2.   Make friends with optimists.

Everyone has disappointments in their lives, but optimists look at failures with humor. By communicating with an optimistic person, you get positive energy yourself. Positive people know how to enjoy every moment of life.

3.   Promote your achievements.

It is a great art that needs to be learned if you want to realize your intentions to reveal your personality. Do not sit in a corner and show no initiative. It is not shameful to demonstrate your achievements and advantages: how else will the people around you believe in you and appreciate what you are capable of? And how else will you find like-minded people?

4.   Do what you like.

Always hope for success. Dare to dream big with a sincere belief in achieving great success. Engage in activities that make you happy. It does not matter if others call you weird. Live your life, not someone else's.

5.   Be thankful.

The result of intellectual, spiritual, and material wealth is gratitude. Be thankful in mind for the goods received. A person with a grateful heart is happy and rich. According to William Shakespeare, "O Lord that lends me life, lend me a heart replete with thankfulness."

6.   Rest in nature.

Take nature walks admiring the trees and flowers, jogging in the morning dew, listening to the chirping of birds and the gurgling stream. In winter, admire the crunch of snow, ski the mountains. All of this dissipates tension and aggression, removes fatigue, restores physical strength, and gives pleasure in continuing to do one's work. All this gives vital energy.

7.   Don't look back.

Let's forget the inconveniences and hurts, let's not remember them. Let's live in the present and not the past and thereby create a glorious future. Let's move from one emotional state to another.

8.   Smile.

A cheerful person seems to attract joy and success; therefore, he is successful. On the other hand, the eternally dissatisfied grump cannot get rid of troubles and problems in any way. The peevish person never finds good luck. To them, everything is always bad, no one wants to communicate with them. They find it difficult to smile.

A smile makes it easier to survive failures. A smile attracts people and strengthens friendships. You see the world in brighter colors. Where there is light, there is also success. They say that laughter costs nothing, so why not laugh? Let's laugh every day and we will feel happier and healthier. When you smile to yourself, your soul will be filled with joy, your muscles will relax, your wrinkles will smooth, your face will become more pleasant and attractive. A smile not only makes our part easier, but also opens the door to other people's hearts. Smile every time you see yourself in the mirror. While looking at it, say, "I am happy. I am doing great. How beautiful I am today." These words spoken out loud give us charm and self-confidence for a long time.

9.   Surround yourself with goodness and beauty.

Success accompanies positive people. Watch comedies and see beautiful things, good people, beloved animals in them. Listen to heartwarming music. Everything brings joy. By letting goodness into your life, you program yourself for happiness and success. Don't indulge in negativity. Avoid horror, keep your home clean, and eschew violent shows and news.

10.   Cultivate creativity.

It has long been proven that favorite activities have a therapeutic effect. Let these hobbies be dancing, music, painting, or other works of art. This is an ideal way to be happy, to experience the joy of creation, the hormone of happiness - beta endorphin - is actively produced.

11.   Don't stand still.

People who are accompanied by success do not stick to one activity. Instead, they move on and try different areas. Professional changes often create a successful turn in life, new opportunities for interesting acquaintances appear. If there is an opportunity to learn something new, you should take advantage of it. Successful people are usually not conservative.

12.   Be proud of yourself.

Rejoice in your every victory and every achievement. Do not underestimate the effort of your achievements, praise yourself and encourage yourself with some kind of gift. Psychologists advise placing that gift in a visible place, then it will be an incentive to try to improve even more.

13.   Unburden yourself.

Declutter from any unnecessary objects, grievances, and burdensome obligations. Clean your computer of unnecessary files. You will be happier and freer.

14.   Have a talisman.

It can be the simplest thing that was with you in the happiest moments. If you deeply believe that it brings success, it will.

15.   Don't get distracted!

This principle means that if you are not successful in something in life - do not be distracted. Try to just trust fate and gratefully accept everything that happens to you. Have one direction and go in that direction and pursue it.

16.   Always hope for success.

Dream boldly and sincerely hope for the best. Never accept you are meant to fail or suffer. Throw such thoughts out of your head!

17.   Play.

Life is not a short fight; it is a game that you cannot stop once you get into it. Many people are too serious and uptight. And for such, the biggest glitch seems like a huge failure. The game is even more interesting when you do not think about winning and when you enjoy the process itself. So, don't lose your excitement!

18.   Don't give up.

Some people have more difficult trials in life, others less, but it is very important for everyone not to lack endurance and perseverance. A person in trouble does not break until he gives up. The British politician Winston Churchill was fond of the saying, "Never, never, never give up."

19.   Travel.

Get to know other countries and other cultures. Travel is an antidote to superstition, blind attachment, and narrow-mindedness.

Chapter One Hundred and Four: A Dream

Dream on. Have your own dreams. Formulate them maximally and concretely.
If your dreams do not scare you, they are not big enough.
- Ellen Johnson Sirleaf, Liberian politician

I dreamt that I was walking in an affluent suburb of Chicago. I approached a very big house where I was supposed to be decorating tables with flowers for a wedding. Inside, I saw a huge single modern open room without a door. There were two wide tables far from each other. On one table there was a bunch of different flowers. Several women were walking around this room. I walked to the left where the flowers were placed and a tall, handsome, and stylishly dressed young man who looked much younger than me came in front of me. I recognized him immediately. Our eyes met as we passed each other. Our glances hit like lightning strikes. We passed and a soft smile came to our faces. We didn't say a single word, we just passed each other by, looking at each other.

I left the house and went out into the yard. I saw the same young man coming towards me again. I gently stroked his cheek with my hand. He touched me gently. We pulled into a tight hug, pressing our bodies together. Kisses flooded our souls. He lifted me up. We turned in a circle and kissed, unable to let go of each other's arms. We kissed long and passionately. He released me from his embrace.

I asked him, "How did you find me?"

"I live near here, Christina. I went for a walk and saw you walking from a distance and knew it was you. Your walk is distinctive, tall, thin, walking very straight with your head held high, proud and confident. I knew that only you could go like that. I'm so happy to have found you again."

I look around and see two young girls sitting on the sand watching us.

I asked him, "Are you married?"

"No. I am still waiting for you."

"But I can't stay. I have to go inside and make bouquet arrangements for the wedding. Will you accompany me?"

"No," he answered. He laid down among the grass and blooming flowers. Flowers covered his beloved face.

I entered the house, now full of people, again in the huge space very nicely arranged with long tables. The people walked around tidying up.

The dog that slept next to my bed started to squeal. I woke up from this wonderful dream in a great mood. I took the dog outside, returned to my bedroom, laid down on the bed, and tried to continue this dream of love. But it was gone. I got up and smiled all day, thinking about the dream. It is a wonderful thing to be loved.

Chapter One Hundred and Five: A Quick Courtship

Find someone who is proud to have you, scared to lose you, fights for you, appreciates you, respects you, cares for you, and loves you unconditionally.
They do not love that do not show their love.
- William Shakespeare, English writer

One day at a store I picked up the free magazine "Singles". In it, I found an advertisement for a dating service. I wrote a letter to the magazine describing myself, my aspirations, and what kind of man I was looking for. I described that I was looking for a professional and financially stable partner. I placed my photo.

A month later, I received a letter from a man who would like to meet me. I gave him my address and phone number. He arrived at the agreed time and parked his car by my house. I saw from the window a tall man with dark hair carrying flowers getting out of the car. I told my mother that he looked a lot like my second husband. He rang the doorbell and presented me with flowers. We sat down for a while and gave him a piece of cake and coffee. Later on, he invited me to a restaurant. At the restaurant, we dined and talked. I told him my history and he told me his.

"I really like you," I said, "but your face reminds me of my second husband. For this reason, I cannot be friends with you."

He laughed, and said, "That's strange, but I understand. I really like you too. You are a beautiful and kind woman. I have a friend, and I will introduce you to him. I think you will really like each other."

He drove me home and I thanked him for the pleasant meeting.

A few hours later his friend called and suggested we go out that very night. I said I was intrigued and invited him to come. That very same evening he arrived at my house. We sat on the sofa and talked all night. At dawn he left, and I went to work. In the evening, he called again and set up a double date at a restaurant in the center of Chicago. He invited his friend who introduced me to him, and I invited my girlfriend. The four of us had a double date.

The four of us spent an extremely nice evening together full of good conversation with humor. After eating and drinking wine, we left the restaurant. My date took my hand and didn't let go when we reached his car.

He said, "I have a proposal to you. First, we will go to my condominium in a skyscraper by the lake. I will change into sports clothes, then we will pick up your son Gabriel. The three of us will go to the western suburbs and I will show you my other property."

We drove to the western suburbs where we arrived at a school by the park with a running track. He said, "Gabriel and I will race on this running track. The first to run two laps wins."

"Okay, let's go," Gabriel said. "Mother, wait for us here."

I kept my fingers crossed, hoping that my son would come in first. After two laps in the end they tied. My friend was a marathon runner.

After a little rest from running, he said, "Sit down on a bench, Cristina."

I sat down next to him, and he took my hand. Looking in my eyes, he boldly asked me, "Are you divorced? If so, tell me when you want to marry me."

"Let me think about it I answered."

"Don't think too long Christina. Okay?"

We sat for another five minutes and then I kissed him and said, "Yes, I'll marry you. I am nothing without love!"